# BESA Studies in Internatio

# Religion in World Conflict

This new book tackles two crucial questions: First, how does religion in its various forms and manifestations influence world politics? Second, how will adding religion to the discourse on international relations modify our theoretical understanding?

Each of these leading authors addresses different aspects of these questions in different contexts providing a diverse and multifaceted view of the topic. Susanna Pearce and Tanja Ellingsen examine the religious causes of conflict on the macro-level. Several of the contributors focus on specific conflicts. Gaurav Ghose and Patrick James examine the Kashmir conflict from the Pakistani perspective and Carolyn James and Özgür Özdamar examine it from the Indian perspective. Similarly Hillel Frisch examines the Palestinian–Israeli conflict from the Palestinian perspective and Jonathan Rynhold examines it from the Israeli perspective. Finally, two of the authors examine other important issues. Stuart A. Cohen examines the evolution of the religious view of war in the Jewish tradition and Yehudit Auerbach examines whether religion can play a role in conflict resolution and reconciliation. These assessments deliver fascinating conclusions.

This book was previously published as a Special Issue of *Terrorism and Political Violence*.

**Jonathan Fox** is currently a senior lecturer in the Political Studies Department of Bar-Ilan University and a senior research fellow at the Begin-Sadat Center for Strategic Studies.

**Shmuel Sandler** is currently The Sara and Simha Lainer Professor in Democracy and Civility, Department of Political Science, Bar-Ilan University, and a senior research fellow at the Begin-Sadat Center for Strategic Studies.

# Religion in World Conflict

Edited by
Jonathan Fox and Shmuel Sandler

Routledge
Taylor & Francis Group

London and New York

First published 2006 by Routledge
2 Park Square, Milton Park, Abingdon, Oxon, OX14 4RN

Simultaneously published in the USA and Canada
by Routledge
270 Madison Ave, New York NY 10016

*Routledge is an imprint of the Taylor & Francis Group, an informa business*

Transferred to Digital Printing 2008

© 2006 Taylor & Francis Ltd

Typeset in Times Roman by AccComputing, South Barrow, Somerset, UK

All rights reserved. No part of this book may be reprinted or reproduced or utilised in any form or by any electronic, mechanical, or other means, now known or hereafter invented, including photocopying and recording, or in any information storage or retrieval system, without permission in writing from the publishers.

*British Library Cataloguing in Publication Data*
A catalogue record for this book is available from the British Library

*Library of Congress Cataloging in Publication Data*
A catalog record for this book has been requested

ISBN10: 0-415-37167-8 (hbk)
ISBN10: 0-415-46434-X (pbk)

ISBN13: 978-0-415-37167-4 (hbk)
ISBN13: 978-0-415-46434-5 (pbk)

**The Begin-Sadat (BESA) Center for Strategic Studies at Bar-Ian University**

The BESA Center is dedicated to the study of Middle East peace and security, in particular the national security and foreign policy of Israel. A non-partisan and independent institute, the BESA Center is named in memory of Menachem Begin and Anwar Sadat, whose efforts in pursuing peace laid the cornerstone for future conflict resolution in the Middle East.

Since its founding in 1991 by Dr Thomas O. Hecht of Montreal, the BESA Center has become one of the most dynamic Israeli research institutions. It has developed cooperative relationships with strategic studies centers throughout the world, from Ankara to Washington and from London to Seoul. Among its research staff are some of Israel's best and brightest academic and military minds. BESA Center publications and policy recommendations are read by senior Israeli decision-makers, in military and civilian life, by academicians, the press and the broader public.

The BESA Center makes its research available to the international community through three publication series: BESA Security and Policy Studies, BESA Colloquia on Strategy and Diplomacy and BESA Studies in International Security. The Center also sponsors conferences, symposia, workshops, lectures and briefings for international and local audiences.

**The Sara and Simha Lainer Chair in Democracy and Civility at the Department of Political Science, Bar-Ilan University**

The Lainer Chair was established in order to promote democracy and civility in Israeli society while maintaining the character of the State of Israel as a Jewish State. One of the central functions of the Chair is to demonstrate that there is no conflict between Jewish values and democracy and that they can coexist in a Jewish state. The Lainer Chair focuses on four fields: civic education, dialogue between the different sectors in Israeli society, civil rights, academic conferences and publications.

# Contents

The Question of Religion and World Politics
   **Jonathan Fox and Shmuel Sandler** . . . . . . . . . . . . . . . . . . . . . . . . . . 1

Toward a Revival of Religion and Religious Clashes?
   **Tanja Ellingsen** . . . . . . . . . . . . . . . . . . . . . . . . . . . . . . . . . . . . . . . . 11

Religious Rage: A Quantitative Analysis of the Intensity of Religious Conflicts
   **Susanna Pearce** . . . . . . . . . . . . . . . . . . . . . . . . . . . . . . . . . . . . . . . . 39

The Changing Jewish Discourse on Armed Conflict: Themes and Implications
   **Stuart A. Cohen** . . . . . . . . . . . . . . . . . . . . . . . . . . . . . . . . . . . . . . . 59

Religion, Postmodernization, and Israeli Approaches to the Conflict with the Palestinians
   **Jonathan Rynhold** . . . . . . . . . . . . . . . . . . . . . . . . . . . . . . . . . . . . . 77

Has the Israeli–Palestinian Conflict Become Islamic? Fatah, Islam, and the Al-Aqsa Martyrs' Brigades
   **Hillel Frisch** . . . . . . . . . . . . . . . . . . . . . . . . . . . . . . . . . . . . . . . . . 97

Conflict over Israel: The Role of Religion, Race, Party, and Ideology in the U.S. House of Representatives, 1997–2002
   **Elizabeth A. Oldmixon, Beth Rosenson, and Kenneth D. Wald** . . . . . . . . . 113

Third-Party Intervention in Ethno-Religious Conflict: Role Theory, Pakistan, and War in Kashmir
   **Gaurav Ghose and Patrick James** . . . . . . . . . . . . . . . . . . . . . . . . . . 133

Religion as a Factor in Ethnic Conflict: Kashmir and Indian Foreign Policy
   **Carolyn C. James and Özgür Özdamar** . . . . . . . . . . . . . . . . . . . . . . . 151

Forgiveness and Reconciliation: The Religious Dimension
   **Yehudith Auerbach** . . . . . . . . . . . . . . . . . . . . . . . . . . . . . . . . . . . . 171

**Index** . . . . . . . . . . . . . . . . . . . . . . . . . . . . . . . . . . . . . . . . . . . . . . . . . 187

# The Question of Religion and World Politics

## JONATHAN FOX AND SHMUEL SANDLER

The purpose of this volume is to examine two central and related issues. First, how does religion in its various forms and manifestations influence world politics? Second, how will adding religion to the discourse on international relations modify our theoretical understanding of international relations? These questions are seemingly simple but, in reality, they are not for a number of reasons. First, until recently social science theory in general—and international relations theory in particular—has overlooked religion as an important social factor. Second, those students of the field who do address religion rarely work from a common conception of the term. Moreover, they often analyze religion in vastly different contexts and pay little attention as to how the findings associated with these particular contexts relate to others. Third, both leading approaches in the discipline of international relations—realism and institutionalism—have not developed any sensitivity to the infusion of religion into their terms of reference.

The authors in this volume necessarily focus on their own particular topics. In one degree or another, however, they also speak to a set of larger questions. The purpose of this introduction is to provide a synoptic view of those larger concerns. Clearly not all of these more specific questions are relevant to each of the studies in this volume, but all of the studies deal with issues that are relevant to at least some of these questions. These questions are discussed below.

This volume is based on papers presented at the conference "Religion and World Politics" held in May 2003 at Bar Ilan University, sponsored by the Begin-Sadat Center for Strategic Studies and the Sara and Simha Lainer Chair in Democracy and Civility. Because of the particular interest of these sponsors in the Middle East, especially Israel and the fact that the Israeli–Palestinian conflict is one of the most high-profile conflicts which includes religious elements, four of the contributions to this volume focus on this conflict. Two of the contributions focus on another high-profile conflict, the Indo-Pakistani conflict over Kashmir. Two of the papers use cross-sectional quantitative methodology and focus on the more general issue of the impact of religion on world conflict. Finally, one of the contributions focuses on the impact of religious identity and belief on voting in the U.S. Congress over foreign policy toward Israel. However, we would like to emphasize that all of these contributions develop theoretical models and have practical findings that are applicable beyond the specific cases which are their focus. This essay is intended to highlight some of these findings.

We proceed in three stages. The first examines the general question of how the social sciences deal with religion in general. The second examines why religion was ignored by the social sciences for most of the twentieth century. The third addresses a set of more specific questions.

## What is Religion and How Can It Be Understood within the Context of the Social Sciences?

Religion is a notoriously difficult term to define. In practice many use the form of definition that has in the past been applied to a notably unreligious topic: I may not be able to define it but I know it when I see it. That approach has no practical value. Only a more precise definition can allow a better understanding of which debates over the topic of religion and world politics are due to differences of opinion over how religion influences world politics, and which are due to different understandings of the multifaceted term "religion" itself.

Since religion can influence all manner of social phenomena, the definition of religion discussed here is not unique to international relations. However, its broader applicability is not a liability.

For practical purposes it is best to avoid theological definitions of religion which focus on the nature of deities. Rather our concern is with how religion can influence human behavior and society. As explaining human behavior and the nature of society is the central goal of social scientists, this approach has the advantage of focusing on the issues relevant in this context and avoiding contentious issues peripheral to the topic at hand.

While each of the authors focuses on different issues in different contexts, five social manifestations of religion can be identified, under which most of their understandings of religion can be placed. At the outset it is important to acknowledge that these five facets of religion often overlap and represent different aspects of a complex whole. Nevertheless, identifying them individually helps to better understand the many ways the concept of religion can be approached by social scientists.

First, religion can be among the bases for identity. The argument that identity issues influence politics is widely accepted. For instance, Samuel Huntington argues that identity-based civilizations will be the basis for world politics in the post–cold war era. Even most of those who dispute his theory acknowledge that identity is important.[1] They instead argue that civilizations will not be the primary basis for identity.[2] The question of identity has become prominent in international relations with the growing influence of constructivism[3] even though it is rarely, if ever, linked up with religion per se. However, the role of religion in identity is not clear. Is it only one basis for identity among many others like language, shared history, place of residence, nationality, and ethnicity? Or is there something unique about the influence of religion on identity?

Second, religion includes a belief system which influences behavior. People's beliefs influence their behavior and few would deny that religion is among the sources of the beliefs of many people. This can apply to leaders as well as the masses. Even if leaders do not themselves believe, they must often give weight to widely held beliefs and prejudices within the populations they govern. In international politics the impact of religiosity has appeared in the analysis of the foreign policy of leaders like Woodrow Wilson and John Foster Dulles. Also, if religious beliefs are involved, the possibility for compromise and accommodation is reduced.[4]

Third, religious doctrine or theology can often influence behaviour. While this facet of religion often overlaps with the previous one, they are not the same thing. Most religions have within them complex and often contradictory doctrines and concepts.[5] These vast bodies of doctrine can provide a resource for those who wish to justify their actions. They also can be where people seek guidance for the proper way to deal with a given situation. Clear aspects of doctrine can also restrict the options of policy makers. The work of Reinhold Niebuhr and his influence on Morgenthau is a primary example in the forgotten intellectual origins of realism.[6]

Fourth, religion is a source of legitimacy. In fact, it can be used to justify nearly any policy or action, even those that may otherwise be considered unjustifiable. For instance, it is used to provide the justification for Muslim suicide bombers who would otherwise be seen as violating religious laws against both murder and suicide. In the past it has also been used to justify both the continued reign of governments as well as their overthrow. Until the Peace of Versailles the divine right of kings to rule was the legitimizing principle of the international system. Despite the fact that religious legitimacy often supports state governments, it is important to remember that it is a source of legitimacy separate from, and often in competition with, the more secular bases for a state's legitimacy.[7]

Finally, religion is generally associated with religious institutions. These institutions can influence politics in a number of ways. To the extent that they are accepted by a population, their moral authority and prominence give their opinion weight. They are authoritative arbiters of religious legitimacy. Religious institutions, like any other established institution, can provide the logistical basis for mass mobilization.[8] On the global scene, religious institutions often act as transnational institutions and as such often interact with other international or transnational actors—and in some cases, such as the Catholic Church, can themselves be defined as international actors.

The identity approach to religion is the most common among the authors of this volume, perhaps because it is the simplest to apply. The quantitative studies in this volume (by Ellingsen, Oldmixon et al., and Pearce) all use religious identity to identify which conflicts are religious. Pearce, in addition to religious identity, also examines whether the presence of religious issues in a conflict influences its level of violence. Oldmixon et al. examine the impact of the religious and ethnic identities of members of the U.S. Congress, as well as that of their constituencies, on their votes with regard to the Israeli–Palestinian conflict. Ellingsen uses religious identity and religiosity to examine the extent to which religion is important in different civilizations and the impact of religion on armed conflict. Ghose and James similarly examine the impact of religious identity, as well as religious belief systems, on international intervention, using Pakistan's 1965 intervention in Kashmir as a case study.

James and Özdamar demonstrate that the Indo-Pakistani conflict over the region of Kashmir involves religious identity issues from the Indian perspective, but from the Pakistani perspective it involves the motivation of defending Islam from India's secular influences. Pakistan also uses Islam to legitimate its actions in the international arena and to mobilize international support for its cause.

Auerbach examines how religious motivations contribute to forgiveness and reconciliation between parties with a history of mutual violence and antagonism. Frisch examines another aspect of religious ideology and doctrine—whether it is truly a motivation for the behavior of Yasser Arafat's Fatah movement or is simply a tool to legitimate the movement and to counter the influence of Palestinian Islamic fundamentalist movements. Rynhold similarly examines whether the religiosity of Israelis impacts on their attitudes toward the Israeli–Palestinian conflict.

Cohen reminds us that the international law of war is based on religious doctrine and examines how Jewish doctrine has evolved to develop a similar set of precepts that guide many Israeli soldiers who must deal with issues of morality and war on a daily basis. This moral code grants legitimacy to many actions taken by these soldiers and is taught and supported in Israel's national religious movement's institutions.

## Why Did International Relations Theory Ignore Religion for Much of the Twentieth Century?

Other than Ellingsen, who focuses less on why religion was ignored than on why the study of religion and religion itself are experiencing a revival, the authors in this volume do not directly address this issue. Nevertheless, it is critically important because it colors all of their topics. All of the authors, to some extent, must grapple with the problem of being among the first to try to integrate religion into international relations and current social science theory. Accordingly, a brief discussion of the history of religion in the social sciences is in order. For reasons which are made clear by this discussion, in order to understand why international relations has ignored religion, it is necessary to first discuss some of the other social sciences.

To a great extent, the social sciences were founded upon the work of luminaries like Durkheim, Freud, Marx, Nietzsche, Voltaire, and Weber, who believed that primordial forces like religion were giving way to more rational and scientific modes of thought which would provide the basis for a new society free of the superstitions and prejudices of the past. This trend is most apparent in sociology. Sociology was born in the context of tensions between religion and liberal culture in Europe. In this struggle against the old status quo which included religious authority, reason and science challenged religion's monopoly on the mind and consciousness. Because of this, the founding generations of sociologists were not disinterested analysts but were advocates for the science and reason which would crush what they saw as the ignorance and superstition caused by religion. Thus the reason most founding sociologists wrote about religion was not because they felt it was to be an important social force in the future but because its perceived death throes were a major issue of their era.[9]

This denial of any real importance of religion by sociologists became formalized into what is now known as secularization theory. This body of theory argues that modern factors like economic development, urbanization, modern social institutions, pluralism, growing rates of literacy and education, and advancements in science and technology would lead to religion becoming an irrelevant force in the world. Modern political and social institutions usurped most of the traditional roles of religion in society. Religious norms of behavior were replaced by technical and rational criteria designated by bureaucratic and scientific sources. Also, the focus of social institutions shifted from communities, a stronghold of religion, to the entire society. Because of this, society devoted less resources to religion.[10] Thus there was little need to deal with religion as an important social factor. When sociologists did address religion, it was as a source of identity—or they focused on what they considered extreme and deviant phenomena.[11]

The origins of the rejection of religion by political scientists is less obvious, but the result was the same. The dominant theory on religion in political science for much of the twentieth century was modernization theory. While this body of theory focused on ethnicity, it was also clearly meant to apply to religion.[12] Its arguments roughly paralleled the arguments of sociologists.

International relations theory, while similarly ignoring religion, is unique among the social sciences for two reasons. First, it has no theory explaining why religion is not important in the modern era. That this is so is simply assumed. If religion must be dealt with it is usually placed within some more secular category such as culture, civilizations, or terrorism.[13] The debate over Samuel Huntington's "clash of civilizations" theory is a case in point. Huntington predicted that conflict in the post–cold war era would be primarily between several "civilizations" which he defined to a large extent based on religion. However, other than in the definitions of his civilizations the term "religion" was rarely used. The detractors of this theory also tended to avoid the term "religion" wherever possible, preferring terms like "culture," "state," "nationalism," and "ethnic group" when referring to the subcivilizational groupings that many of them felt would remain the basis for world conflict.[14] Thus, while many religious factors were discussed, they were rarely discussed overtly.

Second, not only was international relations theory (like the other social sciences) founded upon the belief that religion was receding from the world as an important factor, it can be argued that the modern context for the relations between states was founded upon intentionally secular principles. The modern concept of the territorial state, the basis for modern international relations, was articulated by the Treaty of Westphalia in 1648. This treaty was designed to end the Thirty Years' War between Protestant and Catholic states. In doing so it developed a format for relations between states which intentionally did not include religion. Some like Phiplott argue that the process of removing religion from international relations actually started with the Protestant Reformation and culminated with the Treaty of Westphalia. It is certainly true that this treaty put an end to any remaining overarching authority of the Catholic Church and the Holy Roman Empire over states and recognized that each state had total sovereignty, a situation that remains true today. It also ended intervention by states in the affairs of other states over matters of religion.[15]

These two factors combine to form a profound rejection of religion in international relations theory. International relations journals rarely directly address the topic of religion.[16] Unlike the other social sciences, which are discussed below, it is unclear whether this is changing. The events of September 11, in which religiously motivated terrorists operating from a transnational network with the support (or at least acquiescence) of some state governments killed over three thousand people, should have served as a wake-up call for international relations theorists and state governments alike, yet it is not clear whether this has actually happened. Reactions have been tentative and ambivalent.

For example, the Bush administration approach is to treat the Al Qaeda terrorists as followers of an illegitimate and abhorrent branch of Islam which is not representative of the "true Islam." Issues of the legitimacy of this interpretation of Islam and the standing of an administration made up mostly of Protestant Christians to decide which interpretations of Islam are legitimate aside, this approach obfuscates the undeniable fact that the perpetrators of these acts were motivated and continue to be motivated by their religious beliefs. Furthermore, the members of Al Qaeda are likely not the only international actors who are motivated at least in part by religious beliefs. On the other side of the coin, the U.S. State Department has recently begun publishing a yearly report on religious human rights around the world. Thus, the U.S. government both admits and denies the importance of religion in international affairs.

The reaction of international relations scholars has been similar. A recent special edition of the international relations journal *Millennium*[17] on religion and international relations (which was published before September 11) exemplifies this ambivalence. Most of the articles in the journal addressed either international relations *or* religion. Few, with some notable exceptions, addressed both.

Sociologists are similarly ambivalent. A recent edition of the journal *Sociology of Religion*[18] was devoted entirely to the debate over whether secularization theory is still valid. The debate centered around two issues. First, whether secularization means that people are becoming less religious or it means that religion is moving from the public sphere to the private one. Second, whether either of these are happening. That secularization theory is being seriously questioned at all is a revolutionary development in sociology, but it is clear that the old guard remains strong.

Political scientists began to recognize religion as an important factor around 1980, if one can put a date to it. Events and processes like the Iranian Revolution, Ronald Reagan's election victory with the support of the religious Right, and the worldwide rise of fundamentalism all contributed to this. Even so, until the 1993 events in Waco, Texas, only a few academics considered religious violence in the West anything other than an epiphenomenon.[19] Also, while the recognition of religion as an important factor is growing, it has not yet reached the mainstream of political science.

Given all of this, scholars who wish to understand the role of religion in world politics must, to a great extent, start from scratch. They must either create new bases for their theories or adopt existing bodies of theory to the topic of religion and world politics. Recent events, including but not limited to those of September 11, have clearly shown that religion is, at the very least, an important intervening variable in international relations. Thus this effort to address the topic is a crucial one. This brings us to the next central question of this volume.

## Some More Specific Questions on Religion, International Relations, and the Social Sciences

This section focuses on a set of more specific questions designed to elicit how well current international relations and social sciences theory deals with religion and what needs to be done so that these disciplines can better address the issue. We first articulate the questions and then examine how the individual authors in this volume deal with the issues raised by these questions.

### *To What Extent are International Relations and Social Science Theory Equipped to Deal with the Issue of Religion and What Aspects of These Bodies of Theory Can Be Applied or Modified in Order to Better Understand the Role of Religion in World Politics?*

This question is particularly pertinent to the study of international relations. This is because unlike the other social sciences, not only was the study of international relations in part founded on the belief that religion was becoming unimportant, the modern Westphalian state system itself (following a bloody religious war that lasted decades) was founded with the precise intention of keeping religion out of international politics. Nevertheless, existing theories can be applied to better understand the role of religion in world politics.

## To What Extent are the Religious Phenomena Being Examined Transnational or Domestic in Origin? If They are Domestic in Origin, to What Extent Do They Have an Impact Beyond the Borders of the State in Which They Originated?

This question relates to the Westphalian origins of international relations. As discussed above, the Treaty of Westphalia tried to keep religion from influencing the relations between states by keeping issues of religion within the arena of domestic politics. This view is echoed in international relations theory. For example, while some realists might admit that religion influences domestic politics they argue that it clearly has no influence on foreign policies—which are based solely on material or international order concerns. Thus both the locality of religious phenomena and their ability to travel across borders are in question.

There are three possible answers to this question. First, a particular religious phenomenon is domestic in origin and has little influence beyond the domestic arena. Second, the religious phenomenon in question is domestic in origin but has an influence beyond the borders of the state in which it originated. Third, some religious phenomena may be transnational in their origin and impact. These types of issues include the overlapping phenomena of fundamentalism, political Islam, and religious terrorism.

At the same time we must remember that the doctrine of just war has religious origins. In the current international system this doctrine is not limited to the international system and crosses into the domestic sphere.

## When Religion is Used to Justify Actions, to What Extent are the Motivations for These Actions Religious and to What Extent are They Nonreligious?

In other words, is religion a causal factor or is it a justification for actions motivated by nonreligious factors? This question is not a new one. The argument that religion serves as a tool for more basic social factors and motivations has deep roots in the social sciences. In fact, it is the essence of Marx's famous argument that religion is the opiate of the masses. This particular argument is an example of a larger school of thought found mostly among sociologists called functionalism. The various forms of this argument have religion as a tool for social control, the social cement that bonds society together, or a means for preventing social conflict.[20] More importantly, this argument is beginning to spread to international relations theorists.[21]

Clearly this does occur. However, it is argued here that while religion may be used to justify actions that are not religiously motivated, this does not mean that religious motivations never influence actions. In fact, to argue that this never occurs is a difficult argument to support and obvious examples of religiously motivated political actions are abundant. The attacks of September 11 are one among many such examples. Nevertheless it is important to differentiate between religion in its capacity as a motivating factor and religion in its capacity as a legitimizing factor. For this reason, the list of ways religion can influence behavior presented earlier in this essay does exactly this.

Also, even if religion is used to justify actions motivated by other concerns, this does not mean religion has no impact. If a politician can "play the religion card," meaning using religion to justify an action or mobilize people around a cause that is not religious in origin, this means that religion can be said to be "in the deck." That is, if religion can be used as a legitimating or mobilizing tool, this means it has some resonance among the masses who are the target of these attempts at legitimation and mobilization.

### *Does the Manifestation of Religion in Question Originate with the Elites or the Masses?*

This question can likely be applied to most issues. That is, are foreign policies driven by the elites or the masses? It certainly applies to religion. Many theories of religion and politics focus on the relationship between religious and political elites.[22] However, others argue that the inclusion of the masses into the political process has also allowed the religious among the masses to influence policy.[23] Religion in comparison to nationalism is even more mass oriented. This question also has larger implications with regard to international relations theory because it raises the question of the extent to which foreign policy is driven by mass sentiment as opposed to elite preferences.

### *Some Answers*

The authors in this volume deal with these issues in different ways. Auerbach notes that the realist paradigm is unequipped to deal with conflict resolution that includes elements beyond material interests, including identity issues. She draws from the socio-psychological literature to explain how religion can be part of the processes of forgiveness and reconciliation. While it is clear that the motivation for this forgiveness and reconciliation is not purely religious, religion can play an important role.

Cohen discussed how *ius ad bellum*, when it is just to go to war, plays out in the context of Jewish law. The concept of applying religion to justify going to war is a transnational one as it exists in most theological traditions and is, in fact, one of the bases for modern international law of war. While the interpretation of Jewish law is primarily in the hands of elites, it is the soldiers on the ground who must apply its precepts. Also, while the motivations for many military actions by Israeli soldiers are driven by nonreligious concerns, many soldiers from the national religious movement rely on these moral precepts to guide their actions.

The quantitative studies in this volume have considerably similar approaches and results. Both of them modify general conflict theory to incorporate religion. Ellingsen shows that people are becoming more religious but some world civilizations are more religious than others. She also shows that both religiosity and religious identity impact on armed conflict but other nonreligious factors remain important (and are likely more important) than the religious ingredient. Pearce shows that religious identity conflicts are common among territorial conflicts and make them more violent, but the presence of religious issues in such conflicts make them less violent. This implies that nonreligious issues can often be more important motivations for violence than religious issues. Thus both of these studies show that religion is an important element in world conflict, but it is clearly not the only element and is often secondary to other aspects of these conflicts.

Oldmixon et al. apply traditional methods of congressional voting analysis to the question of whether religion influences votes in the U.S. Congress on an important foreign policy issue, the Israeli–Palestinian conflict. This approach focuses both on the attitudes of elites (the representatives) and on the impact of the American voter. It also provides an excellent example of how international diasporas can influence domestic politics as well as how domestic and often subdomestic religious factors can influence foreign policy decisions.

James and Özdamar also look at the links between the domestic and international, focusing on the foreign policies of India and Pakistan with regard to the conflict over Kashmir. From the Indian perspective, the conflict involves domestic factors including religious identity, nonreligious economic and political factors, and ethnic and cultural factors which overlap, but are not synonymous with, religion. India's motivations also include elite-driven nation-building policies, and more recently Hindu nationalism. From the Pakistani perspective the conflict involves resisting India's secular influence in the region, which conflicts with Pakistan's Islamic ideology (including its desire to include Kashmiri Muslims in an Islamic homeland), as well as religious identity issues. Pakistan also uses religion to legitimate its actions in the international arena. Yet even for Pakistan, the conflict involves more secular issues like territorial integrity and economic issues. Also, the entire conflict has been influenced by nonreligious processes including cold war and post–cold war alliances, but the conflict began with the British partition of the two states based on religious identity. Thus domestic and systemic religious factors contribute to interstate conflict, but they are certainly not the only issues involved in the conflict.

Ghose and James build a model that can account for the impact of religious identity and religious belief systems on international intervention at the domestic, regional, and international levels of analysis and apply this model to Pakistan's intervention in India in 1965. Their model also integrates the impact of nonreligious factors including institutional constraints, national leadership, and regional and international hierarchies and organizations. They find that while religion, along with many nonreligious factors, impacts on the regional and domestic aspects of the conflict, it did not impact on the international aspects.

Frisch and Rynhold both use traditional comparative analyses to examine the Israeli–Palestinian conflict. Frisch focuses on the question of whether the religious symbolism used by Yasser Arafat and his Fatah movement is truly motivated by religion or whether it is a more cynical attempt to use religion to mobilize the masses and counter the influence of his political opponents, the Palestinian Islamic fundamentalist movements. He concludes that the latter is the case. Rynhold examines the impact of religion in Israeli attitudes toward the Israeli–Palestinian conflict. He concludes that the ideologies and behavior of secular and religious Israelis are impacted by their religiosity, among both the "hawks" and "doves." While both of these analyses focus primarily on domestic issues, the impact of the conflict dynamics of the Israeli–Palestinian conflict has considerable international implications.

Overall, the contributions to this volume show that with some ingenuity, social science and international relations theory can and must be adopted to address the impact of religion on world politics. Religion's impact on world politics includes both domestic aspects which can cross borders and transnational issues which impact multiple states, if not the entire world. While religious motivations are often important, world politics is complicated and these religious motivations rarely exist in a vacuum. That is, religious motivations and causes of conflict and other political phenomena are generally mixed with other secular motivations and causes, with the religious aspects often being less important than the nonreligious ones. These motivations and causes are sometimes elite-driven but also often originate at the level of mass politics. Finally, all of the contributions to this volume provide further evidence that, despite predictions to the contrary, religion remains a vibrant and important element of world politics. Nevertheless, the task of theory building and rigorous research is still ahead of us. The answers we provided are limited and partial in terms of scope and profoundness. We call upon students of international relations to continue to investigate the role of religion in world politics, a pattern we don't see disappearing any time soon.

**Notes**

1. Samuel P. Huntington, "The Clash of Civilizations?" *Foreign Affairs* 72, no. 3 (1993): 22–49; Samuel P. Huntington, *The Clash of Civilizations and the Remaking of the World Order* (New York: Simon and Schuster, 1996).

2. Fred Halliday, "A New World Myth," *New Statesman* 10, no. 447 (1997): 42–43; Stephen N. Walt, "Building Up New Bogeymen." *Foreign Policy* 106 (1997): 177–89.

3. Alexander Wend, *Social Theory of International Politics* (Cambridge: Cambridge University Press, 1999).

4. Kenneth D. Wald, *Religion and Politics in the United States* (New York: St. Martins, 1987).

5. R. Scott Appleby, *The Ambivalence of the Sacred: Religion, Violence, and Reconciliation* (New York: Rowman and Littlefield, 2000).

6. M. Benjamin Mollov, *Power and Transcendence: Hans J. Morgenthau and the Jewish Experience* (Lanham, MD: Lexington Books, 2002), 3–8.

7. Mark Juergensmeyer, *The New Cold War?* (Berkeley: University of California, 1993).

8. Jonathan Fox, "Do Religious Institutions Support Violence or the Status Quo?" *Studies in Conflict and Terrorism* 22, no. 2 (1999): 119–39.

9. Jeffrey K. Hadden, "Toward Desacralizing Secularization Theory," *Social Forces* 65, no. 3 (1987): 589–91.

10. Bryan R. Wilson, *Religion in Sociological Perspective* (Oxford: Oxford University Press, 1982).

11. Kenneth Westhus, "The Church in Opposition," *Sociological Analysis* 73, no. 4 (1976): 314.

12. R. Scott Appleby, Religious Fundamentalisms and Global Conflict. Foreign Policy Association Headline Series 301 (New York: Foreign Policy Association, 1994), 7–8; Jeff Haynes, *Religion in Third World Politics* (Boulder, CO: Lynne Rienner, 1994), 21–23.

13. Vendulka Kabalkova, "Towards an International Political Theology," *Millennium* 29, no. 3 (2000): 682–83.

14. Huntington's detractors also made a number of other arguments—that the world is uniting into a single society, that he got his facts wrong, and that he ignored some other important factors which contradict his theory. For a full discussion of Huntington's theory and the debate surrounding it, see Jonathan Fox, "Ethnic Minorities and the Clash of Civilizations: A Quantitative Analysis of Huntington's Thesis," *British Journal of Political Science* 32, no. 3 (2002): 415–34; Jonathan Fox, *Religion, Civilization, and Civil War Since 1945* (Lanham, MD: Lexington Books, 2004).

15. Daniel Philpott, "The Challenge of September 11 to Secularism in International Relations," *World Politics* 55, no. 1 (2002): 66–95.

16. Daniel Philpott, *Revolutions in Sovereignty: How Ideas Shaped Modern International Relations* (Princeton: Princeton University Press, 2001).

17. *Millennium*. Religions in International Relations [Special Issue]. 29, no. 3 (2000).

18. *Sociology of Religion* 60, no. 3 (1999).

19. Jeffrey Kaplan, "Introduction," *Terrorism and Political Violence* 14, no. 1 (2002): 2.

20. Jonathan Fox, *Ethnoreligious Conflict in the Late 20th Century: A General Theory* (Lanham, MD: Lexington Books, 2002), 65–68.

21. For example, at a recent symposium on religion and international relations at Lewis and Clark College in Portland, OR, on April 14, 2003, Jonathan Gallagher made precisely this argument.

22. See, for example, Anthony Gill and Arang Keshavarzian, "State Building and Religious Resources: An Institutional Theory of Church-State Relations in Iran and Mexico," *Politics and Society* 27, no. 3 (1999): 431–65; Bruce Lincoln, ed., *Religion, Rebellion and Revolution* (London: Macmillin, 1985).

23. Barry Rubin, "Religion and International Affairs," in *Religion, the Missing Dimension of Statecraft*, ed. Douglas Johnston and Cynthia Sampson (Oxford: Oxford University Press, 1994), 23.

# Toward a Revival of Religion and Religious Clashes?

TANJA ELLINGSEN

> The assumption we live in a secularized world is false.... The world today is as furiously religious as it ever was.
> —Berger, The Desecularization of the World

## Introduction

Cultural studies and an emphasis on culture (and thus also religion) were in the mainstream of the social sciences in the 1940s and 1950s.[1] However, with the stunning success of the Marshall Plan in Europe and the rebuilding of Japan, optimism abounded and most social scientists seemed to believe that modernization would lead to a decline in ethnic and religious identities, to be replaced by loyalties to larger communities.[2] The argument was that ethnicity and religion were traditional forms of social identity that would pass away with the advent of modernity.[3]

With the exception of a short honeymoon following the fall of the iron curtain, this optimism has been tempered. The result has been a renaissance in cultural studies in general, and religious studies in particular, over the last fifteen years.[4]

Within this literature on religion, two issues seem to receive a lot of attention: (a) a resurgence or revival of religion as an important factor in people's daily life, and (b) religion and religious differences as conflict-generating factors.[5] Finally, several scholars combine the two issues and argue that since the end of the cold war we are witnessing an increase in religious clashes.[6]

But to what extent do these claims have real validity to them? This is the central question asked in this article. As such, the article focuses on the importance of religion to people, over time and across various cultures. More specifically, I investigate the importance of religion to people in terms of their daily life, as well as in terms of their motivations for warfare. Is religion more important to people now than earlier? If so, is this a worldwide trend or is it limited to specific regions and cultures? To what extent do religious differences translate into hostility and even domestic armed conflicts?

In the following pages I start with a review of the arguments put forth as to *why we are witnessing a revival* of religion as a source of identity to people. From this literature I derive four hypotheses that are tested by data from the WVS in 1981–84, 1990–93, and 1995–97. I then move on to the arguments as to *why religious differences would cause conflict*. From this literature I end up with three additional hypotheses, which are subsequently tested by data for the period 1946–2002 from the Uppsala Conflict database. Finally, I make a conclusion and suggest implications for the policy community.

## Why a Revival of Religion?

The answer to this question is oftentimes based on two types of explanations. One is that *religion always has mattered for world politics* and that the advocates of modernity and secularization theory failed to see this because their perceptions have been clouded by their theories. Further, the superpower rivalry during the cold war era left scholars with the impression of the realist paradigm being the only "game in town."[7] Thus, as the cold war ended, scholars finally become attuned to what has always been an important factor in international affairs: culture—and in particular religion.

The second, and possibly most powerful, explanation for why religion has become more important to people is ironically enough related to *the process of modernization*. This is the very same factor which according to "modernization theorists" should result in cultural factors becoming irrelevant, creating a "global village" oriented beyond national and cultural boundaries.[8] In contrast to the modernization theorists, these scholars argue that the more a society is exposed to modernization, the more its people may yearn for a deeper meaning to life. This is a result of modernization contributing to a breakdown in community values, lifestyles, and traditions, causing widespread feelings of dislocation, alienation, and disorientation.[9]

Since globalization is usually considered as the latest stage of modernization, this argument has also found its way into the globalization literature. Harvey, for instance, suggests that today's globalization, associated with the most recent times-pace compression, might lead to the need to discover or manufacture deeper meanings and interpretations.[10] The same conclusion is found in Beyer, who focuses on the grand religious traditions of the world and theorizes on the ways these might be affected by globalization processes. He describes the implications of globalization for religion as follows:

> If particular cultures are to survive in altered form in the modern global context, the religious traditions are facing the serious challenge of the relativized context. Given that religion deals with absolutes, this adjustment should result in significant crises within those traditions.[11]

Instead of adjusting to these changes, possible consequences of globalization are an increased focus on religion, a new search for authenticity and authority in politics (growing nationalism), a revival of interest in basic institutions (family and community), or a new emphasis on tradition. This relationship is evident in the most secular and modernist country in the world, the United States, which is believed to have about 60 million evangelicals who crave a return to more traditional religious values in governmental as well as social practices.[12] This development also seems to confirm Dobbelaere's and Lambert's arguments that religion is moving from the public to the private sphere.[13]

Modernization (and thus globalization) may pose further problems for societies whose cultures do not constitute the principal medium through which development takes place.[14] A lack of economic development, combined with increased levels of urbanization and education, is one of the ways in which modernization poses a problem. As large numbers of people are uprooted from their traditional life but do not benefit from development, they face a crisis of identity. The result is relative deprivation, which generates feelings of frustration and hence aggression.[15] In other words, it is *the failure of modernization* within these societies that causes grievances.

Such grievances are evident in Africa, Asia, the Middle East, and parts of Latin America, and in most cases modernization is closely associated with Westernization and cultural imperialism. According to Huntington, for instance, the naive faith in a "global village" has been based on the belief that Western civilization is embracing the whole world and becoming universal. This has mainly been a Western conception, Huntington says, as Westerners have perceived as universal what non-Westerners have considered as something Western. Although cultural imperialism admittedly might lead to homogenization in some areas (mostly limited to commercial products such as *Baywatch*, Levis, Coca-Cola, McDonald's, etc.), for the most part it leads to counterreactions, increasing levels of hostility, and dislike toward the West and Western values.[16]

Alternative discourses of power, which may appear irrational on the basis of conventional notions of scientific rationality, may emerge among groups to challenge the modernist agenda in such societies. Religion (especially in the form of religious fundamentalism) is a strong candidate in that regard, providing people a way to define, restore, and reinforce their personal and communal identity, which has been destroyed by modernist aspirations. Such groups tend to gain more strength the more people are excluded from the benefits of modernization and the more they are convinced that there is a rich cultural alternative to fall back on. This can be seen in East Asia where processes of indigenization, Asianization, re-Islamization, and rejection of Western values are occurring.[17]

Globalization and modernization have further resulted in increased contact between people of different religions, languages, and ethnicities. While some argue that this should lead to greater understanding and tolerance toward others, Huntington argues that such contact increases the awareness of cultural differences, and hence also reinforces such differences.[18]

Finally, modern communications and technology have also increased the ability of religious movements to organize, coordinate, and share ideas on a global scale. Communication through the Internet, increased tourism and refugee flows, and bank transfers all make the organization of religious diasporas—as well as international terrorist cells—much easier. In this sense, modernization and globalization facilitates the construction and consolidation of religiously based social identities.[19]

Obviously a number of propositions or hypotheses could be put forward in order to test the religious revival thesis properly. Four issues seem, nevertheless, particularly central to it: (a) that religion continues to be important to people in their daily lives and that to some extent it also has become more important to people now, than ever; (b) that religion is more important in certain cultures/civilizations than in others; (c) despite this, religion still is important to people in the West; (d) it is in the countries where modernization has failed that religion is particularly important.

These issues are stated as the following four hypotheses:

Hypothesis 1 ($H_1$): Religion is as (or even more) important to people now than ever.
Hypothesis 2 ($H_2$): Religion is less important in the West than in other civilizations.
Hypothesis 3 ($H_3$): However, religion is still important in the West.
Hypothesis 4 ($H_4$): Poor countries find religion more important than rich countries.

In order to test these hypotheses, one has to connect them to some relevant data. The WVS consist of a number of issues including political attitudes, economic income, trust in government, life satisfaction, values, and identities. In this paper I only look at the aspect of religion. More specifically, when testing hypothesis 1 I use five different variables to measure the importance of religion:[20]

(1) Whether people believe in God or not (0 = "No," 1 = "Yes")
(2) Whether people find comfort in religion or not (0 = "No," 1 = "Yes")
(3) The importance of religion to people (on a scale from 1–4, where 4 is "very important")
(4) The importance of God to people (on a scale from 1–10, where 10 is "very important")
(5) The level of church attendance (on a scale from 1–7, where 7 is "more than once a week")

As is evident from Table 1, hypothesis 1 is supported. When comparing the proportion of respondents who find religion and religious issues to be highly important to them over time, this number has increased slightly from 1981 to 1996. This is true for all five dependent variables except church attendance, which is almost as high in 1996 as it was in 1981. For the variable "belief in God" the increase is so small that it is not significant at the .05 level. However, the increase in the number of respondents that find comfort in religion, as well as those who consider religion and God to be very important, is significant even at the .01 level. This is interesting and one possible interpretation is that although people do not necessarily attend church more, and though the overall proportion of people who believe in God is not increasing, people generally find more comfort in religion and thus find God and religion to be more important in their lives. Since most of the changes are quite small, however, the results should be interpreted with caution. The overall conclusion is nevertheless that religion is at least as important as it used to be, and in some respects might have become more important to people over time.[21]

Hypothesis 2 was that *religion is less important in the West than in other civilizations.* Figure 1 shows the effect of civilization on the mean national level of religiosity. To have a sample covering as many civilizations as possible, this analysis is limited to the third wave of WVS conducted in 1995–1997.[22]

**Table 1.** The proportion of respondents who find religion and religious issues to be highly important to them, by wave

|  | 1981 | 1990 | 1996 | Total |
|---|---|---|---|---|
| Belief in God | **85.8** (12,335) | **83.9** (14,180) | **85.9** (10,916) | **85.1** (37,431) |
| Comfort in Religion | **65.1** (8,639) | **60.3** (9,990) | **67.8** (8,398) | **64.0** (27,027) |
| Importance of Religion |  | **30.6** (11,938) | **36.6** (13,534) | **33.5** (25,472) |
| Importance of God | **30.3** (4,676) | **30.5** (5,539) | **36.9** (5,275) | **32.4** (15,490) |
| Level of Church Attendance | **28.1** (4,592) | **23.1** (3,865) | **27.8** (4,065) | **26.3** (12,522) |

Note: The proportion of respondents reported as "highly religious" refers to the proportion of respondents who said that they believed in God, that they found comfort in religion, that they found religion to be very important (value 4), that God received a score of 8 or higher in importance to them on a scale from 1 to 10, and that they attended church once a week or more (score 6 or 7). The proportion is reported in percent (in bold) and in number of respondents in parentheses.

There are 12 countries included in all three waves. As the number of total respondents varies for each of the variables, this is not reported here due to space limitations. For a list of countries and respondents see appendix 1.

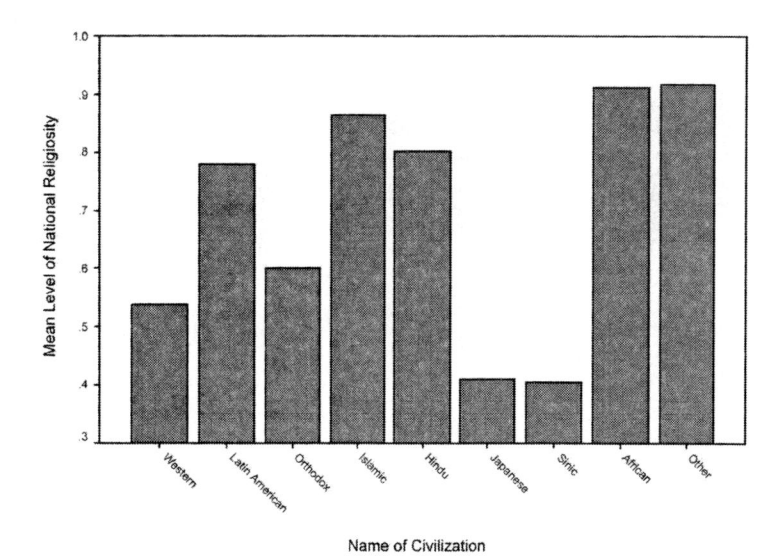

**Figure 1.** Mean level of national religiosity by civilizational belonging, 1996. Note: The category for "Other" refers to the Philippines. Classification of countries into civilizations is based on information from the *CIA World Factbook* of the majority religion within the country where the respondents live. For additional information see appendix 2. Number of total countries included is 63.

As Figure 1 shows, the civilizations which have the highest mean level of national religiosity are the African and the Islamic civilizations.[23] Furthermore, the mean level of national religiosity is lower in the Western civilization than in most other civilizations. The exceptions are the Japanese and the Sinic civilization where the national level of religiosity is even lower than in the West. This is not quite as anticipated, but of all the civilizations outside the West, the Japanese and the Sinic are the ones where the modernization process has been most successful, and the socioeconomic levels within these areas could thus explain why religion is not as important in these civilizations.[24] Further, the fact that the number of countries included in the Japanese and Sinic civilization actually is two (Japan and China), while the Western civilization includes twenty-seven countries (some which score high and some which score low on religiosity) has to be taken into consideration.[25] Thus, although not fully supported, hypothesis 2 gets partial support.

My third hypothesis was that *religion is still important in the West*. As Figure 1 shows, the mean level of national religiosity within the West is .537. This means that over 50 percent of the population within the Western civilization considers religion or religious issues very important to them. This must be seen as a support of hypothesis 3, especially since the other 47 percent do not necessarily consider religion as something unimportant. Furthermore, although there are some variations between the countries within the Western civilization, most countries within the Western civilization fall within the range of .4–.6 as depicted in Figure 2.

Both of these findings are further confirmed in the multivariate analysis in Table 2. As Table 2 shows, the national level of religiosity in most civilizations outside the West is higher than the West, even when controlling for economic and political conditions. However, it is only the estimates for the Islamic, African, and Latin American civilizations which are positive and significant at the .05 level. The coefficients for the Hindu

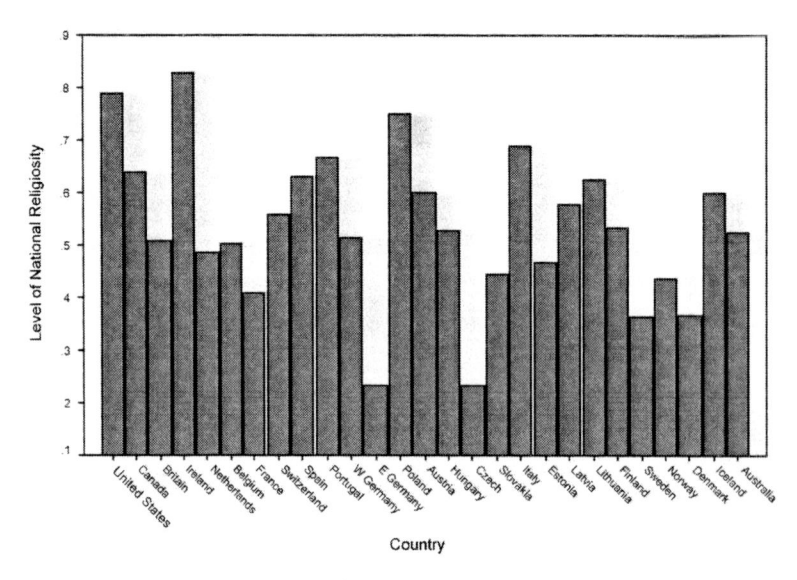

**Figure 2.** Level of national religiosity within the Western civilization, 1996. Note: The number of countries included in the Western civilization is 27.

civilization (India) and the Orthodox civilization are positive, but not significant even at the .10 level. The estimates for the Sinic and Japanese civilization are negative, but not significant.

Turning to my fourth hypothesis, Table 2 also shows that rich countries seem to find religion less important than poor countries (close to significant at the .05 level). This is in line with several other studies of political values which find that the economic conditions within a country are an important factor as respondents from poor countries are far more likely to stress traditional values such as material wellbeing, strong leaders, military strength, and religion than respondents from rich countries.[26]

The type of political regime has also been argued to have an effect on the level of national religiosity.[27] As political participation and freedom of speech results in broader political discussion where different views and values are expressed and exchanged, and as most democracies are economically better off, traditional values such as religion become less important to people. Despite this, the coefficient for polity score is small but positive, indicating that the higher the score the more democratic the country and the more religious the country.[28] However this finding is not significant.

Looking at how much the different variables explain the national level of religiosity, the Adjusted $R^2$ shows that civilizations alone explain .540 of the dependent variable, while Gross Domestic Product (GDP) per capita and polity score together explain .383. The economic, political, and civilization variable together explain .561 of the variance of the national level of religiosity. Thus, the national level of religiosity is more dependent upon which civilization (religion) a country belongs to, rather than economic and political conditions. This is in direct contrast to the arguments put forth in modernization theory literature.

In sum, although most of these findings indicate that there is a slight tendency that religion has become more important to people than previously, the clearest

**Table 2.** Level of national religiosity by civilization and control-variables, wave 3 (1995–97)

|  | Importance of religion (index) | | |
|---|---|---|---|
|  | B | Robust St. error | Sig. |
| Economic and Political Conditions | | | |
| GDP per capita (ln) | −.081 | .041 | .057 |
| Polity score (ln) | .012 | .007 | .114 |
| Civilizations | | | |
| Latin American | .204 | .055 | .000 |
| Orthodox | .026 | .055 | .640 |
| Islamic | .239 | .088 | .009 |
| Hindu | .114 | .147 | .445 |
| Japanese | −.102 | .125 | .419 |
| Sinic | −.101 | .086 | .245 |
| African | .312 | .101 | .003 |
| (Constant) | 1.203 | 0.361 | 0.002 |
| Adj. $R^2$ (Economic and Political Conditions) | .383 | | |
| Adj. $R^2$ (Civilizations) | .540 | | |
| Adj. $R^2$ (All Variables) | .561 | | |

Note: I use ordinary least squares (OLS) estimation. Total number of countries included 62. The omitted variables in Civilizations are Western countries and the Philippines. Civilizational belonging is based on information from the *CIA World Factbook*. GDP per capita is obtained from the World Bank's 2003 World Development Indicators CD-Rom for 1994, the year before wave three (1995–97) was conducted. Polity score is based on the Polity IV data set from Marshall, Jaggers, and Gurr (2003) and varies from 10 (most democratic) to −10 (most autocratic). Here I have only used the 1994 data.

finding is that of stability. Thus, rather than seeing a radical resurgence of religion, the impression is that religion continues to be an important factor in peoples lives—as it has been for ages. This is true for most civilizations, including the West. But how and why does religion (and religious differences) translate into conflict?

## Why Do Religion and Religious Differences Cause Conflict?

It is increasingly asserted that religion and religious differences cause conflict.[29] The arguments as to why this is so are partly based on the more general debate over the culture-conflict nexus, and partly based on the nature of religion in particular.

When it comes to the culture-conflict nexus, three perspectives have dominated the debate. On the one hand we have the *primordialists* who consider religion and ethnicity a deeply rooted cultural, psychological, and affective attachment to historical and ancestral ties.[30] Cultural divisions and tensions are "natural," and the latter are ultimately rooted in the first. As Isaacs puts it:

> Basic group identity consists of the ready-made set of endowments and identifications that every individual shares with others from the moment of birth by the chance of the family into which he is born.[31]

One recent example of the primordial perspective—and one of the most controversial—is Huntington's 1993 article in *Foreign Affairs* titled "Clash of Civilizations?" Here (as well as in his book of 1996) Huntington predicts that culture and cultural identities are the key elements shaping the patterns of peace and conflict in the post–cold war world. While people belonging to the same culture (civilization) will remain at peace with each other, people with different cultural backgrounds will clash. Since a civilization is the broadest level of cultural identity a person might have, the new world order is best described as one of "civilizational clashes."[32] As he puts it:

> In the modern world, religion is central, perhaps the central, force that motivates and mobilizes people... What ultimately counts for people is not political ideology or economic interest. Faith and family, blood and belief, are what people identify with and what they will fight and die for.[33]

The most frequent criticism of this approach is its assumption of fixed identities and its failure to account for variations in the level of conflict over time and place. In short, this perspective treats culture as a static phenomenon, and thus fails to explain the emergence of new and transformed identities. In doing so, it also fails to account for long periods in which culture is not a salient political characteristic, or where the relations between different cultural groups are comparatively peaceful.[34]

In contrast, *instrumentalists* argue that whether culture and cultural differences become salient issues is dependent upon whether the elites see it in their interest to use religion and ethnicity as tools to mobilize support for conflict or not. Thus, in this perspective, culture and cultural differences lead to conflict only if the elites see these factors as valuable instruments for obtaining access to social, political, and material resources.[35] Critics of this approach counter that the effectiveness of this tool or instrument is dependent upon other factors within the society—i.e., to what degree culture and cultural differences coincide with other cleavages within the society. This perspective, which is an attempt to synthesize the previous two, is known as the *constructivist* view and is reflected in the work of several scholars.[36]

Turning to why religion in particular would lead to conflict, Thomas argues that religions can be described as "closed" belief systems, and that they—like other ideologies and belief systems—frequently resist change. Furthermore, religious adherents often see other religious beliefs as a threat, leading to a continued struggle of primacy, thus increasing levels of hostility and conflict.[37] Religious conflicts are also considered to be more intractable because religious differences are said to be more fundamental than, for instance, ideological or economic differences. The argument is that religion is the main source of individual and social identity. Additionally, religious differences exclude—almost by definition—the possibility of compromise, coexistence, or the finding of common ground to resolve disputes. Thus, unlike territorial disputes and economic conflicts, conflict over ideas and religious beliefs cannot be solved.[38] According to Kegley and Wittkopf it is the irresolvable character of religion and religious differences that increases the risk—as well as the duration—of conflict.[39] Relating this to the claimed resurgence of religion as a source of identity, several scholars claim to see a revival of religious and ethnic conflicts, especially after the cold war.[40]

A number of hypotheses and propositions could be derived from this literature. Again, however, I choose to focus on a more narrow set of issues. More specifically I am interested in investigating three issues, all of which are central to the above literature: (a) that we are witnessing an increase in the number of conflicts over identity, (b) that religious differences cause conflict, and (c) that this is something new to the post-cold war era. I have formulated these issues into the following hypotheses:

Hypothesis 5 ($H_5$): The number of armed conflicts over identity is increasing throughout the world.

Hypothesis 6 ($H_6$): Religious heterogeneous countries have a higher risk of armed conflict than religious, homogeneous countries.

Hypothesis 7 ($H_7$): Religious, heterogeneous countries have a higher risk of armed conflict than religious, homogeneous countries—but only after the end of the cold war.

When testing these hypotheses, I use the Uppsala Conflict database which is presented annually in the *Journal of Peace Research*.[41]

When it comes to the validity of hypothesis 5, previous studies have shown that war today is rarely international. By far the largest number of wars today are internal wars.[42] This does not necessarily imply more cultural conflicts, though, as many of these internal conflicts actually take place between parties that are religiously or ethnicly similar. Figure 3 provides an overview of the number of intrastate cultural conflicts compared to noncultural ones. The black line shows the total number of ongoing intrastate conflicts in a given year.[43]

First, as Figure 3 shows, conflicts over identity are a continuing, and not a new, trend. Secondly, since the 1960s identity conflicts have been the dominant form of conflict within the world. Thirdly, although identity conflicts flourished—especially after the cold war—since 1996 they have decreased, and have currently stabilized around the level found in the mid-1970s. Thus, although conflicts over religion and ethnicity still seem to be an important issue, the increased focus on these conflicts might be better explained by the decrease in other types of conflict. In other words, it is not so much a resurgence of cultural conflict, as a persistence of it.

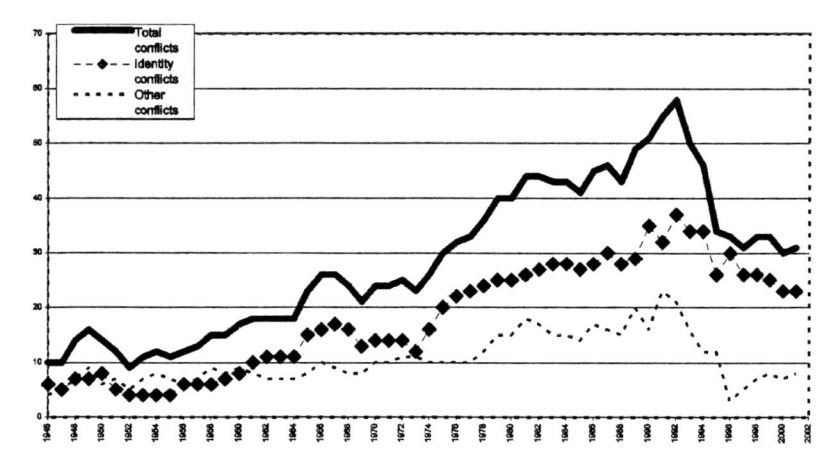

**Figure 3.** Number of armed intrastate conflicts by type, 1946–2002. Note: The conflict data is available at http://www.prio.no/cwp/armedconflict. The classification of conflicts into identity conflicts or not is based on Buhaug and Gates (2002) who define an armed conflict over identity as "one where the rebels originate from different ethnic and/or religious group than the government." For a list of all intrastate identity conflicts see appendix 3.

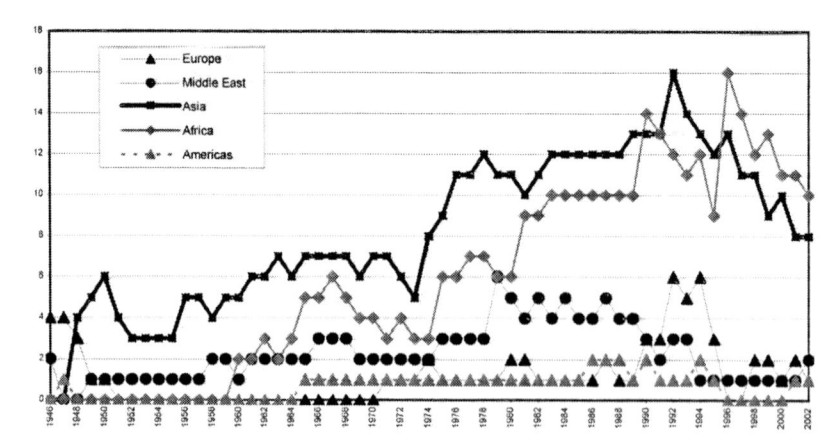

**Figure 4.** Number of armed intrastate identity conflicts by region, 1946–2002. Note: For classification of countries into regions see Michael Eriksson et al. "Armed Conflicts, 1989–2002," *Journal of Peace Research* 40, no. 5 (2003): 593–607.

Looking more specifically at the distribution of intrastate identity conflicts between regions in Figure 4, we can further question the idea of a cultural revival. Although identity conflicts occur in all regions, most of them have been taking place in Asia and Africa. This is as expected as these are the regions with the largest number of ethnic and religious divisions. However, while all regions did see an increase of these conflicts at the end of the cold war, in the last couple of years the numbers have been declining to about the level of identity conflicts seen in the 1970s. Thus, to the extent that we have been witnessing a cultural revival, it may seem as if it is fading again. Further more, Asia and Africa are not only the regions with the largest number of ethnic and religious divisions; they are also the poorest ones. Thus, although conflicts are channeled through ethnic and religious differences, these might not be the actual reasons for fighting.

When testing whether religious differences cause conflict (hypotheses 6 and 7), ran a multivariate analysis in Table 3. My dependent variable was intrastate armed conflicts as defined by the Uppsala Conflict database (see note 10), while my independent variable is *religious differences*, indicating if the country is split between two or more religious denominations (coded as 1 if it is and 0 if it is not).[44] This information is based on the *CIA World Fact Book/Handbook of the Nations*, the *Britannica Book of the Year*, and *the Demographic Yearbook*.

I also include a number of control variables, most of which have been found in previous studies to have an important effect on the propensity of intrastate armed conflict.

1. *Level of National Religiosity*: Whether religious differences cause intrastate armed conflict or not may be dependent upon the level of national religiosity. If religion generally is considered of less importance within the society, then it is less likely that such differences will create conflict. In order to control for this, I included the composite variable described in detail in note 8.
2. *Democracy*: Measures of regime type have proven remarkably robust, both in cross-measurement comparisons and in assessment of both national as well as dyadic conflict behavior. The standard democracy data used in quantitative studies

**Table 3.** Religious differences, control variables, and intrastate conflict during and after the cold war

| Variables | 1979–88 Model 1A | 1979–88 Model 2A | 1989–98 Model 1B | 1989–98 Model 2B |
|---|---|---|---|---|
| Religious Differences | .043 (.195) | −.002 (.359) | .502*** (.193) | .537* (.291) |
| Level of Religiosity | 2.636**** (0.546) | 1.352 (1.037) | 1.072** (0.500) | .513 (0.784) |
| Regime Type (lagged) | .036*** (.013) | .029 (.026) | .012 (.014) | −.005 (.021) |
| Regime Type, sq (lagged) | −.014**** (.002) | −.008 (.006) | −.011**** (.003) | −.005 (.004) |
| Socioeconomic Level (ln + lagged) | −.190 (.079) | .042 (.161) | −.255**** (.073) | −.037 (.117) |
| Growth (lagged) | −1.237 (1.281) | 1.464 (2.221) | −2.312* (1.382) | .084 (1.993) |
| Population (ln + lagged) | .556**** (.066) | .370*** (.134) | .300**** (.056) | .139 (.089) |
| Natural Resource Dependence | 2.068 (1.774) | 2.657 (2.843) | −6.575*** (1.691) | −4.331* (2.517) |
| Natural Resource Dependence (sq) | −2.801 (3.664) | −4.530 (3.970) | 8.482*** (2.924) | 5.055 (4.448) |
| Mountanious Terrain (ln) | .180*** (.063) | .221** (.129) | .189*** (.061) | .121 (.092) |
| Peace-Years | | −2.097**** (0.239) | | −1.819**** (0.203) |
| Spline | | −.057**** (.009) | | −.045**** (.007) |
| Spline 1 | | .013**** (.002) | | .009**** (.002) |
| Spline 2 | | −.001* (.0005) | | −.0001 (.0003) |
| Constant | −7.031**** (1.114) | −3.067 (2.218) | −2.703*** (0.968) | −.038 (1.456) |
| N | 1,231 | 1,231 | 1,193 | 1,193 |
| Log-likelihood | −519.353 | −181.007 | −524.656 | −268.177 |
| LR chi² | 222.64 | 899.33 | 193.92 | 706.88 |
| Pseudo R² | .177 | .713 | .156 | .569 |

Note: Logistic regression estimation. Standard error is reported in parentheses. * = $p < .10$, ** = $p < .05$, *** = $p < .01$, **** = $p < .0001$, two-tailed tests.

of the democratic peace is the Polity IV data. I have included a variable for polity score varying from 10 (most democratic) to −10 (most autocratic). Earlier findings show that democracies are least likely to experience civil war or internal armed conflict, followed by autocracies in the middle, and finally semi-democracies as being the most prone to these types of conflict.[45] To capture this inverted-U-curve relationship I have added a squared term of the polity scale. The regime type variable and its squared term have been lagged one year in order to determine causality.

3. *Socioeconomic Level*: Several studies of the causes of intrastate conflicts show poor countries are far more likely to experience intrastate conflict than affluent countries.[46] To measure the socioeconomic level I have used figures for GDP per capita obtained from the World Development Indicators (WDIs) of the World Bank.[47] Again, the variable has been log-transformed and varies between 5 (low socioeconomic level) to 11 (high socioeconomic level). The variable has further been lagged one year in order to determine causality.

4. *Economic Growth*: Worsening or improving economic conditions within a country also is known to affect the likelihood of conflict.[48] While negative economic growth may increase economic grievances and thus also aggression, economic improvements are expected to increase the level of life satisfaction and thus reduce the risk of intrastate armed conflict. This variable has also been lagged one year and has been taken from the WDIs.

5. *Natural Resource Dependence*: Collier and Hoeffler, as well as de Soysa, further find that natural resource dependence is related to intrastate armed conflict. In their view this is due to natural resources being a ready means for financing rebels. According to de Soysa, though, at very high levels of natural resource dependence, the government is able to control the population either by repressing or buying off its citizens.[49] In line with Collier and Hoeffler, natural resource dependence is operationalized as the ratio of primary commodity exports to GDP (in current U.S. dollars). This information was also obtained from the WDI information. To test for the inverted-U-curve relationship, I also added a squared term for primary commodity exports. Both variables were lagged one year.

6. *Mountainous Terrain*: The geographical characteristics of a country are also argued to have an effect on the risk of intrastate conflict.[50] The existence of swamps, forests, mountains, and jungles make it easier for rebel groups to hide, and thus may affect the risk of insurgents taking up arms. Like Fearon and Laitin, I thus include a variable for the proportion of a country that consists of mountains, information obtained from the World Bank Development Economics Research Group (DECRG) project on civil wars. This variable is also log transformed.

7. *Population*: The size of a state's population is also likely to affect the likelihood of conflict for two reasons: (1) more people implies more potential constellations for conflict and (2) large populations generally imply large geographical areas, meaning that obtaining control over the territory is probably more difficult. This information is taken from Penn World Tables 6.1.[51] This variable was also lagged one year and, like GDP per capita, log transformed.

8. *Time Since Last Conflict*: My dependent variable is the incidence of intrastate armed conflict over the period 1979–98. This raises problems of autocorrelation. A country which is in intrastate armed conflict in a given year is intrinsically more likely to be in intrastate armed conflict the next year, too. One way of dealing with this problem is to include a variable for whether or not the country was in

intrastate armed conflict the previous year. Critics argue that the lagged conflict variable is an inappropriate correction in the incidence model, because it is almost a deterministic predictor of the dependent variable y = 1. Further, it only includes information about whether the country was in conflict or not the previous year, and not the time since last conflict. In order to correct for autocorrelation as well as these other issues, Beck, Katz, and Tucker suggest that one should include peace-years and splines into the model, rather than conflict history.[52]

Finally, I have limited the data to the period 1979–98 so that I can compare between two decades—ten years during the cold war, and ten years after. Models 1A and 2A refer to the period 1979–88, while models 1B and 2B refer to the period 1989–98. In both cases model 1 includes all explanatory variables except the controls for autocorrelation (peace-years and splines), which are added in the second models.

Starting with the period 1979–88, Table 3 shows that religious differences do have a positive, but small and nonsignificant, effect on the probability of armed conflict incidence when not controlling for autocorrelation. Once including these controls the coefficient even becomes negative, although still insignificant (model 2A). Thus, for the period 1979–88 religious differences seem to be unimportant for explaining armed conflict incidence.

What about the period after the cold war? Model 1B shows that religious differences again indicate a positive—and this time *significant*—effect on the probability of armed conflict incidence. This relationship even seems to be close to significant (at the .10 level) when including peace-years and splines into the model (model 2B). *This indicates that although religious differences previously did not have a significant effect on the risk of intrastate conflict, these types of differences have become more important for explaining armed conflict after the end of the cold war.* Hence, hypothesis 5 is not supported, but hypothesis 6 is.

The national level of religiosity also affects the propensity of intrastate armed conflict—whether during or after the cold war. *The higher the level of religiosity, the higher the risk of intrastate armed conflict incidence.* This is true also when controlling for peace-years and splines, but the estimates become insignificant at the .05 level. The same relationship is found for several of the other control variables. Socio-economic level and type of political regime, for instance, do affect the risk of intra state armed conflict when not controlling for peace-years and splines. The coefficient for socioeconomic level is negative and highly significant. This supports the notion that rich countries are far less likely to have intrastate conflict than poor countries.

This is in line with my expectations, which were based on findings from earlier studies. The effect of regime type on conflict takes the commonly found inverted-U-shape, meaning that the semi-repressive regimes are the most conflict prone. However, like with the level of national religiosity, once controlling for peace-years and splines these effects—although mostly in the same directions—become nonsignificant at the .05 level. This is not surprising, as we know that most of the peaceful countries are rich democracies.

The coefficient for growth is negative in the models without controlling for time since last conflict, but positive (and thus as anticipated) once these control variables are included. In three of four models the estimates are insignificant though, which indicates that growth does not really matter that much (in a positive or negative direction) for intrastate armed conflict. Population, on the other hand, has a positive and significant effect on the propensity of internal conflict, meaning that populous countries have a higher risk for conflict both during and after the cold war, and regardless of the amount of time since the country has experienced internal conflict.[53]

Natural resource dependence and mountainous terrain also affect the propensity of a country experiencing intrastate armed conflict. However, for both variables, the estimates are only significant at the .05 level after the end of the cold war. While rough terrain increases the risk of intrastate armed conflict, I find an inverted-U-curve for the relationship between natural resource dependence and intrastate armed conflict.

Finally, the coefficient for peace-years is highly negative, which indicates that the longer the time since the last intrastate conflict, the less likely the country is to experience conflict this year.

In summary, these findings indicate that while religious differences play, at best, a minor role in the prediction of country-years of intrastate conflict during the cold war, it does seem to matter in the post-cold war era. Further more, once controlling for time since last conflict, only a few factors seem to have a significant explanatory power on intrastate armed conflict incidence. These are religious differences, the level of natural resource dependence, population, and rough terrain.

This does not necessarily mean that factors such as the level of national religiosity, socioeconomic level, and regime type are irrelevant for conflict. Rather, the relative size of the coefficients (evident in models 1A and 2A) for these variables indicates that they have a large effect on the propensity for conflict within the country.[54] When these effects disappear when controlling for peace-years and splines, it is thus probably because of two factors: (1) poor countries tend to have shorter wars than, for instance, middle-income countries and (2) socioeconomic and political conditions probably affect the variable time since last conflict, creating problems of endogeneity.

In conclusion, this means that poverty and lack of democracy do not necessarily bring on longer wars, but they certainly increase the risk of outbreak of such conflicts, and to a larger extent than religious factors. Nevertheless, religious differences seem to increase the risk not only of intrastate armed conflicts, but also the duration of them.[55]

## Conclusions

As a result of modernization and globalization, people have been increasingly faced with different kinds of cultural habits, values, and norms. What effect these changes have on people's lives is less certain. While the optimists are confident that the growth and spread of urbanization, education, economic development, scientific rationality, and social mobility will combine to diminish the sociopolitical position of religion, other scholars take the quite opposite view: arguing that the modernization and globalization process makes people feel more insecure and alienated, increasing the importance of traditional values as well as the level of hostility. As a result, we will be witnessing a resurgence of religion and religious clashes.

This paper has investigated the religious pattern of people, aiming at contributing to this debate. The findings clearly show that the optimistic scenario is not well founded. Religion has and continues to be an important source of identity to people—especially outside the more "globalized world." In addition, there is some evidence that during the last decades we have witnessed a resurgence of the impact of religion upon the question of identity, as well as the question of warfare. This is in line with "the religious revival/religious clashes thesis." Moreover, although the relative explanatory power of socioeconomic and political factors are higher for the occurrence of intrastate armed conflict than that of religious differences, when relatively rich countries do have conflicts, they tend to last longer. These are interesting findings, which also lead to some important policy implications.

First, improving socioeconomic and political conditions within a country are important tasks when laying the ground for peace. Secondly, religious differences and a high level of religiosity within a country make the conflict more intractable, and thus more complex to resolve. Finally, in some of these cases of religious clashes, it might actually be the relatively high socioeconomic level that keeps the conflict going, since the warring parties have means of financing the conflict. Hence, although partition generally is not a realistic alternative (nor the most desirable one) in some cases it may very well be the only solution, at least if one wants to accomplish long-term peace.

## Notes

1. MaxWeber's book *The Protestant Ethic and the Spirit of Capitalism* (New York: Charles Scribner's Sons, 1958) is probably the most famous articulation of a relationship between culture (religion) and national development in his examination of the rise of European capitalism.

2. See Ted Robert Gurr, "Peoples against the State: Ethnopolitical Conflict and the Changing World System," *International Studies Quarterly* 38, no. 3 (1994): 347–77; Lawrence E. Harrison, 'Foreword' in *Culture Matters: How Values Shape Human Progress*, ed. Lawrence E. Harrison and Samuel P. Huntington (New York: Basic Books, 2000): i–vii.

3. See i.e., David Apter, *The Politics of Modernization* (Chicago: Chicago University Press, 1965), Daniel Bell, *The End of Ideology* (New York: Collier, 1962).

4. See for instance, Ali A. Mazrui, *Cultural Forces in World Politics* (New York: Heineman, 1990) and Gurr, "People against the state," as well as his book *Peoples Versus States, Minorities at Risk in the New Century* (Washington DC: United States Institute of Peace Press, 2000). See also the work of David Carment, "The International Dimensions of Ethnic Conflict: Concepts, Indicators, and Theory," *Journal of Peace Research* 30, no. 2, (1993): 137–150; also his work *Wars in the Midst of Peace*, with Patrick James, "Ethnic Conflict at the International Level: An Appraisal of Theories and Evidence," in ed. David Carment and Patrick James (Pittsburgh, Pennsylvania: Pittsburgh University Press, 1997): 32–59. Errol A. Henderson and Tanja Ellingsen's articles in *Journal of Conflict Resolution*: Errol A. Henderson, "Culture or Contiguity: Ethnic Conflict, the Similarity States, and the Onset of War 1820–1989," *Journal of Conflict Resolution* 41, no. 2 (1997): 649–68; Tanja Ellingsen, "Colorful Community or Ethnic Witches Brew? Multiethnicity and Domestic Conflict during and after the Cold War," *Journal of Conflict Resolution* 44, no. 2 (2000): 228–49. See also the work by Jonathan Fox, "Is Islam More Conflict Prone than Other Religions? A Cross-Sectional Study of Ethno-Religious Conflict," *Nationalism and Ethnic Politics* 6, no. 2 (2000); 1–23; "Religious Causes of International Intervention," *International Politics* 38, no. 4 (2001); 515–32. Two other valuable studies are Marta Reynal-Querol, "Ethnicity, Political Systems, and Civil Wars," *Journal of Conflict Resolution* 46, no. 1 (2002): 29–54; James D. Fearon and David D. Laitin, "Ethnicity, Insurgency, and Civil War," *American Political Science Review* 97, no. 1 (2003): 75–90.

5. For more information about the relationship between religion and conflict, see Jonathan Fox and Josephine Squires, "Threats to Primal Identities: A Comparison of Nationalism and Religion as Impacts on Ethnic Protest and Rebellion," *Terrorism and Political Violence* 13, no. 1 (2001): 87–102; Jonathan Fox, *Ethnoreligious Conflict in the Late 20th Century: A General Theory* (Lanham, MD: Lexington Books, 2002). See also Ken R. Dark, ed., *Religion and International Relations* (New York, Palgrave, 2000).

6. One of the most famous studies is Samuel P. Huntington, "The Clash of Civilizations?" *Foreign Affairs* 72, no. 3 (1993): 22–49; later transformed into a book, *The Clash of Civilizations*

*and the Remaking of World Order* (New York: Simon and Schuster, 1996). Also famous is the article by Benjamin Barber, "Jihad vs. McWorld," *Atlantic Monthly* 269, no. 3 (1992): 53–65. This article is available electronically at http://www.theatlantic.com/ politics/foreign/barberf. htm and was also transformed into a book, *Jihad versus McWorld: How Globalism and Tribalism Are Reshaping the World* (New York: Ballantine Books, 1997). See also Peter Berger, ed. *The Desecularization of the World: Resurgent Religion in World Politics* (Los Angeles: William B. Eerdmans, 1999); Mark Juergensmeyer, "Terror in the Mind of God: The Global Rise of Religious Violence," *Comparative Studies in Religion and Society* 13 (Berkeley: California Press, 2000).

7. Again see Jonathan Fox, *Ethnoreligious conflict.*

8. Examples of these arguments are found in Bell, *The End of Ideology*; Charles Kerr et al., *Industrialism and Industrial Man: The Problems of Labor and Management in Economic Growth* (London: Heineman, 1962), Marshall McLuhan's *Understanding Media: The Extensions of Man* (New York: McGraw-Hill, 1964).

9. For more information, see Jeff Haynes, *Religion in Third World Politics* (Boulder, Co: Lynne Rienner 1994). See also Fox, *Ethnoreligious conflict.*

10. David Harvey in his book *The Condition of Postmodernity: An Enquiry into the Origins of Cultural Change* (Oxford : Blackwell, 1980), 350–52.

11. See Peter Beyer, *Religion and Globalization* (London: Sage, 1994), 9.

12. Ibid, 10, and 133.

13. See Karel Dobbelaere, "Towards an Integrated Perspective on the Processes Related to the Descriptive Concept of Secularization," *Sociology of Religion* 60, no. 3 (1999): 229–47; Yves Lambert, "Religion in Modernity as a New Axial Age: Secularization or New Religious Forms," *Sociology of Religion* 60, no. 3 (1999): 303–33.

14. Again this argument is found in Haynes, *Religion*.

15. For some of the classical studies of this, see Dollard et al., *Frustration and Aggression* (New Haven: Yale University, 1939); Ted Robert Gurr, *Why Men Rebel* (Princeton: Princeton University Press, 1970), Ivo Feierabend and Rosalind Feierabend, "Aggressive Behaviors within Politics: 1948–1962: A Cross-National Study," *Journal of Conflict Resolution* 10, no. 3 (1972): 249–71.

16. See Huntington, *Remaking*, 58–78 for more details. See also Haynes, *Religion in Third World*, Religion, and Jeff Haynes, *Religion, Globalization and Political Culture in the Third World* (New York: Palgrave, 1999).

17. This argument is mentioned by a number of studies besides Huntington "Clash of Civilizations," and Huntington, *Remaking*. Examples are the work of Martin E. Marty and Scott R. Appleby, *Fundamentalism Comprehended* (Chicago: University of Chicago Press, 1995); Barber, "Jihad Vs. McWorld"; Barber, *How Globalism*; Giles Kepel, *The Revenge of God: The Resurgence of Islam, Christianity and Judaism in the Modern World*, Trans. Alan Braley (Cambridge: Polity Press, 1994).

18. Huntington, "Clash of Civilizations," 66.

19. This argument is found in Scott M. Thomas, "Religion and International Conflict," in *Religion and International Relations*, ed. Ken R. Dark (New York: Palgrove, 2002). Similar arguments are also found in Anson Shupe, "The Stubborn Persistence of Religion in the Global Arena," in *Religious Resurgence and Politics in the Contemporary World*, ed. Emilie Sahliyeh (Albany: State University of New York Press, 1990): 71–98.

20. The WVS is a worldwide investigation of sociocultural and political change. It builds on the European Values Surveys, first carried out in 1981 when they included twenty-two independent countries. A second wave of surveys was completed in 1990–91 (forty-three countries), a third wave was carried out in 1995–97 (fifty-three countries), and a fourth wave took place in 1999–2001 (sixty-five countries). As the fourth wave was not yet fully released at the time of writing I only have data for the first three waves. For more information on each of the variables see http://www.worldvaluessurvey.org/

21. I also reran these analyses looking at the twenty-eight countries included in waves two and three of the WVS and found the same pattern—to some extent even stronger (not reported here). Thus, the results seem to hold when including additional non-Western countries into the analyses.

22. For countries where I did have information from 1981 or 1990, but not for 1996, the information was interpolated in order to include as many countries as possible. In this way I ended up with an $N = 63$.

23. The "Other" category refers to the Philippines.

24. For information on the effects of globalization in different cultures, see David Dollar and Paul Collier, *Globalization, Growth and Poverty: Building an Inclusive World Economy* (Washington DC: Oxford University Press, 2001).

25. The minimum value on the national level of religiosity in the Western civilizations is .232 (Czech Republic) while the maximum value is .827 (United States).

26. I.e., Ronald Inglehart, "Changing Values, Economic Development and Political Change," *International Social Science Journal* 1,007 (1995) 379–404; Ronald Inglehart, *Modernization and Postmodernization* (Princeton: Princeton University Press, 1997); Ronald Inglehart and Wayne E. Baker, "Modernization, Cultural Change and the Persistence of Traditional Values," *American Sociological Review* 65, no. 1 (2000): 19–51; Pippa Norris and Ronald Inglehart, *Islam & the West: Testing the Clash of Civilizations Thesis*, John F. Kennedy School of Government Harvard University Faculty Research Papers Series, RWP02-015, 2002.

27. Again, see Inglehart, "Changing Values"; Inglehart and Baker, "Modernization." The data is obtained fromthe Polity IV data by Monty G. Marshall, and Keith Jaggers, (2003). *Polity IV Project: Political Regime Characteristics and Transitions 1800–2002. Dataset Users Manual.* Data and codebook is available at http://www.cidcm.umd.edu/inscr/polity/index.htm

28. While I use the five different variables above as my dependent variables in the cross tabulations, for the multivariate analysis I only use one dependent variable which I have called "Level of National Religiosity." This variable is a composite measure of each of the five different variables in the crosstabulations. This variable was constructed by first transforming each of the five variables into national measures, adding the number of respondents within each of the variable's values multiplied with the value signified, then divided by total number of respondents multiplied by the total number of values. Once transformed into national measures, I then added the country's score on each of the five variables and divided it by the number of variables (5). For instance, if 137 of the 989 respondents in France found religion very important (value 4), 283 found it rather important (value 3), 274 found it not very important (value 2), and 289 did not find it important at all (value 1), the calculation is: $\sum \frac{[137 \times 3 + 283 \times 2 + 274 \times 1 + 289 \times 0]}{[989 \times 4]}$ which is .420. This way I ended up with a composite measure of the level of national religiosity which varies on a scale from 0–1, where 1 is the highest possible level of national religiosity. The composite measure had a mean correlation of .907, and a Crombach's $\alpha$ of 952, which indicates a reliable index.

29. See Thomas, "International Conflict," 4.

30. Examples of this perspective are found in Clifford Geertz, *Old Societies and New States* (New York: Basic Books, 1963); Harold Isaacs, "Basic Group Identity: Idols of the Tribe," *Ethnicity* 1 (1975) 15–41; Anthony D. Smith, *The Ethnic Origins of Nations* (Oxford: Basil Blackwell, 1986); Robert D. Kaplan, *Balkan Ghosts: A Journey through History* (New York: St. Martin's Press, 1993); Walker Connor, *Ethnonationalism: The Quest for Understanding* (Princeton: Princeton University Press, 1994).

31. Isaacs, "Basic Group Identity," 38.

32. Civilizations are mainly defined by religion. As a result, Huntington divides the world into eight possible civilizations: Western, Latin American, African, Islamic, Sinic, Hindu, Orthodox, and Japanese.

33. Huntington, "Clash of Civilization," 27.

34. See David A. Lake and Donald Rothchild, *The International Spread of Ethnic Conflict* (Princeton: Princeton University Press, 1998), 5.

35. Lake and Rothchild, *International Spread*, 6.

36. See, for instance, Benedict Anderson, *Imagined Communities: Reflections on the Origin and Spread of Nationalism* (London: New Left Books, 1983); Virginia Dominguez, *People as Subject, People as Object: Selfhood and Peoplehood in Contemporary Israel* (Madison: University of Wisconsin Press, 1989); Rogers Brubacker, "National Minorities, Nationalizing States, and External National Homelands in the New Europe," *Daedalus, 3*, no. 1 (1995): 107–32.

37. This view is reflected in Thomas, "International Conflict," 4.

38. See i.e., Huntington, *Remaking*, 28.

39. Charles Kegley and Eugene Wittkopf, *World Politics: Trend and Transformation*, 6th ed. (New York: St. Martin's Press, 1997).

40. I.e., Huntington, "Clash of Civilization," and Huntington, *Remaking*. Also see Juergensmeyer, "Mind of God".

41. The dataset differs between four types of armed conflict: (1) extra-systemic, (2) interstate, (3) intrastate, and (4) intrastate with foreign intervention. Here I only investigate intrastate armed conflict. Originally the data included only the post–cold war years, but it has recently been dated back to 1946 (Nils Petter Gleditsch et.al. "Armed Conflict 1946–2001: A New Dataset," *Journal of Peace Research* 39, no. 5 [2002]: 615–37) and includes data for all member states of the international system as defined by Kristian S. Gleditsch and Michael D. Ward for the period 1946–2002, in "A Revised List of Independent States Since 1816," *International Interactions* 25, no. 2 (1999): 393–413. The criterion is either that the state (1) has a population ⩾250,000/or diplomatic connections to two major powers or (2) is a member of the United Nations (UN) during the period. The Uppsala Conflict database also distinguishes between major armed conflict (resulting in 1,000 battle deaths or more per year) intermediate armed conflict (resulting in at least 25 battle-deaths per year and 1,000 battle-deaths or more throughout the duration of the conflict) and minor armed conflict (with a minimum of 25 annual battle-deaths, but less than 1,000 battle-deaths during the duration of the conflict). In this analysis I define an armed conflict as an armed conflict resulting in 25 battle-related deaths or more within a year. See Håvard Strand, Lars Wilhelmsen, and Nils Petter Gleditsch, (2003). *Armed Conflict Dataset Codebook*; http://www.prio.no/page/ Project_detail//9244/42133.html

42. See Gleditsch et al., "Armed Conflict."

43. Each country may have numerous conflicts going on within the same year. See Strand, Wihelmsen, and Gleditsch, *Armed Conflict Dataset*.

44. The second largest religious group had to be 5 percent or more of the total population for the country to be considered split between religious denominations.

45. See Ellingsen (2000) (note 4), Hegre et al., "Towards a Democratic Civil Peace? Democracy, Political Change, and Civil War 1816-1992," *American Political Science Review* 95, no. 1 (2001): 33–48; Fearon and Laitin (2003) (note 4); Paul Collier et al., *Breaking the Conflict Trap: Civil War and Development Policy* (Washington DC: Oxford University Press, 2003).

46. See, for instance, Terry Bosswell and William Dixon, "Dependency and Rebellion: A Cross-National Analysis," *American Sociological Review* 45, no. 4 (1990): 540–59; Edward N. Muller and Erich Weede, "Cross National Variation in Political Violence. A Rational Action Approach," *Journal of Conflict Resolution* 34, no. 6 (1990): 624–51.

47. World Development Indicators CD-ROM, 2003.

48. I.e., Paul Collier and Anke Hoeffler, "Greed and Grievance in Civil War," http://www.worldbank.org/research/conflict/papers.

49. For more information about the arguments, see Ibid. Also see Indra de Soysa, "Paradise Is a Bazaar? Greed, Creed, and Governance in Civil War," *Journal of Peace Research* 39, no. 4 (2002): 395–416.

50. See i.e., Fearon and Laitin 2003, Halvard Buhaug and Scott Gates, "The Geography of Civil War," *Journal of Peace Research* 39, no. 4 (2002): 417–33.

51. The data for the Penn World Tables 6.1 was collected by Alan Heston, Robert Summers, and Bettina Aten, *Penn World Tables Version 6.1.*, Center for International Comparisons at the University of Pennsylvania (CICUP, 2002).

52. See the article by Nathaniel Beck, Jonathan N. Katz, and Richard Tucker, "Taking Time Seriously: Time-Series-Cross-Section Analysis with a Binary Dependent Variable," *American Journal of Political Science* 42, no. 4 (1998): 1260–88.

53. In model 2B the population is not significant at the .05 level, however.

54. Although the size of the coefficients might seem small, these variables are continuous variables and thus the decrease in risk of conflict going from being a poor to being a rich country is much higher than going from a country with religious differences to one without.

55. I also ran models with conflict in the previous year, and interaction terms between this variable and the others seem to support these findings. Due to space limitations these models are not reported here.

**Appendix 1.** Countries and numbers of respondents included in each wave of the world value surveys

| Country | 1981 | 1990 | 1995–97 | Total |
|---|---|---|---|---|
| France | 1,200 | 1,002 | | 2,202 |
| Britain | 1,231 | 1,484 | 1,093 | 3,808 |
| W Germany | 1,305 | 2,101 | 1,017 | 4,423 |
| Italy | 1,348 | 2,018 | | 3,366 |
| Netherlands | 1,221 | 1,017 | | 2,238 |
| Denmark | 1,182 | 1,030 | | 2,212 |
| Belgium | 1,145 | 2,792 | | 3,937 |
| Spain | 2,303 | 4,147 | 1,211 | 7,661 |
| Ireland | 1,217 | 1,000 | | 2,217 |
| United States | 2,325 | 1,839 | 1,542 | 5,706 |
| Canada | 1,254 | 1,730 | | 2,984 |
| Japan | 1,204 | 1,011 | 1,054 | 3,269 |
| Mexico | 1,837 | 1,531 | 1,510 | 4,878 |
| S Africa | 1,596 | 2,736 | 2,935 | 7,267 |
| Hungary | 1,464 | 999 | | 2,463 |
| Australia | 1,228 | | 2,048 | 3,276 |
| Norway | 1,246 | 1,239 | 1,127 | 3,612 |
| Sweden | 954 | 1,047 | 1,009 | 3,010 |
| Iceland | 927 | 702 | | 1,629 |
| Argentina | 1,005 | 1,002 | 1,079 | 3,086 |
| Finland | 1,003 | 588 | 987 | 2,578 |
| S Korea | 970 | 1,251 | 1,249 | 3,470 |
| Poland | | 938 | 1,153 | 2,091 |
| Switzerland | | 1,400 | 1,212 | 2,612 |
| Puerto Rico | | | 1,164 | 1,164 |
| Brazil | | 1,782 | 1,149 | 2,931 |
| Nigeria | | 1,001 | 2,769 | 3,770 |
| Chile | | 1,500 | 1,000 | 2,500 |
| Belarus | | 1,015 | 2,092 | 3,107 |
| India | | 2,500 | 2,040 | 4,540 |
| Czech | | 930 | | 930 |
| E Germany | | 1,336 | 1,009 | 2,345 |
| Slovenia | | 1,035 | 1,007 | 2,042 |
| Bulgaria | | 1,034 | 1,072 | 2,106 |
| Romania | | 1,103 | | 1,103 |
| Pakistan | | | 733 | 733 |
| China | 90 | 1,000 | 1,500 | 2,500 |
| Taiwan | | | 1,452 | 1,452 |
| Portugal | | 1,185 | | 1,185 |
| Austria | | 1,460 | | 1,460 |
| Turkey | | 1,030 | 1,907 | 2,937 |

(*Continued*)

**Appendix 1.** Continued

| Country | Wave 1981 | Wave 1990 | Wave 1995–97 | Total |
|---|---|---|---|---|
| Lithuania |  | 1,000 | 1,009 | 2,009 |
| Latvia |  | 903 | 1,200 | 2,103 |
| Estonia |  | 1,008 | 1,021 | 2,029 |
| Ukraine |  |  | 2,811 | 2,811 |
| Russia |  | 1,961 | 2,040 | 4,001 |
| Peru |  |  | 1,211 | 1,211 |
| Venezuela |  |  | 1,200 | 1,200 |
| Uruguay |  |  | 1,000 | 1,000 |
| Ghana |  |  | 96 | 96 |
| Philippines |  |  | 1,200 | 1,200 |
| Moldova |  |  | 984 | 984 |
| Georgia |  |  | 2,593 | 2,593 |
| Armenia |  |  | 2,000 | 2,000 |
| Azerbaijan |  |  | 2,002 | 2,002 |
| Dominic Rep |  |  | 417 | 417 |
| Bangladesh |  |  | 1,525 | 1,525 |
| Colombia |  |  | 6,025 | 6,025 |
| Serbia |  |  | 1,280 | 1,280 |
| Montenegro |  |  | 240 | 240 |
| Macedonia |  |  | 995 | 995 |
| Croatia |  |  | 1,196 | 1,196 |
| Slovakia |  | 466 |  | 466 |
| Bosnia Herzegovina |  |  | 1,200 | 1,200 |
| Total | 29,165 | 57,853 | 72,365 | 159,383 |
| Number of Countries | 22 | 42 | 50 |  |

Note: The survey also includes some areas that are not independent nation-states (i.e., Basque, regions Moscow, Tambov, etc.). These have been excluded from the analysis and thus this list.

Countries included in all waves (total = 12): Britain, West Germany, Spain, United States, Japan, Mexico, South Africa, Norway, Sweden, Argentina, Finland, South Korea.

Countries included in waves one and two (total = 21): France, Britain, West Germany, Italy, Netherlands, Belgium, Denmark, Ireland, Spain, United States, Canada, Japan, Mexico, South Africa, Norway, Sweden, Argentina, Finland, Hungary, Iceland, South Korea.

Countries included in waves two and three (total = 28): Britain, West Germany, Spain, United States, Japan, Mexico, South Africa, Norway, Sweden, Argentina, Finland, South Korea, Poland, Switzerland, Brazil, Nigeria, Chile, Belarus, India, East Germany, Slovenia, Bulgaria, China, Turkey, Lithuania, Latvia, Estonia, Russia.

Countries included in waves one and three (total = 13): Britain, West Germany, Spain, United States, Japan, Mexico, South Africa, Norway, Sweden, Argentina, Finland, South Korea, Australia.

Countries included only in one wave (number of wave in brackets): Czech (2), Romania (2), Slovakia (2), Austria (2), Portugal (2), Puerto Rico (3), Pakistan (3), Taiwan (3), Ukraine (3), Peru (3), Venezuela (3), Uruguay (3), Ghana (3), Philippines (3), Moldova (3), Georgia (3), Armenia (3), Azerbaijan (3), Dominican Republic (3), Bangladesh (3), Colombia (3), Serbia (3), Montenegro (3), Macedonia (3), Croatia (3), Bosnia Herzegovina (3). (total = 21 in wave two and 21 in wave three) Source: http://www.worldvaluessurvey.org/services/index.html.

## Appendix 2: Classification of Countries into Civilizations

### Western Civilization

- 2 United States
- 20 Canada
- 200 Britain
- 205 Ireland
- 210 Netherlands
- 211 Belgium
- 220 France
- 225 Switzerland
- 230 Spain
- 235 Portugal
- 260 W Germany
- 265 E Germany
- 290 Poland
- 305 Austria
- 310 Hungary
- 316 Czech
- 317 Slovakia
- 325 Italy
- 366 Estonia
- 367 Latvia
- 368 Lithuania
- 375 Finland
- 380 Sweden
- 385 Norway
- 390 Denmark
- 395 Iceland
- 900 Australia

### Latin American Civilization

- 42 Dominic Rep
- 70 Mexico
- 100 Colombia
- 101 Venezuela
- 135 Peru
- 140 Brazil
- 155 Chile
- 160 Argentina
- 165 Uruguay

### Orthodox Civilization

- 343 Macedonia
- 344 Croatia
- 346 Bosnia
- 347 Montenegro
- 347 Serbia
- 349 Slovenia
- 355 Bulgaria
- 359 Moldova
- 360 Romania
- 365 Russia
- 369 Ukraine
- 370 Belarus
- 371 Armenia
- 372 Georgia

### Islamic Civilization

- 373 Azerbaijan
- 640 Turkey
- 770 Pakistan
- 771 Bangladesh

### Hindu Civilization

- 750 India

### Japanese Civilization

- 740 Japan

### Sinic Civilization

- 710 China
- 713 Taiwan
- 732 S Korea

### African Civilization

- 452 Ghana
- 475 Nigeria
- 560 S Africa

### Other Civilization

- 840 Philippines

Appendix 3. Intrastate armed conflict over identity, 1946–2002

| Begin | End | Location | Incomp | Territory | Intensity | Type | Cow_a | Cow_b | Cow_loca | Continen | Identity |
|---|---|---|---|---|---|---|---|---|---|---|---|
| 1946 | 1946 | Iran | 1 | Kurdistan | 1 | 4 | 630 | 365 | 630 | 2 | 1 |
| 1966 | 1968 | Iran | 1 | Kurdistan | 2 | 3 | 630 | | 630 | 2 | 1 |
| 1979 | 1990 | Iran | 1 | Kurdistan | 3 | 3 | 630 | | 630 | 2 | 1 |
| 1993 | 1993 | Iran | 1 | Kurdistan | 2 | 3 | 630 | | 630 | 2 | 1 |
| 1946 | 1946 | Iran | 1 | Azerbaijan | 1 | 4 | 630 | 365 | 630 | 2 | 1 |
| 1946 | 1948 | Soviet Union | 1 | Estonia | 2 | 3 | 365 | | 365 | 1 | 1 |
| 1946 | 1947 | Soviet Union | 1 | Latvia | 2 | 3 | 365 | | 365 | 1 | 1 |
| 1946 | 1948 | Soviet Union | 1 | Lithuania | 3 | 3 | 365 | | 365 | 1 | 1 |
| 1946 | 1950 | Soviet Union | 1 | Ukraine | 3 | 3 | 365 | | 365 | 1 | 1 |
| 1947 | 1947 | Paraguay | 2 | | 3 | 3 | 150 | | 150 | 5 | 1 |
| 1948 | 2002 | Burma | 1 | Karen | 3 | 3 | 775 | | 775 | 3 | 1 |
| 1948 | 1988 | Burma | 1 | Arakan | 1 | 3 | 775 | | 775 | 3 | 1 |
| 1991 | 1994 | Burma | 1 | Arakan | 1 | 3 | 775 | | 775 | 3 | 1 |
| 1948 | 1963 | Burma | 1 | Mon | 1 | 3 | 775 | | 775 | 3 | 1 |
| 1990 | 1990 | Burma | 1 | Mon | 1 | 3 | 775 | | 775 | 3 | 1 |
| 1948 | 1951 | India | 2 | | 3 | 3 | 750 | | 750 | 3 | 1 |
| 1967 | 1972 | India | 2 | | 1 | 3 | 750 | | 750 | 3 | 1 |
| 1989 | 2002 | India | 2 | | 1 | 3 | 750 | | 750 | 3 | 1 |
| 1949 | 1949 | Burma | 1 | Kachin | 1 | 3 | 775 | | 775 | 3 | 1 |
| 1961 | 1992 | Burma | 1 | Kachin | 3 | 3 | 775 | | 775 | 3 | 1 |
| 1965 | 1995 | Guatemala | 2 | | 1 | 3 | 90 | | 90 | 5 | 1 |
| 1949 | 2002 | Israel | 1 | Palestine | 1 | 3 | 666 | | 666 | 2 | 1 |
| 1950 | 1950 | China | 1 | Tibet | 1 | 3 | 710 | | 710 | 3 | 1 |
| 1956 | 1956 | China | 1 | Tibet | 3 | 3 | 710 | | 710 | 3 | 1 |
| 1959 | 1959 | China | 1 | Tibet | 3 | 3 | 710 | | 710 | 3 | 1 |

(Continued)

**Appendix 3.** Continued

| Begin | End | Location | Incomp | Territory | Intensity | Type | Cow_a | Cow_b | Cow_loca | Continen | Identity |
|---|---|---|---|---|---|---|---|---|---|---|---|
| 1950 | 1950 | Indonesia | 1 | South Moluccas | 3 | 3 | 850 | | 850 | 3 | 1 |
| 1956 | 1968 | India | 1 | Nagalard | 1 | 3 | 750 | | 750 | 3 | 1 |
| 1989 | 1997 | India | 1 | Nagalard | 1 | 3 | 750 | | 750 | 3 | 1 |
| 1957 | 1957 | Burma | 1 | Kaya | 1 | 3 | 775 | | 775 | 3 | 1 |
| 1992 | 1992 | Burma | 1 | Kaya | 1 | 3 | 775 | | 775 | 3 | 1 |
| 1996 | 1996 | Burma | 1 | Kaya | 1 | 3 | 775 | | 775 | 3 | 1 |
| 1959 | 1959 | Iraq | 2 | | 1 | 3 | 645 | | 645 | 2 | 1 |
| 1982 | 1984 | Iraq | 2 | | 1 | 3 | 645 | | 645 | 2 | 1 |
| 1987 | 1987 | Iraq | 2 | | 1 | 3 | 645 | | 645 | 2 | 1 |
| 1991 | 1996 | Iraq | 2 | | 3 | 3 | 645 | | 645 | 2 | 1 |
| 1958 | 1958 | Lebanon | 2 | | 3 | 3 | 660 | | 660 | 2 | 1 |
| 1975 | 1990 | Lebanon | 2 | | 1 | 4 | 660 | 652,666 | 660 | 2 | 1 |
| 1960 | 1970 | Burma | 1 | Shan | 1 | 3 | 775 | | 775 | 3 | 1 |
| 1976 | 1988 | Burma | 1 | Shan | 2 | 3 | 775 | | 775 | 3 | 1 |
| 1994 | 2002 | Burma | 1 | Shan | 3 | 3 | 775 | | 775 | 3 | 1 |
| 1960 | 1962 | Congo/Zaire | 1 | Katanga | 1 | 3 | 490 | | 490 | 4 | 1 |
| 1960 | 1962 | Congo/Zaire | 1 | South Kasai | 1 | 3 | 490 | | 490 | 4 | 1 |
| 1997 | 2002 | Nepal | 2 | | 1 | 3 | 790 | | 790 | 3 | 1 |
| 1961 | 1993 | Iraq | 1 | Kurdistan | 3 | 3 | 645 | | 645 | 2 | 1 |
| 1962 | 1991 | Ethiopia | 1 | Eritrea | 1 | 3 | 530 | | 530 | 4 | 1 |
| 1963 | 1966 | Malaysia | 1 | North Borneo | 1 | 3 | 820 | | 820 | 3 | 1 |
| 1963 | 1972 | Sudan | 1 | Southern Sudan | 3 | 3 | 625 | | 625 | 4 | 1 |
| 1983 | 2002 | Sudan | 1 | Southern Sudan | 3 | 3 | 625 | | 625 | 4 | 1 |
| 1964 | 1965 | Congo/Zaire | 2 | | 3 | 3 | 490 | | 490 | 4 | 1 |
| 1967 | 1967 | Congo/Zaire | 2 | | 1 | 3 | 490 | | 490 | 4 | 1 |
| 1977 | 1978 | Congo/Zaire | 2 | | 1 | 3 | 490 | | 490 | 4 | 1 |

| | | | | | | | | |
|---|---|---|---|---|---|---|---|---|
| 1996 | 2002 | Congo/Zaire | 2 | | 4 | | 490 | 4 | 1 |
| 1965 | 1965 | Burundi | 2 | | 3 | | 516 | 4 | 1 |
| 1990 | 1992 | Burundi | 2 | | 3 | | 516 | 4 | 1 |
| 1995 | 2001 | Burundi | 2 | | 3 | | 516 | 4 | 1 |
| 1965 | 1990 | Chad | 2 | | 4 | | 483 | 4 | 1 |
| 1991 | 1994 | Chad | 2 | | 3 | | 483 | 4 | 1 |
| 1997 | 2001 | Chad | 2 | | 3 | | 483 | 4 | 1 |
| 1965 | 1965 | Indonesia | 1 | West Papua | 3 | | 850 | 3 | 1 |
| 1976 | 1978 | Indonesia | 1 | West Papua | 3 | | 850 | 3 | 1 |
| 1966 | 1968 | India | 1 | Mizoram | 3 | | 750 | 3 | 1 |
| 1966 | 1966 | Nigeria | 2 | | 3 | | 475 | 4 | 1 |
| 1966 | 1988 | South Africa | 1 | Namibia | 3 | | 560 | 4 | 1 |
| 1979 | 1982 | Syria | 2 | | 3 | | 652 | 2 | 1 |
| 1967 | 1970 | Nigeria | 1 | Biafra | 3 | | 475 | 4 | 1 |
| 1970 | 1988 | Philippines | 1 | Mindanao | 3 | | 840 | 3 | 1 |
| 1994 | 2002 | Philippines | 1 | Mindanao | 3 | | 840 | 3 | 1 |
| 1971 | 1971 | Pakistan | 1 | East Pakistan | 3 | | 770 | 3 | 1 |
| 1981 | 1991 | Uganda | 2 | | 3 | | 500 | 4 | 1 |
| 1994 | 2002 | Uganda | 2 | | 3 | | 500 | 4 | 1 |
| 1971 | 1993 | United Kingdom | 1 | Northern Ireland | 3 | | 200 | 1 | 1 |
| 1998 | 1998 | United Kingdom | 1 | Northern Ireland | 3 | | 200 | 1 | 1 |
| 1972 | 1979 | Rhodesia | 2 | | 3 | | 552 | 4 | 1 |
| 1974 | 1992 | Bangladesh | 1 | Chittagong Hill Tracts | 3 | | 771 | 3 | 1 |
| 1974 | 1974 | Cyprus | 1 | Northern Cyprus | 4 | 640 | 352 | 1 | 1 |
| 1974 | 1977 | Pakistan | 1 | Baluchistan | 3 | | 770 | 3 | 1 |
| 1974 | 1982 | Thailand | 2 | | 3 | | 800 | 3 | 1 |
| 1975 | 2001 | Angola | 2 | | 4 | 560,490 | 540,40 540 | 4 | 1 |
| 1975 | 1983 | Ethiopia | 1 | Ogaden | 4 | | 530,40 530 | 4 | 1 |

*(Continued)*

## Appendix 3. Continued

| Begin | End | Location | Incomp | Territory | Intensity | Type | Cow_a | Cow_b | Cow_loca | Continen | Identity |
|---|---|---|---|---|---|---|---|---|---|---|---|
| 1996 | 2002 | Ethiopia | 1 | Ogaden | 1 | 3 | 530 | 530 | 530 | 4 | 1 |
| 1975 | 1989 | Indonesia | 1 | East Timor | 3 | 3 | 850 | 850 | 850 | 3 | 1 |
| 1992 | 1992 | Indonesia | 1 | East Timor | 2 | 3 | 850 | 850 | 850 | 3 | 1 |
| 1997 | 1998 | Indonesia | 1 | East Timor | 2 | 3 | 850 | 850 | 850 | 3 | 1 |
| 1975 | 1989 | Morocco | 1 | Western Sahara | 3 | 4 | 600,435 | | 600 | 4 | 1 |
| 1978 | 1978 | Afghanistan | 2 | | 3 | 3 | 700 | | 700 | 3 | 1 |
| 1989 | 2001 | Afghanistan | 2 | | 3 | 3 | 700 | | 700 | 3 | 1 |
| 1978 | 1988 | India | 1 | Tripura | 1 | 3 | 750 | | 750 | 3 | 1 |
| 1993 | 2002 | India | 1 | Tripura | 1 | 3 | 750 | | 750 | 3 | 1 |
| 1981 | 1996 | Somalia | 2 | | 1 | 3 | 520 | | 520 | 4 | 1 |
| 1979 | 1988 | Afghanistan | 2 | | 3 | 4 | 700,365 | | 700 | 3 | 1 |
| 1979 | 1980 | Iran | 1 | Arabistan | 1 | 3 | 630 | | 630 | 2 | 1 |
| 1980 | 1981 | Spain | 1 | Basque | 1 | 3 | 230 | | 230 | 1 | 1 |
| 1987 | 1987 | Spain | 1 | Basque | 1 | 3 | 230 | | 230 | 1 | 1 |
| 1991 | 1992 | Spain | 1 | Basque | 1 | 3 | 230 | | 230 | 1 | 1 |
| 1981 | 1993 | South Africa | 2 | | 1 | 3 | 560 | | 560 | 4 | 1 |
| 1982 | 1994 | India | 1 | Manipur | 1 | 3 | 750 | | 750 | 3 | 1 |
| 1997 | 2000 | India | 1 | Manipur | 1 | 3 | 750 | | 750 | 3 | 1 |
| 1983 | 1993 | India | 1 | Punjab/Khalistan | 1 | 3 | 750 | | 750 | 3 | 1 |
| 1983 | 2001 | Sri Lanka | 1 | Eelam | 1 | 3 | 780 | | 780 | 3 | 1 |
| 1984 | 2002 | Turkey | 1 | Kurdistan | 1 | 3 | 640 | | 640 | 2 | 1 |
| 1986 | 1988 | Surinam | 2 | | 1 | 3 | 115 | | 115 | 5 | 1 |
| 1989 | 1991 | Ethiopia | 1 | Afar | 1 | 3 | 530 | | 530 | 4 | 1 |
| 1996 | 1996 | Ethiopia | 1 | Afar | 1 | 3 | 530 | | 530 | 4 | 1 |
| 1989 | 2001 | India | 1 | Kashmir | 1 | 3 | 750 | | 750 | 3 | 1 |
| 1989 | 2001 | India | 1 | Assam | 1 | 3 | 750 | | 750 | 3 | 1 |

| | | | | | | | |
|---|---|---|---|---|---|---|---|
| 1989 | 1991 | Indonesia | 1 | Aceh | 3 | | 850 | 3 | 1 |
| 1999 | 2002 | Indonesia | 1 | Aceh | 3 | | 850 | 3 | 1 |
| 1989 | 1996 | Papua New Guinea | 1 | Bougainville | 3 | | 910 | 3 | 1 |
| 1990 | 1990 | Mali | 1 | Air and Azawad | 3 | | 432 | 4 | 1 |
| 1994 | 1994 | Mali | 1 | Air and Azawad | 3 | | 432 | 4 | 1 |
| 1990 | 1994 | Niger | 1 | Air and Azawad | 3 | | 436 | 4 | 1 |
| 1997 | 1997 | Niger | 1 | Air and Azawad | 3 | | 436 | 4 | 1 |
| 1990 | 1994 | Rwanda | 2 | | 3 | | 517 | 4 | 1 |
| 1998 | 2001 | Rwanda | 2 | | 3 | | 517 | 4 | 1 |
| 1990 | 1991 | Soviet Union | 1 | Nagorno-Karabakh | 3 | | 365 | 1 | 1 |
| 1990 | 1990 | Soviet Union | 1 | Azerbaijan | 3 | | 365 | 1 | 1 |
| 1990 | 1990 | Trinidad and Tobago | 2 | | 3 | | 52 | 5 | |
| 1991 | 1991 | Yugoslavia | 1 | Slovenia | 3 | | 345 | 1 | 1 |
| 1991 | 1991 | Yugoslavia | 1 | Croatia | 3 | | 345 | 1 | 1 |
| 1992 | 2002 | Algeria | 2 | | 3 | | 615 | 4 | 1 |
| 1992 | 1997 | Angola | 1 | Cabinda | 3 | | 540 | 4 | 1 |
| 1992 | 1994 | Azerbaijan | 1 | Nagorno-Karabakh | 4 | 371 | 373 | 1 | 1 |
| 1992 | 1995 | Bosnia & Herz. | 1 | Serb | 4 | 345 | 346 | 1 | 1 |
| 1992 | 1995 | Croatia | 1 | Serb | 3 | | 344 | 1 | 1 |
| 1992 | 1998 | Egypt | 2 | | 3 | | 651 | 2 | |
| 1992 | 1993 | Georgia | 1 | Abkhazia | 3 | | 372 | 1 | 1 |
| 1992 | 1992 | Georgia | 1 | South Ossetia | 3 | | 372 | 1 | 1 |
| 1992 | 1992 | Moldova | 1 | Dniestr | 3 | | 359 | 1 | 1 |
| 1992 | 1996 | Tajikistan | 2 | | 3 | | 702 | 3 | 1 |
| 1998 | 1998 | Tajikistan | 2 | | 3 | | 702 | 3 | 1 |
| 1993 | 1995 | Bosnia & Herz. | 1 | Bihac | 3 | | 346 | 1 | 1 |
| 1993 | 1994 | Bosnia & Herz. | 1 | Croat | 4 | 344 | 346 | 1 | 1 |
| 1993 | 1993 | India | 1 | Jarkhand | 3 | | 750 | 3 | 1 |

(Continued)

## Appendix 3. Continued

| Begin | End | Location | Incomp | Territory | Intensity | Type | Cow_a | Cow_b | Cow_loca | Continen | Identity |
|---|---|---|---|---|---|---|---|---|---|---|---|
| 1994 | 1994 | Mexico | 2 | | 1 | 3 | 70 | | 70 | 5 | 1 |
| 1994 | 1996 | Russia | 1 | Chechnya | 1 | 3 | 365 | | 365 | 1 | 1 |
| 1999 | 2002 | Russia | 1 | Chechnya | 3 | 3 | 365 | | 365 | 1 | 1 |
| 1995 | 1996 | Pakistan | 2 | | 1 | 3 | 770 | | 770 | 3 | 1 |
| 1996 | 1999 | Ethiopia | 1 | Somali | 1 | 3 | 530 | | 530 | 4 | 1 |
| 1996 | 1997 | Niger | 1 | Toubou | 1 | 3 | 436 | | 436 | 4 | 1 |
| 1998 | 1999 | Yugoslavia | 1 | Kosovo | 3 | 3 | 345 | | 345 | 1 | 1 |
| 1999 | 2001 | Ethiopia | 1 | Oromiya | 1 | 3 | 530 | | 530 | 4 | 1 |
| 1999 | 1999 | Russia | 1 | Dagestan | 1 | 3 | 365 | | 365 | 1 | 1 |
| 2000 | 2000 | Uzbekistan | 2 | | 1 | 4 | 704,703 | | 704 | 3 | 1 |
| 2001 | 2001 | Macedonia | 2 | | 1 | 3 | 343 | | 343 | 1 | 1 |
| 2001 | 2002 | United States | 2 | | 3 | 4 | 2,900,20,220 255,325,740 663,210,290 365,640,200 | | 2 | 5 | 1 |

# Religious Rage: A Quantitative Analysis of the Intensity of Religious Conflicts

## SUSANNA PEARCE

As the daily headlines of any newspaper illustrate, it is a popular stereotype that there is something about religious conflicts that makes them more violent. Images of suicide bombers in the Middle East, of pipe bombs and punishment killings in Northern Ireland, of the near genocide in southern Sudan, of violent riots over the institution of sharia law in North Africa, and of the possibility of nuclear war regarding Kashmir are typical conceptions of religious conflicts—and these are only a few examples from within the last decade alone. Go further into history and almost inconceivable examples spring to mind—the genocide of Jews in the Holocaust and massacre of Muslims in the Crusades. From these and other events, the collective belief is that combining religion with conflict—either sincerely or manipulatively—escalates a conflict to a greater intensity than would otherwise be present. Is this reputation deserved? Are conflicts involving religion really more intense than other types of conflicts or are these just a few visible exceptions to the rule? This study evaluates this question using a statistical analysis of 278 interstate and intrastate territorial conflicts since World War II.

## Literature Review

The scholarly research is not short on attempts to explain religious violence, and spans several fields of study including psychology, anthropology, sociology, theology, and political science. Many scholars have focused on religion as the primary cause of conflict, but the result is often an overemphasis on its importance that is not supported by empirical evidence. The most potent example is the secularist theories often connected with Marxist perspectives of religion.[1] This group of theories holds that as the world modernizes, religion will become less important in individuals' lives, and thus a less frequent cause of conflict.[2] However, as the world has continued to modernize the frequency of religious conflict has not decreased but has arguably increased,[3] and thus this group of theories has largely been discredited. Currently, more scholars have emphasized the increasing importance of religion that appears to accompany modernization.[4] The effect of modernization on the importance of religion (and on religion in conflict) remains unknown, but research continues.

Conflict studies often focus on psychological or institutional causes of conflict, relegating religion to an indirect cause.[5] Ted Gurr's theory of relative deprivation is an example of a sociopolitical theory of conflict in this vein.[6] Gurr's theory explains conflict in terms of the satisfaction of expected outcomes for individuals. At its most basic, Gurr's theory argues that discrimination causes grievances which cause a group to organize to fight the discriminating party. Jonathan Fox has followed up on Gurr's study and put forward a model that places the role of religion in the formation of grievances, as well as in causing increased discrimination and repression.[7] In terms of grievance formation, Fox tested his hypotheses using the Minorities at Risk Dataset and concluded that religious legitimacy has an influence on grievance formation, but the influence was not consistent.[8] Religious legitimacy encouraged the development of grievances when religion was not an issue, yet discouraged the formation of grievances when religion was an issue.

Many theological studies focus on the central principle of peace and harmony in religious traditions as a foundation for preventing or ending conflict.[9] Given the frequency of religious conflict, however, the evidence shows that there are circumstances under which religion can, in fact, provoke rather than resolve conflict. What is increasingly being studied is the dual nature of religious theology in inciting and resolving conflict.[10] This strand of research suggests that the presence of a religious group is not a sufficient cause of conflict (or peace), and its role as a contributing factor continues to be explored.

Scott Appleby is the most prominent of these authors outlining the ambivalence of religion in conflict. Among the factors that Appleby identifies as the most important in the determination to use religion to legitimize violence or peace is the education of the believers. He argues that extremist religious leaders must convince their followers to ignore the religion's teachings of peace in order for the extremist movement to gain widespread support. Such leaders will be unsuccessful, however, if their followers "are well formed spiritually and informed theologically."[11] Appleby calls those who are not "sufficiently grounded in the teachings and practices of their own tradition"[12] followers of a "folk religion." These followers are unable "to counter arguments based on scriptures and doctrines carefully chosen for their seeming endorsement of violence or ambivalence about its use"[13] and are ultimately swayed by the arguments of extremist religious leaders. Appleby argues that without a strong religious education, believers are vulnerable to the teachings of extremists in which violent traditions legitimize the use of violence. Conversely, when believers are properly educated, the violent traditions do not serve to encourage violence.

Determining the proper education of believers, however, is extraordinarily problematic for a social researcher. Who decides if a set of followers is "well formed spiritually and informed theologically"? Very few people would argue that the Al Qaeda terrorists were not well-versed in Islamic teaching, nor are scholars quick to deny the Christian Crusaders' knowledge of the Bible.

If religious involvement can serve as a proxy for spiritual education, Gary Marx's study of African Americans in the 1960s provides support for Appleby's argument.[14] Marx used a 1964 survey of African Americans to see if militants were more or less involved in their faith. He concludes that "the greater the religious involvement, whether measured in terms of ritual activity, orthodoxy of religious belief, subjective importance of religion, or the three taken together, the lower the degree of militancy."[15] Jon P. Alston, Charles W. Peek, and C. Ray Wingrove followed up Marx's study with one using a 1969 survey of African Americans that found comparable results to those of Marx's study. The most significant difference was that Alston, Peek, and Wingrove found age, sex, and denominational differences in the degree of militancy not uncovered in Marx's study. Both studies conclude overall that a higher religiousness is related to lower levels of militancy. Religious involvement, however, does not entirely measure what Appleby intended by "well formed spiritually and informed theologically." It fails to measure the level of education by measuring only the attendance and involvement of followers.

Marx provides an alternative explanation of the dual nature of religion in conflict. He argues that religion often espouses contradicting values—particularly the value placed on rewards in the afterlife or the value placed on action on behalf of a deity in the present life. When stress is put on the temporal, the faithful are encouraged to do what they can for social change. On the other hand, if stress is put on the afterlife, adherents feel less of a need to try to change society. Marx's evidence from the 1964 survey of African Americans seems to support this claim, though more empirical evidence would surely be needed to accept Marx's explanation.

Charles Kimball, like Appleby, has argued that authentic religion does not result in violence and destruction because such actions violate the central tenets of love and peace found in every major religion.[16] Kimball argues that the frequent violence carried out by seemingly religious people is evidence that a religion has been corrupted, similar to Appleby's notion of folk religion. According to Kimball, a corrupted religion can be identified by its claim to absolute truth, the blind obedience of its adherents, its description of the perfect life or an "ideal" time, its belief that the end justifies any means necessary, and by its call for a holy war to defend the faith. According to Kimball, when any of these five characteristics exhibit themselves in a religion, the religion is corrupted and violence is an inevitable consequence unless something is done to revive the authentic religion.

However, Kimball goes to great lengths to argue that corrupted religion is not beyond repair. In his view, it is the responsibility of the uncorrupted faithful to take a stand against the distortion of their faith. For example, in response to Islamic extremists' call for jihad against America, Kimball urges moderate Muslims to remind the extremists of the "greater jihad" (as labeled by Muhammad) to struggle to do the right thing in everyday life or to point out that the high threshold required to justify violence in Islam has not been reached.

The discussion of the peaceful influences of religion is usually done in a normative sense, in which suggestions and arguments are made about how religion *should* be involved in conflicts in order to bring them to a peaceful end—rather than on what the dominant way is in which religion is involved in conflicts. Although religion clearly has the capacity to be a peaceful influence in a conflict, this potential does not address the current reality or describe the observable relationship between religion and conflict.

Outside of these normative doctrinal studies, there is a great deal of literature regarding the role of religious identities in conflict. In particular, there is an ongoing debate about the primordial versus instrumental role of identities in initiating and perpetuating a conflict. Those who take a primordial perspective argue that the identities are innately in opposition to each other and conflicts are only contained through institutional structures. A common example is the ethnic divisions in Yugoslavia that began to manifest themselves following Tito's death and which ultimately culminated in the bloody breakup of the state. Tito's regime maintained relative peace among the various ethnic and religious identities through its suppressive institutions. After his death when the system underwent reforms, the tenuous balance that kept the peace disintegrated. Instrumentalists, on the other hand, argue that it was not the removal of the suppressive structures that caused the disintegration of the state, but that strategic elites used the ethnic and religious identities to mobilize support for their cause—namely gaining access to power for themselves. Though the differing identities may not be created by the elites, they are used as a strategic tool that enables them to gain power—and thereby cause or fuel a conflict.

Closely related to the primordial-instrumental debate is the controversy surrounding Samuel Huntington's "clash of civilizations" thesis.[17] According to Huntington, the world system is evolving along civilization fault lines that will increasingly become intense battle lines between civilizations. Huntington identifies these civilizations largely by their religious or ethnic traditions, which has ignited efforts by many to disaggregate civilizational factors to determine the legitimacy of Huntington's thesis.

Errol Henderson, for instance, uses the Correlates of War Dataset to determine the influence of cultural factors on the likelihood of war between 1820 and 1989. Henderson separates the ethnic similarity and religious similarity of the dyads and includes contiguity of the participants in a logistical regression. The results indicate that religious similarity is a major determinant of the likelihood of war—the more religiously similar the dyad the less likely there would be a war, and the less religiously similar the more likely there would be a war. Rudolph Rummel picks up the question of an association between religion and the likelihood of political violence by taking account of the religious pluralism in the state. While Henderson's approach is international, Rummel's is domestic. Rummel, too, finds a relationship between pluralism (dissimilarity in Henderson's study) and political violence, but concludes that other characteristics such as level of development, political stability, age, size, and region have a greater influence on the likelihood of violence. Marta Reynal-Querol also addresses the question of the likelihood of civilizational conflicts by separating ethnic and religious divisions and evaluating the likelihood of civil war. Her study finds that ethno-religious divisions are more likely than ethnolinguistic divisions to lead to civil war. To explain why all ethno-religiously divided states are not embroiled in a civil war, Reynal-Querol finds that consociational political systems serve to mediate tensions in divided populations.

The quantitative studies testing Huntington's thesis largely agree that religious differences are a contributing factor to the likelihood of conflict, though they disagree on the centrality of these divisions as well as the characterization that these civilizational conflicts are increasing in frequency and will become the fault line for conflicts in the future. These studies have not attempted to characterize the level of violence of civilizational conflicts. Although they have separated out religious identities from other identities and determined their influence on the probability of various forms of violent conflict, they do not provide any insight on the impact these identities have on the *intensity* of violent conflict. Each of these studies, as well as the theories summarized previously, generally focuses on the cause, likelihood, or resolution of conflict. Very little research has directly investigated the consequences on the intensity of a conflict caused by involving religion, regardless of the reason for its involvement. The underlying assumption is often that religion's involvement is associated with greater violence and longer-lasting conflicts in which the annihilation of the other side is each party's goal. A great deal of research has focused on explaining *how* religion creates such intense conflict and has relied heavily on case studies to develop the explanation without testing the underlying assumption.

Michael Sell's analysis of the Serb-Bosnian conflict, for instance, identified how the Christ-killer tradition was brought into the conflict and perpetuated the violence.[18] The Serbian Christians were able to graft the tradition into their own national history and thereby hold the Bosnian Muslims responsible for Christ-killing figuratively despite their nonexistence at the time of Christ. Holding the Muslims responsible for the "death of the Serb nation" (though the Serb nation exists to this day) and figuratively attacking Christ in the form of the Serb nation left the ordinary Serbs with little option than to defend themselves against the vicious Muslim aggressors.

Mark Juergensmeyer as well argues that religious extremists see the world as being involved in a cosmic war in which good fights to eliminate all evil.[19] A cosmic war worldview is unique to religious violence because God's success demands one's obedience and defense in present circumstances. Though one may argue that the Marxist guerilla or nationalist rebel also see themselves in a fight of good versus evil, their struggle lacks the metaphysical element that incorporates that battle within a context of spiritual warfare. According to Juergensmeyer, this is one explanation of the excessive violence observed in religious conflicts. Juergensmeyer illustrates how the cosmic war worldview exacerbates a conflict in examples such as the antiabortionists in the United States, unionists in Northern Ireland, Jewish extremists in Israel, Islamic terrorists throughout the world, Sikhs in Punjab, and the Aum Shinrikyo cult in Japan. In Juergensmeyer's illustrative cases, the participants truly believe that evil is threatening good and that it is their responsibility to defend good.

David Rapoport, too, supports Juergensmeyer's and Sell's view that the religious beliefs themselves are important influences of the use of violence. Although Rapoport sees little difference in religious and secular doctrines, he argues that these doctrines drive the level of terrorist activity much more than technological advances that make weapons and targets more accessible.[20] Specifically concerning messianic terrorists, Rapoport argues that when believers think that a day of final judgment is coming soon and "that their actions can or must consummate the process,"[21] the religious belief in the end of the world when good fights evil and triumphs can encourage violence in six ways. According to Rapoport, "They are (1) the nature of the desired action, (2) the cause or character of messianic aspiration, (3) the proof that believers think may be necessary to demonstrate sufficient faith, (4) the moral qualities ascribed to participants in the messianic struggle, (5) the 'signs' or 'portents' of a messianic intervention, and (6) the character of the diety's involvement."[22] But Rapoport emphasizes that terrorism is not only inherent in the religious belief systems of those who ascribe to a messianic view, but is appealing because it falls outside socially accepted behavior. Messianists are disillusioned and reject their orthodox co-religionists, who they believe are corrupted. They want to break with the past to usher in the coming time of judgment and triumph of good. Terrorism then epitomizes "the antinomianism or complete liberation which is the essence of the messianic expectation."[23] For Rapoport, though, messianic terrorists do not differ significantly from their secular counterparts as both are driven by an intense devotion to their cause.

Paul Brass's analysis of riot events in India offers a more cynical accounting of religious violence in which the elites in the community use appeals to communal identities to incite their supporters and ensure power for themselves. Brass argues that the communal riots in India are perpetuated and aggravated by the constructed interpretation of events by elites in the community. The precipitating events according to Brass are often not "inherently ethnic/communal in nature" but are transformed into communal incidents by interpretations publicized by elites and the "further reinterpretation by the press and extralocal politicians and authorities. The 'official' interpretation that finally becomes universally accepted is often, if not usually, very far removed, often unrecognizable from the original precipitating events."[24] By contextually analyzing five riot events in modern India, Brass finds support for his argument—concluding that appeals to faith and sentiment (whether sincere or manipulated) were guises used by elites to increase their power and consequently perpetuate a communal riot.

As with any case study, however, this support for Brass's model is limited because of the small number of cases and selection bias. A more reliable test would require the analysis of a large number of randomly selected cases. Furthermore, Brass's study does not address why *religious* conflicts are more intense, but rather evaluates communal conflicts in general. One could argue that religious conflicts are a special subcategory of communal conflicts in which the religious identities serve as the basis of the communal identities and division. In the five cases examined by Brass, the communal riots are characterized by their religious division—Hindus versus Muslims—and are thus categorized as "religious conflicts" in this study. This, however, lumps together religious, ethnic, and other identity conflicts and cannot address the unique intensity of religious conflicts that is often assumed.

Andreas Hasenclever and Volker Rittberger offer an explanation of why religious conflicts are more violent, before turning their attention to how religion can be used to de-escalate a conflict. In their model, religion is an important influence to the extent that it modifies the strategic choices of elites in the conflict. In order to sustain a violent strategy, elites need members to carry out actions, as well as broad societal support that provides resources and morale for the group. According to Hasenclever and Rittberger, the mobilization and societal support is determined by four characteristics of the conflict, each in turn influenced by the involvement of religion in the conflict: the nature of the conflict, the willingness to make sacrifices, the relationship between the parties, and the legitimacy of violence. The involvement of religion creates value conflicts, as opposed to conflicts over scarce resources, that "are more prone to violence than conflicts about interests."[25] Religion also creates a following that is more willing to make sacrifices by "idealizing suffering in this world and promising rewards in another."[26] Furthermore, religious perceptions of the value conflict create an environment in which the other party cannot be trusted to follow through with any promises made in negotiations, thereby preventing a compromise and ultimate resolution to the conflict. And finally, the involvement of religion grants moral superiority to a group that embarks on a violent strategy that legitimizes their actions and provides the requisite societal support. Hasenclever and Rittberger do not test their model with empirical data, but rather use it as a foundation for exploring religion's capacity for de-escalating a conflict.

Underpinning these theoretical and case study explanations of how religion serves to intensify a conflict is the assumption that religion is associated with a higher level of violence that demands an explanation. Two studies in particular have quantitatively addressed this assumption to test its validity. Philip Roeder approaches the question within the "clash of civilizations" debate by attempting to determine how much religious division influences the intensity of a conflict. Roeder counts as a civilizational conflict any conflict in which the "dominant religion of the ethnic group belongs to a different civilization than that of the majority of the country's population."[27] Roeder uses a dataset of over one thousand domestic ethno-political conflicts between 1980 and 1999 in part to determine whether these civilizational conflicts are any more intense than other cultural conflicts. Using a logistical model, Roeder concludes that civilizational differences are a significant determinant of both the intensity and increase of intensity in a conflict, thereby supporting the assumption that religious differences are associated with more intense conflicts.

More recently, Fox addresses the question of the intensity of religious conflicts in a quantitative study using the State Failure Dataset that includes "1135 conflict years between 1950 and 1996."[28] By using a t-test that compares the average intensity of religious and nonreligious conflicts, Fox concludes that religious conflicts are more intense than nonreligious conflicts, although he notes the ambiguity of the results. Like this study, Fox relies on an identity-oriented definition, though no effort was made to account for the relevance of religion to a conflict. An earlier study of Fox's that tested the role of religious legitimacy on the formation of grievances, however, indicates that relevance is an important component in the relationship between religion and conflict.[29]

The plethora of case studies, some of which are cited in the literature review, leaves one with the impression that religious conflicts are inevitably more violent *because* of the involvement of religion, even if normatively religion has the capacity to bring peace rather than violence. Although Fox's and Roeder's studies cannot establish causality, they do demonstrate an association between religion and intensity which is assumed in the causal explanations developed in the theoretical and case studies. This study will take an approach similar to that used by Fox and Roeder, while building on their results by including a measure of the relevance of religion and comparing the intensity of conflicts involving the world's five major religions.

## Data and Methodology

In order to do this, a dataset of 278 cases of territorial conflict phases occurring between 1946 and 2001 in all parts of the world are compared statistically. The data was originally compiled by the International Peace Research Institute in Oslo, Norway (PRIO) in collaboration with Uppsala University and the Norwegian University of Science and Technology. According to PRIO, "An armed conflict is a contested incompatibility that concerns...territory where the use of armed force between two parties, of which at least one is the government of a state, results in at least 25 battle-related deaths."[30] The conflicts are broken down into phases when the number of battle deaths each year changes significantly.

The data include both interstate and intrastate conflicts provided that at least one party is a state and there is a territory that is disputed. Such conflicts ranging from the Chechnyan conflict in Russia to the Falkland War between Argentina and Britain are thus included. Furthermore, the data include conflicts that might generally be classified as "terrorist" as well as those that would be classified as "war," thereby including the Omagh bomb in Northern Ireland as a separate conflict phase as well as the Sudanese civil war (from 1983 to present). One might argue that these divergent cases are not comparable and the study should limit itself to one classification or the other because they are essentially different phenomena. While this is a valid argument, these are all instances of political violence and the purpose of this study is to determine the impact of religion on the intensity of *political violence*. Limiting the data to one particular form of this violence, then, would cause the study to fail in its objective.

There are two characteristics of the conflict phase that are pertinent to test the relationship between religion and the intensity of a conflict. First it is necessary to distinguish between religious conflicts and other types of conflicts. A religious conflict could be one in which the primary issue between the parties is a religious issue (issue-oriented definition) or a religious conflict could be one in which the two parties have differing religious identities (identity-oriented definition). Both definitions are legitimate, yet limited, measures of what is intended by religious conflict in this study.

In regards to the issue-oriented definition, it is often difficult to ascertain the central issue in a complex web of disputes and propaganda that surround a conflict. The list of issues is seemingly endless and often leaves a specific case belonging to multiple categories. The discrepancies are a result of the varying ways to identify the central issue of a conflict. For instance, a conflict over the sovereignty of a given territory that is claimed by two competing groups would generally be categorized as secessionist because the sovereignty or authority over the area is the primary issue for both sides. It could also be categorized as nationalist if the minority group is a somewhat coherent ethnic group (or claims to be such) and wishes to establish a homeland for their nation. Or if the minority was a coherent economic class wishing to install a government that favors their class, the conflict may best be described as a class conflict.

An additional problem is that there are often many goals for one group and determining which one defines a conflict can be difficult. In Northern Ireland, for instance, Sinn Fein is equally committed to removing British control of Northern Ireland and to creating a Marxist state.[31] It would be difficult to determine which goal comes before the other as they are so intertwined in Sinn Fein's ideology. Thus, Sinn Fein and the Northern Ireland conflict could be categorized as either a conflict over territory or as a Marxist conflict.

Furthermore, many groups see themselves involved in a conflict of which the other party is unaware. The Al Qaeda movement is an excellent example. In 1996 (long before the United States recognized a war against Al Qaeda and terrorism), Osama bin Laden issued a fatwa (or religious declaration) that described the American actions in the Gulf War as a "clear declaration of war on God, His Messenger and Muslims."[32] Yet the American government saw their actions as defending Kuwait's sovereignty (or more likely defending Western access to Kuwait's oil) from a more terrestrial enemy, Saddam Hussein. From bin Laden's perspective the conflict between the United States and Iraq was religious, while from the American perspective the conflict was territorial.

Because of these limits to the issue-oriented definition, it may seem more accurate to use the identity-oriented definition. The identity-oriented definition classifies a conflict as religious when the two sides have differing religious identities, whether or not those identities are explicitly pertinent to the conflict. Quantitative studies of the clash of civilizations thesis have relied on an identity-oriented definition as they are essentially interested in whether these identities are increasingly becoming the dividing lines in conflicts. This definition allows for an exploration of the effect that these identities have on the dynamics of the conflict, even when the identities are not a primary cause of (or issue in) the conflict. The identity-oriented definition, however, is also limited precisely because it does not take into account the relevance of religion to the conflict. Such a definition lumps together the Bosnian wars and the Falkland War, which clearly involve religion to different degrees.

In this study, the identity-oriented definition is used as it permits a more reliable measure of religious conflict, however, the relevance of religion to the conflict is included as a control variable to correct for the limits of this definition.[33] As such, a conflict is determined to be religious when 80 percent of the population in the territory differs from 80 percent of the state with which the territory is in dispute. The relevance variable evaluates the importance of religion relevant to other issues in the conflict. It takes into account the proximity and awareness of the parties of their religious identity in relation to the other party, and particularly takes into account the parties' appeals based on that identity.

Using this identity-oriented definition, the dataset takes a very broad definition that results in the inclusion of more cases than might be included if the issue-oriented definition were used. As such, the dataset used in this study includes more "religious" conflicts than "nonreligious" conflicts. Furthermore, it should be noted that there are a disproportionate number of conflicts involving Christianity and Islam rather than Buddhism, Hinduism, and Judaism. Again, adopting the relevance of religion as a control variable allows one to determine if this broad definition potentially biases the results of the study.

The second variable needed for a test of the intensity of religious conflicts is one that measures the intensity of each conflict phase. The PRIO Armed Conflict Dataset documents the number of deaths (on a three-point scale) as well as the duration of the conflict (in years). In one sense, the level of violence is the best measure of the intensity and, in fact, the number of deaths is often used as a proxy of intensity in quantitative evaluations of conflicts. But intensity is not just the number of people that die in a conflict. More people died on September 11 than in the over thirty-five years of the Northern Ireland "Troubles." Intensity includes not just the level of violence, but also the length of time that violence is sustained. Therefore, this study combined the two measures to document the intensity of each conflict phase.[34]

There are multiple statistical tests that would allow for a comparison of the intensity of religious conflicts to that of other conflicts, each test appropriate and yet limited. As the lowest level of measurement for the variables is nominal ("religious conflict"), a nominal test such as a chi-square test would generally be the most appropriate. It is also possible, however, to treat a dichotomous nominal variable as an ordinal variable, as order is reversible with two categories. Thus, it is possible to use an ordinal test of association such as Kendall's tau-b or Gamma. Generally an ordinal test would be preferred to a nominal test because it takes advantage of the ordering rather than disregarding this information, but there are also circumstances under which a nominal test would provide a stronger test of association between the two variables. Specifically, if the relationship does not have a single overall positive or negative trend, but is better described as a curvilinear relationship, the ordinal test will cancel out the opposing trends and mask the existence of a relationship.[35] As discussed in the following section, the data indicates a curvilinear relationship and is therefore more accurately tested using the chi-square test than an ordinal measure of association.

## Results

The results of the chi-square test of the PRIO armed territorial conflicts are displayed in Table 1. As expected, this test confirms that religious conflicts are in fact more intense than other types of conflicts, as is reflected in the significantly positive chi-square value. The chi-square value, while indicating a significant relationship between religion and conflict intensity at a 90 percent confidence level, nevertheless demonstrates a weak result and is not the overwhelming proof one might have expected from previous research. In fact, if one were to use another commonly used significance level (95 percent), the results would indicate a lack of relationship between the involvement of religion and conflict intensity. Like Fox's results, the results of this test are far from conclusive.

**Table 1.** Religious conflicts and intensity

|  | % of nonreligious conflicts | % of religious conflicts |
|---|---|---|
| Low Intensity | 33 | 21 |
| Somewhat Low Intensity | 21 | 25 |
| Moderate Intensity | 22 | 34 |
| Somewhat High Intensity | 15 | 16 |
| High Intensity | 9 | 4 |
| N | 67 | 211 |
| Chi-value | 7.7327 | |
| Probability | 0.102 | |

It is worth noting that there are more cases of religious than nonreligious territorial conflicts. Although a broad definition of religious conflict is used, this nevertheless indicates that territorial conflicts are more often than not divided along religious lines as well as land boundaries. This observation, however, does not make any pretenses about the importance of religion or religious issues in territory conflicts, as the relevance of religion has not been taken into account in the Table 1 results.

A closer look at the cell values offers a more detailed description of the nature of this relationship. Over 50 percent (54 percent) of nonreligious conflicts had either low or somewhat low intensities while 50 percent of religious conflicts exhibited moderate to somewhat high intensities, indicating that religious conflicts are characterized by a slightly higher intensity than nonreligious conflicts—as suggested by the significant chi-square value. The distribution, however, does not follow a single trend. Rather, religious conflicts dominate the moderate intensity category, while nonreligious conflicts fall to the extremes with either higher or lower intensities. Notice that 54 percent of nonreligious conflicts fall into the lowest two categories of intensity as compared to only 46 percent of religious conflicts. The other extreme demonstrates the same relationship: 24 percent of nonreligious conflicts fall into the two highest categories of intensity as compared to only 20 percent of religious conflicts. On the other hand, in the moderate intensity category are 34 percent of religious conflicts and only 22 percent of nonreligious conflicts. Though one can clearly see the pattern indicated by the chi-square values in the intensity distribution of religious and nonreligious conflicts, the evidence is not as overwhelmingly convincing as one might have expected. This confirms the conclusion drawn from the borderline significance of the chi-square value.

Why are the results not as convincing as one would have expected? Although limited to the realm of speculation in this study, one possible explanation is that religious conflicts are only more intense under specific conditions. As Appleby suggested, the education of the religious faithful may be an important determinant of the relationship. Or as Marx proposed, the emphasis in the religion placed on the afterlife may be an important component of the relationship. Furthermore, religious identity may only intensify a conflict when it exists in conjunction with discrimination against the religious identity, a meddling international diaspora, a tight community network to organize the faithful, or a highly regarded religious hierarchy. Without considering religious conflicts in the context of these and countless other hypothetical factors, the overall relationship between religion and conflict intensity may appear weak or nonexistent when in reality it is contingent on specific conditions.

The incongruence between the Table 1 results and expectations may also be because of the broad definition of religious conflict used in this study. As described at the start, there are two broad categories of definitions, one focusing on the identities of the parties involved and the other on the issues at the heart of the conflict. Each definition comes with its unique limitations. This study took advantage of the broader (and measurably, more reliable) definition and determined that the oftassumed relationship with conflict intensity is weak at best. There are undoubtedly many cases categorized as "religious" that will raise an eyebrow and draw valid objection. Would altering the definition, and thus altering the categorization of "religious conflicts," alter the results of this study? Ideally, the results would be rigorous enough to withstand minor modifications, but the question here is: does choosing an issue-oriented definition over the identity-oriented definition cause a major modification that alters the results?

As mentioned previously, incorporating the relevance of religion to the conflict is one way to address the limits of the identity-oriented definition used in this study. By evaluating the changes between the initially observed relationship with that observed after incorporating relevance, one can determine the importance of relevance to the relationship between religion and intensity of a conflict. If relevance significantly alters the observed relationship, it suggests that the identity-oriented definition is not only limited, but leads to potentially biased results. The results of the test of religion and conflict intensity controlling for relevance are displayed in Table 2.

The results presented in Table 2 demonstrate that controlling for relevance alters the initially observed relationship between religion and conflict intensity. In cases of low relevance, the relationship does not wholly disappear but weakens below an accepted level of significance, whereas in cases of high relevance the relationship vanishes entirely. Relevance clearly does not have a uniform effect on the two categories of cases. This suggests that relevance is interacting with the religious

**Table 2.** Religion and intensity controlling for relevance of religion to a conflict

|  | Low relevance |  | High relevance |  |
| --- | --- | --- | --- | --- |
|  | % of nonreligious conflicts | % of religious conflicts | % of nonreligious conflicts | % of religious conflicts |
| Low Intensity | 42 | 23 | 17 | 20 |
| Somewhat Low Intensity | 21 | 31 | 21 | 23 |
| Moderate Intensity | 14 | 27 | 38 | 36 |
| Somewhat High Intensity | 12 | 10 | 21 | 18 |
| High Intensity | 12 | 8 | 4 | 3 |
| N | 43 | 48 | 24[36] | 163 |
| Chi-value | 5.622 |  | 0.3629 |  |
| Probability | 0.229 |  | 0.985 |  |

conflict variable which supports the expectation that relevance is an important element of the relationship between religious conflicts and the intensity of conflicts.

It was expected, though, that the more relevant religion is to a conflict, the more "religious" the conflict and the more likely it would exhibit a higher intensity. If this were true, one would minimally expect an evident relationship (captured in a significant chi-square value) in cases where religion is highly relevant. The results in Table 2, however, leave no doubt that there is no relationship in these cases. Interestingly, the results are much closer to being significant for cases when religion is less relevant to the conflict than in cases where religion is more relevant to the conflict. In other words, there is a suggestion that relevance has the opposite effect on the relationship between the involvement of religion and intensity of a conflict than was expected. The less relevant religion is in a religious conflict, the more likely religious conflicts are related to the intensity of conflicts. The relationship does not display a single positive or negative trend, though, so one cannot say that the less relevant religion is, the more likely a religious conflict will be more intense than a nonreligious conflict. The results of the partial table for cases of low relevance exhibit the same pattern observed for all cases: nonreligious conflicts fall at the extremes, while religious conflicts dominate the moderate intensity category.

Another way to address the question about the importance of the relevance of religion to the relationship between religion and conflict intensity is by asking specifically how introducing relevance changes the distribution of cases in Table 1. If relevance is unimportant to the analysis, one would expect that the partial tables for cases of both low and high relevance would mirror Table 1. On the other hand, if relevance has a systematic effect on religious conflicts, one would expect to see a decrease in low intensity religious conflicts and increase in high intensity religious conflicts when relevance was high.

The distribution of the intensity of religious conflicts changes with the introduction of the relevance of religion, though less dramatically than one might expect. About 46 percent of religious conflicts were in the lowest two categories of intensity, which increased by 8 percentage points (54 percent of cases) in cases where religion was less relevant and declined by 3 percentage points (43 percent of cases) in cases where religion was more relevant. About 34 percent of religious conflicts had a moderate intensity, which decreased by 7 percentage points (27 percent of cases) when relevance was low and increased by 2 percentage points (36 percent of cases) when relevance was high. And finally, 20 percent of religious conflicts fell into the highest two categories of intensity, which dropped by 2 percentage points (18 percent of cases) when relevance was low and increased by 1 percentage point (21 percent of cases) when relevance was high.

This analysis is particularly concerned with the impact of relevance on the intensity of cases of religious conflicts, as the expectation is that the relevance increases the "religiousness" of a conflict and thereby increases its intensity. There does seem to be some support for this hypothesis as the percentage of religious conflicts in the two highest intensity categories is 6 points higher when relevance is high than when relevance is low. Conversely, the percentage of religious conflicts in the two lowest intensity categories is 11 points lower when relevance is high than when relevance is low. In other words, the higher the relevance, the higher the intensity of religious conflicts; the lower the relevance, the lower the intensity of religious conflicts. However, this evidence—like the chi-square values—is weak and only hazily indicates the expected relationship.

Both a close examination of the change in distribution of the cell values and an in-depth analysis of the change in chi-square values indicate that the relevance variable interacts with the religious conflict variable in relation to the intensity of a conflict. Like Fox's study of grievance formations, this study indicates that relevance of religion is an indispensable element of the relationship between religion and conflict.

There are two important implications of the Table 2 results. First, relying solely on an identity-oriented definition potentially biases any tests of the relationship between religion and conflict intensity. As was demonstrated, leaving relevance out of the analysis indicates a significant, though weak, relationship—though the relationship is clearly insignificant when this vital component is included. In order to accurately assess the nature of religion in conflict, one should not rely on a strict identity-oriented definition.

A second implication of this result is that this analysis can only be considered a necessary first step as there are countless other variables that potentially and logically interact with religion to alter the observed relationship. This study is merely concerned with establishing an association between religion and conflict intensity and not on defining a causal relationship between the two variables. Although the analysis found only a weak relationship between religion and conflict intensity, it cannot rule out the reasonable possibility that when the education of believers and their theology (or the discrimination against a particular religious identity, or countless other potentially interacting variables) are accounted for, the relationship will more closely meet expectations derived from the large number of case studies. As yet, a list of widely agreed-upon interacting variables has not developed.

There is currently, however, much public discussion about the potential for excessive violence within specific religious traditions suggesting that the result displayed in Table 1—that religious conflicts are more intense—exists only when a particular religion is involved in the conflict. The implication is that one religion may be more likely to be involved in a higher intensity conflict than another religion. Specifically, the images of an Islamic suicide bomber and a Gandhian peace protestor lead some to believe that the type of religion involved in the conflict is an important control variable when analyzing the intensity of the conflict that has yet to be included in this analysis.

Every religious tradition has at its disposal violent myths and precedents with which a violent strategy can be justified and persistence to the death can be encouraged. Within Islam, the concept of jihad (struggle) has been widely discussed as a mobilizer for those willing to sacrifice themselves and others in a conflict. Yet for many Muslims, this form of jihad—the lesser jihad according to Muhammad—should only be used in extreme and specific conditions. Rather, the everyday jihad—called the greater jihad by Muhammad—is a daily struggle against impurity within oneself.

Christianity, as well, has its traditions of violence that serve to inspire some of its adherents to engage in violence. The first half of Christianity's sacred text, the Bible, chronicles battle after battle in which the Israelites (God's chosen people) succeeded when they obeyed God and lost when they disobeyed God. In one particularly grisly passage, God commanded Moses and the Israelites to attack and kill all the Midianites—including women and young boys—because they had corrupted the Israelites.[37] Many current mainstream Christians interpret events such as the massacre of theMidianites as no longer relevant to modern Christians. While they believe such events occurred and believe in the biblical interpretation of those events, they believe that the events occurred before Jesus lived. They believe Jesus's teachings prioritize love and peace over such violence. Jesus's teachings and the theology of the second half of the Bible is often referred to as the "New Covenant" that overrides the agreement between God and man in the first half of the Bible. "Love one another"[38] and "Turn the other cheek"[39] are dominant themes within this new covenant. In fact, by the fourth century, the just war doctrine was developed within Christianity to limit the acceptance of violence and war.

Even Hinduism—associated with Gandhi and the peaceful protests for independence in India—is not devoid of violent traditions on which justifications for the use of violence can be built. One of the sacred texts of Hinduism, the Bhagavad Gita, opens with a description of an ensuing battle.[40] On the one side were the Pandavas and on the other were the Kauravas, cousins of the Pandavas. At stake in the battle was land the Pandavas deemed they were entitled to and which the Kauravas refused to hand over. The Bhagavad Gita describes a conversation that took place between the leader of the Pandavas, Arjuna, and the god Krishna just before the battle was to begin. Arjuna was hesitant to go to war because he saw family members on the other side. Krishna, however, implored Arjuna to go to war as his duty as a soldier and in order to protect the Pandava people. Ultimately Arjuna heeded Krishna's advice and successfully led the Pandavas to victory over the Kauravas.

The quantitative tests of the use of violence by groups following these religious traditions are limited. Jonathan Fox addressed this stereotype of Islam in his crosssectional study of ethno-religious conflicts.[41] Using 105 cases of current ethno-religious conflicts, Fox used a mean comparison technique to compare Islam, Christianity, and other religions. Contradicting a few prominent historical examples, Fox found that Islamic minority groups were no more conflict prone than any other ethno-religious minority group. However, religion seemed to be a more important issue when Islamic minority groups were involved. Fox also found that there was very little difference in the intensity of conflicts involving the different religions. Fox's evidence, in other words, seems to shatter the image of Islam being more violent than other religions.

Interestingly, Hector Avalos compared the violence in the Bhagavad Gita to that in the Christian Bible in an effort to determine which sacred text was more violent.[42] He found that the Bible recounted significantly more acts of violence than the Bhagavad Gita and the biblical justification for violence was much more pronounced in the interpretations of the two texts. The Bhagavad Gita is generally interpreted as an allegory for humanity's internal struggle or as a historical precedent for the very limited use of violence. The Bible, on the other hand, is first interpreted as a precedent that justifies violence and only secondarily (if at all) interpreted as an allegory. In other words, the story of Arjuna is first interpreted by Hindus as an example of a soul's struggle, while the story of the destruction of the Midianites is primarily read as a historical event by Jews and Christians.

The data in this study provides an opportunity to test the violence in practice of the various religious traditions. The 278 conflict phases in the dataset of this study are subjected to chi-square tests. In these tests, conflicts involving one religion are compared to all other conflicts (i.e., Buddhist conflicts compared to all conflicts not involving Buddhism, Christian conflicts compared to all conflicts not involving Christianity, etc.). The chi-square value then represents the difference between the intensity distribution of each religion against all others. Thus a significant chi-square value indicates that the specified religion differs in its intensity from all other religions. The results are displayed in Table 3.

The results are somewhat surprising. Buddhist, Christian, and Islamic conflicts do not display intensities that are significantly different than the other religions. Hindu and Jewish conflicts, on the other hand, do have significantly different intensities than the other religions. A glance at the average intensity of these two types of conflicts shows that they are associated with higher intensity conflicts. In the results concerning both Hinduism and Judaism, however, the tests are susceptible to bias due to a very small number of cases.

The association of Hindu conflicts with a higher intensity is unanticipated. Often the first image roused by the mention of Hinduism is that of meditating monks or, in the context of political violence, of Gandhi and the peaceful protests that brought India its independence in 1947. Avalos's analysis of the doctrinal justifications of violence in the two religions leads one to expect Hinduism to be associated with lower intensities. Yet this analysis that considers postindependence India suggests that this popular image needs to be modified. Hinduism displays a significant relationship with higher conflict intensity when subjected to a chi-square test. The result, however, is potentially biased by limits in the data. There are only a small number of cases involving Hinduism in the dataset, and all conflicts are those in which India was a participant (with the exception of the Sri Lankan Tamil conflict). It is possible that another characteristic of India other than its religious identity is the cause of excessive violence, though the data in this study cannot differentiate between the two.

Though in the present context of the festering Middle East conflict the result that Judaism is associated with higher intensity conflicts may not be as unexpected as the Hindu finding, the result of the chi-square test is also potentially biased due to the small number of Jewish conflicts—all involving Israel.

This study is limited to the data available to test these hypotheses; however, it is possible to use an alternative method that better accounts for the number of cases and can provide an indication of any biases in the chi-square value due to the number of cases. The chi-square is calculated using the number of cases in each category only to determine the expected frequency for each cell. There is no measure incorporated into the test that takes account of the accuracy of these expected frequencies. Therefore, the test is not sensitive to the varying number of cases and particularly in this study to the low frequency of Hindu and Jewish conflicts. A difference of means t-test corrects for this by comparing the average intensity, while taking into account the standard deviation (that is dependent on the number of cases in the category). The number of cases in a category is thus a determinant of the accuracy of the means. Although the difference of means t-test is potentially biased because it depends on a mean (that is biased for ordinal variables), the test offers another perspective that is not available with the chi-square tests.

In these tests, the average intensity of conflicts involving one religion is compared to the average intensity of all other conflicts. The t-value then represents the difference between the average intensity of conflicts involving one specific religion to the average intensity of conflicts involving all other religions. A positive and significant t-value indicates that the average intensity of conflicts involving that religion is higher than conflicts involving all other religions. The results are presented below the chi-square results in Table 3.

Clearly the difference of means t-test demonstrates that no one religion is

Table 3. Intensity and type of religion

| | % not Buddhist | % Buddhist | % not Christian | % Christian | % not Hindu | % Hindu | % not Islamic | % Islamic | % not Jewish | % Jewish |
|---|---|---|---|---|---|---|---|---|---|---|
| Low Intensity | 23 | 30 | 25 | 21 | 26 | 6 | 23 | 25 | 24 | 9 |
| Somewhat Low Intensity | 24 | 18 | 22 | 27 | 21 | 43 | 25 | 23 | 24 | 9 |
| Moderate Intensity | 31 | 30 | 31 | 31 | 30 | 37 | 31 | 32 | 30 | 73 |
| Somewhat High Intensity | 16 | 15 | 15 | 18 | 17 | 9 | 15 | 16 | 16 | 9 |
| High Intensity | 5 | 6 | 7 | 3 | 5 | 6 | 7 | 4 | 6 | 0 |
| N | 245 | 33 | 178 | 100 | 243 | 35 | 137 | 141 | 267 | 11 |
| Chi-value | 1.2199 | | 3.3244 | | 13.4210 | | 1.0400 | | 9.2996 | |
| Probability | .875 | | .505 | | .009 | | .904 | | .054 | |
| Average Intensity | 3.56 | 3.48 | 3.56 | 3.55 | 3.54 | 3.66 | 3.58 | 3.52 | 3.54 | 3.82 |
| Standard Deviation | 1.16 | 1.25 | 1.21 | 1.10 | 1.20 | 0.94 | 1.19 | 1.16 | 1.18 | 0.75 |
| T-value | .3611 | | .0422 | | −.5577 | | .4208 | | −.7642 | |
| Probability | .7183 | | .9664 | | .5775 | | .6742 | | .4454 | |

systematically involved in conflicts of a higher or lower intensity than all other religions. Not only are the t-values very near zero for all cases, but also the probability of those values is very far from any acceptable level of significance. Taken in combination with the chi-square test results, there is substantial reason to believe that the initially evident relationship between Hinduism, Judaism, and higher conflict intensity resulted from a bias due to the limited number of cases of these types of conflicts in the dataset used in this study.

## Conclusion

This article has addressed the conventional wisdom and widespread perceptions about the intensity of religious conflicts. Based on the statistical analysis of 278 interstate and intrastate territorial conflict phases occurring worldwide between 1946 and 2001, the evidence indicates that conflicts involving religion are significantly more intense than other types of conflicts, though the evidence is statistically much weaker than expected. Using the broad definition of a religious conflict also found that the great majority of territorial conflicts involved religious divisions.

When the relevance of religion to the conflict is incorporated to address the limits of the identity-oriented definition of a religious conflict used in this study, the relationship between the involvement of religion and conflict intensity weakens below an accepted level of significance. The analysis found that relevance is an important component of the relationship as it interacts with the "religious conflict" variable. The implication of this result is that studies that are dependent on the identity-oriented definition are potentially biased because of the limits of the definition.

Furthermore, this study initially found that Hinduism and Judaism are related to higher conflict intensity, although it was concluded that this result was likely due to the small number of cases of Hindu and Jewish conflicts in the dataset.

## Notes

1. See David Apter, *Ideology and Discontent* (New York: Free Press, 1964); Jeffrey R. Seul, "'Ours Is the Way of God': Religion, Identity, and Intergroup Conflict," *Journal of Peace Research* 36, no. 5 (1999): 553–69; Hizkias Assefa, "Religion in the Sudan: Exacerbating Conflict or Facilitating Reconciliation?" *Bulletin of Peace Proposals* 21, no. 3 (1990): 255–62.

2. See Harvey Cox, *The Secular City* (London: SCM Press, 1965). Otto Maduro countered this view with a modified Marxism that is in line with liberation theology in Latin America in his book, *Religion and Social Conflict* (Maryknoll, NY: Orbis Books, 1982).

3. Jonathan Fox, "Religion and State Failure: An Examination of the Extent and Magnitude of Religious Conflict from 1950 to 1996," *International Political Science Review* 25, no. 1 (2004): 55–76; Errol A. Henderson, "Culture or Contiguity: Ethnic Conflict, the Similiarity of States, and the Onset of War, 1820–1989," *Journal of Conflict Resolution* 41, no. 5 (1997): 649–68; Marta Reynal-Querol, "Ethnicity, Political Systems, and Civil Wars," *Journal of Conflict Resolution* 46, no. 1 (2002): 29–54; Rudolph J. Rummel, "Is Collective Violence Correlated with Social Pluralism?" *Journal of Peace Research* 34, no. 2 (1997): 163–75; Philip G. Roeder, "Clash of Civilizations and Escalation of Domestic Ethnopolitical Conflicts," *Comparative Political Studies* 36, no. 5 (2003): 509–40.

4. For examples of this type of research, see: Mark Juergensmeyer, *Terror in the Mind of God: The Global Rise of Religious Violence* (Berkeley: University of California Press, 2000); Samuel P. Huntington, *The Clash of Civilizations and the Remaking of World Order* (London: Simon and Schuster, 1997); Rodney Stark and William Sims Bainbridge, *The Future of Religion: Secularization, Revival and Cult Formation* (London: University of California Press, 1985); Daniel H. Levine, ed., *Churches and Politics in Latin America* (London: Sage Publica-

tions, 1980); John H. Kautsky, *The Political Consequences of Modernization* (London: John Wiley and Sons, 1972); Elie Halevy, *A History of the English People in 1815* (London: Ark Paperbacks, 1924); Mark Juergensmeyer, *The New Cold War? Religious Nationalism Confronts the Secular State* (London: University of California Press, 1994); Giles Kepel, *The Revenge of God: The Resurgence of Islam, Christianity and Judaism in the Modern World*, Trans. Alan Braley (Cambridge: Polity Press, 1994); John R. Hall, Philip D. Schuyler, and Sylvaine Trinh, *Apocalypse Observed: Religious Movements and Violence in North America, Europe and Japan* (London: Routledge, 2000).

5. See Paul R. Brass, *Theft of an Idol: Text and Context in the Representation of Collective Violence* (Princeton: Princeton University Press, 1997); Donald Eugene Smith, *Religion, Politics, and Social Change in the Third World: A Sourcebook* (London: Collier-MacMillan, 1971); Alan D. Falconer, "The Role of Religion in Situations of Armed Conflict: The Case of Northern Ireland," *Bulletin of Peace Proposals* 21, no. 3 (1990): 273–80; Andreas Hasenclever and Volker Rittberger, "Does Religion Make a Difference? Theoretical Approaches to the Impact of Faith on Political Conflict," *Millenium: Journal of International Studies* 29, no. 3 (2000): 654–659.

6. Gurr's earliest theory was presented in *Why Men Rebel* (Princeton: Princeton University Press, 1971). He has modified this theory to include elements of organization. The revised theory is presented in *Minorities at Risk: A Global View of Ethnopolitical Conflict* (Washington DC: United States Institute of Peace, 1993).

7. Jonathan Fox, "Towards a Dynamic Theory of Ethno-Religious Conflict," *Nations and Nationalism* 5, no. 4 (1999): 431–63.

8. Jonathan Fox, "The Influence of Religious Legitimacy on Grievance Formation by Ethno-Religious Minorities," *Journal of Peace Research* 36, no. 3 (1999): 289–307.

9. See especially Marc Gopin, *Between Eden and Armageddon* (New York: Oxford University Press, 1999).

10. See R. Scott Appleby, *The Ambivalence of the Sacred* (New York: Rowman and Littlefield Publishers, 2000), Guenter Lewy, *Religion and Revolution* (New York: Oxford University Press, 1974); David C. Rapoport, "Comparing Militant Fundamentalist Movements and Groups," in *Fundamentalisms and the State: Remaking Polities, Economies, and Militance*, ed. Martin E. Marty and R. Scott Appleby (London: University of Chicago Press, 1993), 429–61.

11. Appleby, *The Ambivalence of the Sacred*, 17.

12. Ibid.

13. Ibid.

14. Gary T. Marx, "Religion: Opiate or Inspiration of Civil Rights Militancy Among Negroes?" *American Sociological Review* 32, no. 1 (1967): 64–72. See also Gary T. Marx, *Protest and Prejudice* (London: Harper and Row Publishers, 1967).

15. Ibid., 72.

16. Charles Kimball, *When Religion Becomes Evil* (New York: Harper Collins, 2002).

17. Samuel P. Huntington, *The Clash of Civilizations*.

18. Michael Sells, *The Bridge Betrayed: Religion and Genocide in Bosnia* (Berkeley: University of California Press, 1998).

19. Juergensmeyer, *Terror in the Mind of God*.

20. David Rapoport, "Fear and Trembling: Terrorism in Three Religious Traditions," *American Political Science Review* 78, no. 3 (1984): 658–77.

21. David Rapoport, "Messianic Sanctions for Terror," *Comparative Politics* 20, no. 2 (1988): 197.

22. Ibid., 197–98.

23. Ibid., 210.

24. Brass, *Theft of an Idol*, 6.

25. Hasenclever and Rittberger, "Does Religion Make a Difference?" 653.

26. Ibid., 656.

27. Roeder, "Clash of Civilizations and Escalation of Domestic Ethnopolitical Conflicts," 516.

28. Fox, "Religion and State Failure."

29. Fox, "The Influence of Religious Legitimacy."

30. Havard Strand et al., (2002). *Armed Conflict Dataset Codebook*. http://www.prio.no/cwp/ArmedConflict.

31. The introduction page of Sinn Fein's Web-site makes clear that union with Ireland is not the sole goal of the party. See http://www.sinnfein.ie (accessed on November 14, 2003). Sinn Fein's President, Gerry Adams, also makes this clear in his book, *Free Ireland: Towards a Lasting Peace* (Niwot, CO: Roberts Rinehart Publishing, 1994).

32. As cited in Juergensmeyer, *Terror in the Mind of God*, 145.

33. The cases classified as "religious" are as follows. The number in parentheses is the relevance score. Keep in mind that these conflicts are broken down into phases based on changes in the annual number of deaths throughout the duration of the conflict. Furthermore, these are defined as "religious" based on a difference in the majority religion of the two sides involved and are defined as "highly relevant" when the sides are in close proximity and make references to the differing identities.

Algeria independence (2), Angola independence (2), Angola-Cabinda (3), Argentina-UK (2), Azerbaijan-Nagorno Karabakh (3), Bangladesh-Chittagong Hill Tracts (3), Bosnia Herzegovina-Serb territories (3), Bosnia Herzegovina-Bihac (3), Bosnia Herzegovina-Croat territories (3), Burkina Faso-Mali (3), Burma-Karen territories (3), Burma-Arakan territories (3), Burma-Kachin territories (3), Cambodia independence (2), Cambodia-Vietnam (1), Cameroon independence (2), Chad-Libya (3), China-Tibet (3), China-Burma (3), China-India (3), China-USSR (3), China-Taiwan Strait (3), China-Vietnam (3), Comoros-Anjouan (1), Croatia-Serb territories (3), Cyprus independence (2), Cyprus-North Cyprus (3), Egypt-UK (2), El Salvador-Honduras (1), Ethiopia-Ogaden (3), Ethiopia-Afar (3), Ethiopia-Somali territories (3), Ethiopia-Somalia (3), Georgia-Abkhazia (3), Guinea Bissau independence (2), Hyderabad-India (3), India-Nagaland (3), India-Mizoram (3), India-Tripura (1), India-Manipur (3), India-Punjab (3), India-Kashmir (3), India-Assam (3), India-Pakistan (3), Indonesia independence (2), Indonesia-South Moluccas (3), Indonesia-West Papua (3), Indonesia-East Timor (3), Indonesia-Aceh (1), Indonesia-Netherlands (2), Iran-Kurdistan (3), Iran-Arabistan (3), Iran-Iraq (1), Israel independence (3), Israel-Palestine (3), Israel-Egypt (3), Israel-Egypt, Iraq, Lebanon, Syria, Jordan (3), Israel-Jordan (3), Israel-Syria (3), Israel, UK, France-Egypt (3), Kenya independence (2), Laos independence (2), Laos-Thailand (3), Madagascar-Malagasy (2), Malaysia independence (2), Malaysia-Indonesia (3), Mali-Air and Azawad (3), Mauritania-Morocco/Mauritania (2), Mauritania-Senegal (1), Morocco independence (2), Morocco-Spanish territories (2), Mozambique independence (2), Nigeria-Biafra (3), North Korea-South Korea (3), Pakistan-Baluchistan (1), Papua New Guinea-Bougainville (3), Philippines-Mindanao (3), Puerto Rico independence (1), Russia-Chechnya (3), Russia-Dagestan (3), Senegal-Casamance (3), South Africa-Namibia (3), USSR-Estonia (3), USSR-Latvia (3), USSR-Lithuania (3), USSR-Ukraine (3), USSR-Azerbaijan (3), Sri Lanka-Tamil (3), Sudan-South Sudan (3), Thailand-France (2), Tunisia independence (2), Tunisia-France (2), UK-Northern Ireland (3), UK-Albania (2), Vietnam independence (2), Yemen-South Yemen (1), Yemen-Aden (2), Yugoslavia-Kosovo (3).

The conflicts categorized as nonreligious are as follows:

Algeria-Morocco (1), Brunei-North Borneo (1), Burma-Mon territories (1), Burma-Kaya territories (1), Burma-Shan territories (1), Cambodia-Thailand (1), Cameroon-Nigeria (1), Chad-Nigeria (3), China-Taiwan (3), Congo/Zaire-Katanga (1), Congo/Zaire-South Kasai (1), Ecuador-Peru (1), Eritrea-Ethiopia (1998–2000), Ethiopia-Eritrea (1), Georgia-South Ossetia (3), Honduras-Nicaragua (1), Iraq-Kurdistan (3), Iraq-Kuwait (1), Malaysia-North Borneo (3), Moldova-Dniestr (1), Morocco-Western Sahara (3), Niger-Air and Azawad (1), Niger-Toubou (1), Oman independence (1), Pakistan-East Pakistan (1), South Vietnam independence (1), South Vietnam-North Vietnam (1), USSR-Nagorno-Karabakh (3), Spain-Basque (1), Turkey-Kurdistan (1), Yugoslavia-Slovenia (3), Yugoslavia-Croatia (3).

34. The duration listed in the PRIO Armed Conflict Dataset was converted to a threepoint scale and added to the number of deaths variable to generate an "intensity" variable ranging from two to six.

35. Alan Agresti, *Categorical Data Analysis*, 2nd ed. (Hoboken, NJ: John Wiley and Sons, 2002).

36. It may strike the reader as illogical for there to be cases of nonreligious conflicts in which religion is highly relevant to the conflict. Keep in mind that "religious conflicts" are defined by the religious identities that divide the two sides in the conflict. In each of these cases, the territory and state shared an identity, but the religious identities were not referenced by one or both of the parties involved in the conflict.

37. Num. 31: 1–18 (King James Version).

38. John 15:17 (King James Version).
39. Matt. 5:39 (New American Standard Version).
40. Bhagavad Gita.
41. Jonathan Fox, "Is Islam More Conflict Prone Than Other Religions? A Cross-Sectional Study of Ethnoreligious Conflict," *Nationalism and Ethnic Politics* 6, no. 2 (2000): 1–24.
42. Hector Avalos, "Violence in the Bible and the Bhagavad Gita," in *Holy War: Violence and the Bhagavad Gita*, ed. Steven J. Rosen (Hampton, VA: A. Deepak Publishing, 2002), 127–44.

# The Changing Jewish Discourse on Armed Conflict: Themes and Implications

## STUART A. COHEN

For the most part, the classic sources of Jewish theological discourse devote very little attention to discussion of the circumstances that might justify a resort to war.

In this respect, Jewish political traditions differ very markedly from those of the West, whose protracted concern with "just war" issues has fueled various detailed definitions of the precise components of a *ius ad bellum*.[1]

That discrepancy is not hard to explain. Although warfare undoubtedly played a crucial role in the formation of Israel's national identity during biblical times, for the past two millennia the dominant motifs of Jewish political history have been exile, subjugation, and powerlessness.[2] Such circumstances alone would have removed the notion of a collective use of force from the practical agenda of Jewish political action. Their impact was buttressed by collective memories of the disastrous Bar Kochba rebellion against Rome in 135 C.E. which entered the canon as a standing warning against the possibility that Jews might "seek national power by their own political and military efforts."[3]

The result has been a distortion in the entire landscape of Jewish religious discourse. Over the course of the generations subsequent to the trauma of exile, numerous aspects of required Jewish behavior (public as well as private) were analyzed and legislated at great length—often in the most minute detail. But of all the classic authoritative exponents of the Jewish tradition, only Maimonides (Rabbi Moses ben Maimon, Egypt, 1135–1204) systematically analyzed the conditions under which military action might receive religious sanction. That titanic exception apart, the topic was virtually ignored in the *halacha*—the generic term applied to the huge corpus of ancient, medieval, and early modern texts that transmit the orthodox Jewish code of conduct.

Such is no longer the case. During the course of the past half century, warfare—broadly defined—has become a subject of intense halachic interest. Questions that for centuries were simply not asked now constitute areas of crucial religious inquiry. What, if anything, do the canonical sources have to say about the justice of warfare in general and about the ethics of specific modes of warfare in particular? Can the received texts accommodate a perspective that regards national security (as opposed to personal safety) as a categorical imperative? Altogether, can the dictates of traditional observances be reconciled to the practicalities of military life?

In embryonic form, some of those questions first began to clamor for rabbinic attention as early as the 1930s, when the Jewish community in mandatory Palestine first debated the pros and cons, moral as well as practical, of an organized Jewish response to the "Arab Revolt."[4] But the need to ascertain the religious validity of military activity became vastly more acute with the establishment of the state of Israel in 1948. Born into war, Israel has ever since had to live by her sword. Efraim

Inbar has argued that this circumstance generates a general (and perhaps politically motivated) wish to grant "religious legitimacy to the secular authorities of the state of Israel in pursuing warlike activities."[5] Closer inspection reveals a much wider phenomenon. The fact that so many orthodox Israeli Jews now enlist in the Israel Defense Force (IDF) also creates an immediate and highly personal need to identify the acts of force that do, or do not, warrant halachic sanction. In Israel, especially, the response has been the appearance of a swelling tide of detailed and erudite analyses of warfare and its conduct. Together such publications have created a dynamic halachic discourse in a field virtually uncharted for centuries.

The present essay outlines the contours of that discourse. My discussion focuses on contemporary analyses of issues that in the Western tradition fall under the rubric of *ius ad bellum*, rather than *ius in bello*. In part that concentration reflects constraints of space. But it is also designed to highlight the intrinsic importance that Judaism attaches to the validity of war initiation. Obviously, only the grant of halachic license to a particular act of organized violence can permit its perpetrators to set aside the otherwise inviolable prohibitions against killing other human beings, and against placing themselves in situations of mortal danger. What also needs to be stressed, however, is that without proof of *ius ad bellum*, in terms dictated by *halacha*, orthodox Jews could find the use of force virtually impractical. After all, they are expected to live their daily lives in accordance with a large number of commandments, strict compliance with which would undoubtedly hinder the war effort (Sabbath observance presents the most obvious instance). Only religious sanction for war initiation can place such obligations in temporary abeyance. Hence, the halachic tradition can never consider *ius ad bellum* analyses to be in any way theoretical, nor even concerned only with the application of abstract principles of conduct. Ultimately, proof of the justice and correctness of the act of war permits (perhaps mandates) the suspension of virtually every act that normally governs everyday Jewish behavior for the duration of hostilities.

The present essay proceeds in four stages.

First, it sketches a portrait of the principal participants in the contemporary halachic discourse on the *ius ad bellum*.
Second, it outlines the format and style of that discussion.
Third, the essay itemizes the principal questions with which the discourse is concerned.
Finally, it discusses some of the potential implications of the developments described.

## Participants

Participation in the contemporary halachic discourse on *ius ad bellum* issues is by no means evenly spread throughout the literati of contemporary orthodox Jewry. Clearly demarcated boundaries of affiliation distinguish between those who seek to break new ground by analyzing the topic and those who refrain from doing so. Overwhelmingly, persons in the former camp are associated with schools of thought generally termed "modern-orthodox" or "religious-Zionist." Although these deliberately hyphenated terms beg some important questions (In what way "modern" or "orthodox"? How "religious" or "Zionist"?), they nevertheless remain serviceable. Not least is this so since they differentiate their subjects from "ultra-orthodox" (*haredi*) society, whose members avow a far more sectarian attitude toward both the secular world and many of its contemporary manifestations. Concentrated in primarily urban communities in Israel and elsewhere, "ultra-orthodox" Jews prefer to retain lifestyles and thought processes that are self-consciously modeled on habits and attitudes embedded in Jewry's premodern past.[6]

It is tempting to attribute the tendency of ultra-orthodox scholars to abstain from participation in current halachic discussions on *ius ad bellum* to their rigidly conservative mindset. In fact, equally powerful (if not more so) is the influence exerted in this particular instance by the deep conviction that religious sanction for a Jewish recourse to military force is in any case impossible. Central to ultra-orthodox tenets is the belief that, in present circumstances, any effort to take up arms would be sinful. This is especially so if action were to be initiated with the purpose of re-establishing Jewish sovereignty over the Holy Land or in defense of the modern, secular state of Israel. Exile from Zion, after all, had been a divine punishment; hence, a return to the Almighty's grace is the necessary precondition for the promised redemption. The true Restoration will signify the resolution of the spiritual dialogue between God and the assembly of Israel. It cannot take place until all Jews bow to the yoke of heaven. Even then, national renewal will have to be divinely inspired and await definitive signs from heaven that the House of Israel has indeed worked its passage home. In the absence of such omens, precipitate communal action of any sort—and certainly military action—rebels against God's plan. Instead of hastening the Messiah's coming, it threatens to postpone his arrival.

Distilled from centuries of rabbinic teachings, sentiments such as these have long constituted the staple diet of much of *haredi* polemical opposition to modern political Zionism.[7] More recently, they have also been drafted into the campaign waged by ultra-orthodoxy in Israel against the enlistment into military service of its youth.[8] True, such sentiments have not prevented intense discussions in ultra-orthodox circles, in Israel and elsewhere, over the ultimate theological meanings of warfare. Several of Israel's victories (and defeats) have been the subjects of particularly acute reflection.[9] But this interest has not been translated into the realm of practical *halacha*. Here, the combined confluence of traditional beliefs and current interests has resulted in a frame of mind that clearly prefers to leave all treatment of the *ius ad bellum* in its traditional abeyance.

Typical, in this respect, are the sentiments expressed in a pithy 1979 communication from New York by Rabbi Moses Feinstein (1895–1985), one of the most widely respected of all recent rabbinic authorities. Replying to an inquiry from an Israeli correspondent about the possible applicability of certain halachic categories to contemporary Israel's wars, Rabbi Feinstein simply dodged the entire issue.

> I have not even considered how to decide—even theoretically, and there would be no point in such a question being addressed to me by those who presently exercise sovereignty in the hand of Israel. *A fortiori* would it be pointless for me to reply. For we trust only in the Almighty, in whose hands all things are, and we pray to Him that He have mercy on us and all Israel and that all will turn out well and that He also send us our righteous Messiah soon.[10]

No spiritual leaders of "national-religious" Jewry could ever take that position. Indeed, central to their entire ideology is a rebellion against the traditionally resistant attitude toward this-world political action that the *haredi* community continues to espouse. Religious Zionism has always maintained that the reconstitution of Jewish independence in 1948 did not merely register a milestone in the mundane political chronology of the nation. Far more fundamentally, it also defined a crucial stage in the teleological process toward the fulfillment of the divine plan. One consequence of this essentially transcendental prism is the teaching that service in the IDF, the army entrusted with the mandate to defend Israel's sovereignty over the Holy Land, will always constitute a religious obligation. Another is that the elucidation of halachic opinion on all aspects of warfare (a category that most definitely includes the rights and wrongs of war initiation), likewise deserves to be considered a sacred enterprise.

In a very personal sense, many of national-religious Jewry's contemporary halachic authorities are uniquely qualified to address this subject. Those who have been born or brought up in Israel have—virtually without exception—undergone some form of (sometimes protracted) military service. Quite apart from distinguishing them from most of their *haredi* counterparts, this experience also sets them apart from any other generation of rabbis in recorded history. True, the differences in background must not be exaggerated. All national-religious rabbis do most certainly undergo a professional training that is essentially traditional in form. Specifically, they acquire their scholarship in conventional academies of Jewish learning (*yeshivot*), and derive much of their authority from their consequent mastery of the Talmud and its commentaries, texts that have for centuries formed the staple diet of the Jewish orthodox academic curriculum. Consequently, as will be seen, the language and style of their analyses of the *ius ad bellum*, as of all other topics of halachic interest, are decidedly—and deliberately—traditional in tone. Even so, the influence exerted by their military backgrounds remains undeniable. By virtue of their personal acquaintance with army life, they are able to achieve an entirely novel twinning of "the scroll" (i.e., scholarship) with "the sword" (martial valor), artifacts that classic Jewish texts tended to depict as diametric opposites.

Undoubtedly the most prominent of the early examples of this new synthesis was Rabbi Shlomo Goren, the IDF's first chief chaplain (he held the office from 1948–71, and by the time he retired was the longest-serving major general (*aluf*) in the entire force). Virtually single-handedly, Goren crafted the accommodation of traditional *halacha* with army life and vice versa. His organizational achievement made it possible for religiously observant conscripts to enlist alongside their secular comrades. By way of example, his unending stream of publications on military-related *halacha* also showed how traditional scholarship could be combined with military service to produce an entirely new type of rabbinical authority.[11] Most second-generation participants in the contemporary *ius ad bellum* discourse have followed Goren's lead. Some have likewise served in the IDF rabbinate; but others have held comparatively senior rank in combat formations. In the most interesting of cases (and often the most prolific too), individuals have gone on to become either a principal or senior teacher at one of the religious academic institutions that enable national-religious conscripts to combine military service with advanced Jewish studies. Thus in virtual daily contact with successive cohorts of troops, this new breed of orthodox Jewish soldier-scholar is particularly well-placed to make halachic research into the *ius ad bellum* relate to the changing nature of Israel's security environment.

## The Style and Format of the Discourse

Similarly novel, secondly, are several of the mediums through which contemporary orthodox analyses of the *ius ad bellum* are transmitted to the public at large.

Many authors retain the time-honored form of halachic communication, known as "responsa," which for centuries has consisted of published replies to specific queries.[12] (Interestingly, of late this epistolary form has increasingly been adapted to the abbreviated and instantaneous style required by e-mail and Internet-based chat groups.)[13] Others, however, prefer to compose analyses on their own initiative. Several such works appear in book form, either as single works of scholarship or in collected volumes of essays, often dedicated to the memory of a fallen soldier.[14] But many more see the light of day as articles in the new journals that now specialize in intra-rabbinic efforts to come to terms with modern Jewish statehood.[15] Combined, these frameworks have created an extended chain of authoritative exposition in an area that has hitherto constituted one of the great lacunae of halachic inquiry.

Although the form of national-religious analyses of the *ius ad bellum* thus exhibits several novel characteristics, it is important to note that the terminology and frameworks of the discourse as a whole remain decidedly traditional. In categorizing types of wars, all participants in that discourse scrupulously retain the usages of the ancient authoritative texts. As a result, the entire discussion is framed in accordance with parameters that are unique to the tradition of which it claims to be a part. Thus, since no canonical source ever explicitly refers to wars as "just/unjust" or "holy/profane," the modern discourse also avoids those attributions. Instead, the preferred distinction is between a war that is mandatory (*milkhemet mitzvah*, "commanded war") and one that is discretionary (*milkhemet reshut*, "permitted").

Scattered references to the mandatory/discretionary taxonomy are to be found in Jewish sources dating as far back as the third century C.E. But it became a definitive topos of halachic classification about a millennium later, when enumerated in the fourteenth volume of Maimonides' great code of Jewish law (*Mishneh Torah*), under a section entitled "Laws of Kings and Their Wars."[16] That source makes it absolutely clear that both mandatory and discretionary wars constitute religiously valid forms of state-initiated military activities. At the same time, however, it also emphasizes the differences in the source of their respective *ius ad bellum*. Wars are "mandatory" when the origin of their license to use force is transcendental, in the sense that it can be traced to an explicit divine command. By contrast, "discretionary" wars respond to impulses decidedly of this world, of which the most generic—in Maimonides' own words—is a monarch's desire "to extend the borders of Israel and enhance his [own] greatness and prestige." Presumably, these differences in motive also underlie the distinctions that he prescribes for the procedures whereby, in each category, the *ius ad bellum* has to be confirmed. According to chapter 5:2 of "Laws of Kings and Their Wars."

> For a commanded war, the king need not obtain the sanction of the court. He may at any time go forth of his own accord and compel the people to go with him.
> But in the case of a discretionary war, he may not lead forth the people save by a decision of the court of 71.

## The Foci of Contemporary Inquiry

Traditional Jewish scholastic convention mandates that all halachic analyses of war initiation, retrospective as well as prospective, must follow Maimonides' template. Hence, all subsequent writings must be harmonized with his rulings, and all contemporary analyses have to accord with his mandatory/discretionary classification. Indeed, the only way in which such analyses might gain any authoritative status at all is by demonstrating that they constitute authentic derivations of either Maimonides' own exposition, or of its interpretation by one or more of the great master's recognized commentators. That convention certainly bounds the contemporary *ius ad bellum* discourse within clear parameters. By the same token, it explains why the need to reconcile present-day circumstances with Maimonidean stipulations has become a primary scholarly preoccupation. Indeed, ever since its inception, the contemporary halachic discourse on the *ius ad bellum* has always been characterized by strenuous intellectual efforts to adapt the Maimonidean template to contemporary conditions.[17]

That is by no means an easy task. One particularly notorious complication arises from the fact that today's Jewish society possesses none of the agencies whose authorization Maimonides requires for the validation of *ius ad bellum*. Ostensibly, this fault is entirely technical. But for a culture obsessed with tradition and precedents, the "agency deficit" in fact constitutes a substantive barrier to any attempt to set in motion the necessary procedures for war initiation. Arguably, both of the Maimonidean categories of warfare could thereby be invalidated. Strictly speaking, until such time as Israel possesses a ruling monarch, no conflict—whatever its motive or origin—could authentically be classified as a "mandatory war." Likewise, absent a duly constituted "court," no governmental call to arms could ever meet the constitutional definition of a "discretionary war."[18]

An obvious solution to any such situation is to recognize modern agencies of government as the legitimate heirs of the presently nonexistent institutions stipulated in the ancient texts. Quite simply, "the king" of the Maimonidean code could be translated as "the executive power," and "the court" as "the legislature." Presumably even those substitutions would leave some matters of detail to be ironed out. But by allowing the mandatory/discretionary dichotomy to remain a valid framework of analysis, they would enable the contemporary *ius ad bellum* discourse to address both categories of conflict.[19]

Contemporary halachic discussions have certainly explored that possibility in some depth. This is particularly so with respect to "the court," unanimously considered by orthodox Jewish scholarship to be a Maimonidean reference to the *sanhedrin*, a tribunal-cum-council of seventy-one rabbinic sages, which tradition invests with supreme authority to interpret Israel's God-given law.[20] Perhaps, it has been suggested, Maimonides would have himself concurred with the depiction of the *sanhedrin* as the mouthpiece of a "general will."[21] If so, then he might have been prepared to forego formal sanction by a body of that name for a discretionary war, provided that there existed some alternative demonstration of the people's unanimous determination to enter into combat.[22] Alternatively, perhaps the *sanhedrin* can be considered a personification of Israel's moral consciousness—"the physical embodiment of what Socrates called 'the conscience of the laws.'" Is this not the position that we would rightly expect to be filled in contemporary Israel by the Knesset (parliament) and the Supreme Court of Justice whose members, working in concert, would be constitutionally empowered to determine whether or not there existed just cause for a resort to force?[23]

All such inquiries have certainly generated fruitful theoretical debates. In practical terms, however, the results have been meager. Modern halachic thought has still not managed to identify an institutional substitute for the Maimonidean "court" and thereby cut the Gordian knot binding the agency of that name to the authorization of a "discretionary war." Indeed, any search for an alternative appears to be invalidated by the virtually totemistic status accorded in Jewry's historical consciousness to the *sanhedrin* of seventy-one sages as the sole, and hence irreplaceable, repository of the divine law's authentic elucidation. Rather than play fast and loose with such notions—especially in the service of something so questionable as a war fought for personal or national aggrandizement—it seems far more appropriate to stick rigidly to Maimonides' requirements. A properly constituted "court" (*sanhedrin*), then, remains an absolute sine qua non for the legal authorization of a discretionary conflict. Absent such a body, no conflict of that name can ever be considered valid, and hence—from a halachic viewpoint—cannot today be undertaken by the IDF.[24]

On the other hand, contemporary halachic exegesis has managed to be far more flexible with respect to Maimonides' references to the role of "the king" in the war-making process. Mainly, this is because on this subject it is possible to appeal to the bar of older authority. Painstaking review of the available sources has revealed that, even in late medieval times, rabbinic authorities were prepared to acknowledge that the term "kingship" can be applied to any sovereign authority: "a king, a judge or whosoever exercises jurisdiction over the people."[25] All possess the powers once invested solely in monarchs—including, presumably (although no medieval authority ever explicitly said so), the power to launch mandatory wars.

Contemporary national-religious halachic thought has had merely to exploit the republican opening thus provided. The initial, crucial steps toward doing so were taken some years before the establishment of the state of Israel by the elder Rabbi Kook (1865–1935), the first chief rabbi of the Ashkenazi (European-origin) Jewish community in mandatory Palestine.[26] But not until Israel's War of Independence in 1948–49 did Kook's disciple and successor, Rabbi Isaac Herzog (1888–1959), specifically apply the necessary inferences to the realm of war-making and conflict mobilization. Herzog admitted that the absence of a court/*sanhedrin* made it impossible to identify any body that might sanction acts of force to which the term "discretionary war" might apply. But "mandatory" conflicts, because they required nothing more than monarchical initiative, presented no such difficulties.

> Even though we have no king, the public in its entirety... has the authority of a king of Israel. And the present law of universal conscription was decreed with the sanction of the vast majority of the [Jewish] community of the land of Israel, which represents the entire Congregation of Israel.[27]

From the purely procedural perspective, therefore, the halachic validity of the *ius ad bellum* could in that case be considered beyond question.

Whether or not the same could be said of every other instance of the IDF's more recent force applications is nevertheless not at all clear. Ultimately, they can only be sanctioned if they too meet the criteria of "mandatory wars." Consequently, attention must now be turned to an examination of those criteria.

In his "Laws of Kings and Their Wars" (chapter 5:2), Maimonides himself cites three instances of mandatory wars:

> The war against the seven nations [i.e., the inhabitants of the land of Canaan prior to its conquest by Joshua]; that against Amalek [the first tribe to attack the Israelites after the exodus from Egypt; Exod. 17:8–14 and Deut. 25:17–19]; [a war] to deliver Israel from the enemy attacking him.[28]

It is tempting to regard each of Maimonides' illustrations as examples of far broader instances of military activity, and hence as prototypes that lend themselves to subsequent elaboration and adaptation. In this reading, his reference to Joshua's "war against the seven nations" could be extended to any campaign fought in order to dispossess whichever non-Jewish population might happen to reside in the Holy Land. Similarly, since "Amalek" has entered traditional Jewish demonology as a generic personification of evil, the commandment "to wage war against Amalek" could be extended to include any foe that might fit that depiction. In fact, however, contemporary as well as medieval commentary has in this respect been exceedingly restrictive. Overwhelmingly, halachic opinion refuses to legitimate contemporary military activities in Israel in terms of the biblical instruction given to Joshua. Similarly, it rejects all attempts to employ the original commandment to wipe out Amalek as a *ius ad bellum* for a war of extermination against any other enemy. Some recent expositions, which have indeed equated contemporary Israel's Palestinian neighbors with the Amalekites of old, are as exceptional as they are notorious.[29]

In short, a sequential process of elimination has thus considerably whittled down the contemporary relevance of Maimonides' original taxonomy. In fact, all that remains available for application is the last of his three instances of a mandatory war: one fought "to deliver Israel from the enemy attacking him." Ostensibly, this phraseology seems clear enough and appears to set out fairly precise conditions as to when the *ius ad bellum* might exist and when not. It undoubtedly provides a general sanction for the use of force in national self-defense, such as is expressly permitted by article 51 of the United Nations (UN) Charter. At the same time, albeit without actually saying so, the same formula seems also to outlaw unprovoked military operations, such as acts of blatant aggression against peaceful neighbors. With the halachic boundaries of permissible and prohibited uses of force thus clearly defined, observers could be excused for assuming that the application of the category of mandatory wars to contemporary conditions presents few problems.

In fact, little could be further from the truth. Modern Israel's military practice has seldom conformed with the tidy categorizations of the rabbinic mind, and closer inspection reveals that the instances in which IDF operations can be said to meet the classic Maimonidean criteria of a mandatory war are in fact few and far between. The principle of self-defense could most obviously (and most justifiably) be invoked as *ius ad bellum* during Israel's War of Independence in 1948–49 and during the Yom Kippur War of October 1973. In both instances, the Jewish state was clearly the victim of armed aggression, and its leaders therefore had little choice other than to respond with violence. But neither situation has been typical. For the most part, the circumstances compelling modern Israel to resort to military force have been far more complex, and her own responses also far more varied.[30] Those circumstances do not necessarily invalidate the Maimonidean category of a mandatory war. They do, however, underscore the need for the exercise of considerable interpretative maneuver in its application.

As part of that exercise, particular attention has been focused on the precise rules of engagement that halachic definitions of the *ius ad bellum* might allow. Here, as J. David Bleich pointed out, the Maimonidean prooftext is especially recalcitrant.[31] At first glance, its sanction for wars waged "to deliver Israel from the enemy attacking him" seems to cover only "reactive-defensive" actions, initiated after the enemy offensive has actually commenced. This is particularly so since the Hebrew term that Maimonides employs (*ve-ezrat*) more precisely translates as "to assist," which itself carries connotations of a reactive response. But this bland ruling is self-evidently fuzzy at the edges. Is it to be taken to imply that operations warrant definition as "mandatory" only when they take the form of a second strike? Or, to put matters another way, does the Maimonidean definition preclude the use of force at a prior stage, when military commanders might wish to nip a prospective danger in the bud by taking the offensive?

That these are not merely theoretical questions is illustrated by the specific contexts in which each is framed. How would Maimonides classify a "preemptive" war, undertaken in order to forestall immediately anticipated enemy aggression, such as was launched by the IDF against Egypt in June 1967? Could his taxonomy accommodate "preventative" operations, such as the Sinai campaign of 1956 and the Israeli air bombardment of Iraq's nuclear facility in 1981, both of which were initiated in order to destroy a putative predator's war-making potential before the threat actually materialized?[32] And what would his ruling be in the case of such "offensive-defensive" actions of the type exemplified by Israel's "reprisal raids" of the 1950s or, on a larger scale, Operation Peace for the Galilee of June 1982? Altogether, need applications of his taxonomy be restricted solely to conditions of conventional warfare, waged against organized armies? Or is it sufficiently flexible also to accommodate subconventional ("low intensity") and asymmetric situations, such as those confronted during both the first intifada (1987–1993) and its even more bloody successor (2000–2005)?

Displaying considerable ingenuity and resounding erudition, contemporary scholars have located in scattered traditional sources at least some of the building blocks from which answers to such questions might be constructed. One product of that enterprise has been the discovery that both ancient and medieval rabbinical authorities seem to have possessed a far more sophisticated appreciation of the potential psychological and political utility of force application than was once thought. Certainly, for instance, they could have accommodated many of the notions embedded in the modern concept of strategic deterrence. As much is evident from the very first extant halachic discussion of permissible conflict scenarios, during the course of which the term "mandatory war" is (in one interpretation) in fact explicitly reserved for preemptive strikes launched "in order to diminish the heathens so that they may not march against [Israelites]."[33] Admittedly, Maimonides did not himself pursue this particular line of thought. But it has been found in some subsequent commentaries, at least some of which articulate sensitivity to both the tactical advantages of military initiative and the wider strategic prudence of timely demonstrations of force.[34]

Since many such sources lend themselves to various interpretations, several aspects of deterrent action still await precise halachic definition. Nevertheless, by way of interim summary it can be said that the span of imponderables is undoubtedly being narrowed. Gradually, but inexorably, the *ius ad bellum* intrinsic to Maimonides' "mandatory" classification is being applied to force applications that are offensive as well as defensive in form, and to operations that are launched within "low-intensity" as well as "high-intensity" contexts. In both categories of conflict, the IDF's apparent predilection for preemptive deterrence ("by denial") seems to be receiving as much halachic sanction as do the more traditional applications of deterrence reactively ("by punishment").[35] Increasingly, the contemporary halachic interpretation tends to be expansive. A growing variety of military actions are now incorporated within the

Maimonidean rubric of wars fought "to deliver Israel from the enemy attacking him."[36]

Undoubtedly that tendency has been influenced by self-conscious sensitivity to the specific theater of battle. For national-religious scholars, especially, the duty "to deliver Israel from the enemy attacking him" carries particularly potent overtones when the need to do so arises in the Holy Land. After all, this portion of the globe possesses an inherent sanctity, derived from its divine designation as the eternal patrimony of the Jewish people. A minority of militants have taken that argument to its logical conclusion, contending that the duty to defend possession of the Holy Land is an individual obligation, incumbent upon each and every Jew when the homeland is in danger. A resort to arms for that purpose, they have suggested, really ought therefore to be considered an instinctive reaction, for which no governmental authorization is required at all.[37] Few rabbinic authorities sanction the apparent license for vigilantism implied in such doctrines. Many, however, concur with its basic premise. Certainly, they endorse the argument that the protection of Jewish sovereignty in the land of Israel (*eretz Israel*) constitutes a religiously valid *ius ad bellum* in its own right.[38]

Interestingly, the required prooftext for the latter contention does not appear in Maimonides' discussion of "Laws of Kings and Their Wars." In fact, that passage of his code draws no distinctions whatsoever between attacks on "Israel" (i.e., the Jewish collectivity) in the Holy Land and anywhere else—thereby permitting the inference that geography might altogether be an inconsequential halachic variable where this particular variety of mandatory war is concerned.[39] However, sharp-eyed students of the texts have managed to locate what appears to be a relevant teaching elsewhere, tucked away in the great master's audit of the complex dos and don'ts of Sabbath observance. There, its specific context is the action to be followed were the obligation to defend Jewish communities from attack to conflict with the commandment to observe the Sabbath. Maimonides' decision, based on talmudic precedents and endorsed by all subsequent rabbinic authorities, is short and to the point. As a rule, he writes, the Sabbath may only be violated when Jewish lives are clearly endangered. However, if the threatened community "is situated close to the borders of the Land of Israel," Jews are permitted to take up arms on the Sabbath—even in order to repel petty thieves.[40] It goes without saying that they are authorized to do so on any other day of the week.

Ever since the outbreak of the first intifada, the precise relevance of this ruling to contemporary circumstances in Israel has become a subject of public debate as well as scholarly scrutiny.[41] Do not Jewish settlements located in the territories conquered in June 1967 meet the Maimonidean criterion of "border communities"? If so, surely their inhabitants possess an obvious license to resort to force in self-defense? In support of such contentions, not only was Maimonides' ruling cited at length in a pronouncement that a group of over two hundred Israeli rabbis first published late in 1993, in the wake of the Oslo Accords. It was also quoted verbatim in a privately funded advertisement that right-wing groups published in both the national-religious daily newspaper *Ha-Tzofeh* on December 15, 1995 (just a month after the assassination of Prime Minister Rabin) and—much more incongruously—in the avowedly secularist daily *Ha-Aretz* on March 5, 1996.

Whether or not Maimonides deserves to be thus dragooned into the service of political polemic can be left for future analysis. Far more germane to the present discussion is the contextual evidence that the citation provides. The deliberate use of texts and terms rooted in the traditional Jewish canon endows that polemic with an aura of traditional religious continuity. It also proclaims a belief that timehonored frameworks of analysis remain resilient enough to be serviceable even under the radically new circumstances in which the modern Jewish discourse on the *ius ad bellum* is now taking place.

## Implications

The implications of the developments described in this essay fall into two distinct categories. For the purposes of the following analysis, the first will be labeled "intellectual" and the second "practical."

The intellectual category of the implications of the new discourse is essentially academic in thrust. The explosion of interest in *ius ad bellum* issues in contemporary Jewish thought has not merely created a whole library of new halachic texts. It has also stimulated the rediscovery of an entire substratum of older materials, most of which have been hidden from view by centuries of scholarly neglect. By subjecting such materials to new forensic analysis, the contemporary *ius ad bellum* discourse has in fact uncovered a complete layer of traditional Jewish writings never before examined. This process has rescued from obscurity *obiter dicta* relating to warfare that have hitherto been tucked away in recondite discussions of other points of ritual law. It has also brought to light passages of biblical commentary previously ignored.[42]

The essentially archeological and antiquarian nature of much of that enterprise must not be allowed to obscure the fact that it also nurtures a creative and even radical scholastic impulse. For many of the participants in the *ius ad bellum* discourse, the object of research is not merely to scour older texts for possible precedents that can, through the application of time-honored rabbinic exegesis, be made to "match" contemporary conditions. In addition, they often look to the ancient texts to help them forge halachic categories of analysis that can help them come to terms with what, from personal experience, many of them appreciate to be situations quite unlike any with which Jewry's spiritual leaders have usually been concerned. To put matters another way, the most advanced of the participants in the modern Jewish discourse on the *ius ad bellum* do not simply query how the traditional sources might help them reconcile a resort to force with other traditional obligations (such as Sabbath observance). Rather, they look to those texts to provide them with a means of granting the *ius ad bellum* its own halachic "space," justified by virtue of the unique moral and spiritual challenges that it poses. Only thus, they argue, can they understand how religious sanction can be accorded to an action that, inevitably, will lead to loss of life on both sides.[43]

As matters stand, all this intellectual huffing and puffing seems hardly likely to have much practical effect on the specific security policies of Israeli governments. However much traditional Jewish themes and motifs might indeed influence some aspects of modern Israel's official attitude toward the external world,[44] the chances that they could become primary considerations in decisions about war and peace seem very slim indeed. It is probably safe to say that, for the foreseeable future, pragmatic realism will remain the dominant characteristic of Israeli security policies.[45] Doubtless, individual rabbis will continue to offer individual ministers the benefit of their advice. But, for better or for worse, other than on matters of essentially ceremonial interest, their opinions will go unheeded.

Matters begin to look very different, however, once the search for policy implications is extended below the very apex of the decision-making pyramid. At a deeper societal level, the practical repercussions of the new *ius ad bellum* discourse in modern orthodox Jewry seem likely to be profound.

In part, that prediction is based upon changing trends in the military service profile of troops in the IDF who come from a "national-religious" background.[46] Until recently, practically the only features about those troops that in any way set them apart from others were their observance of ritual practices and their adherence to a singular dress code. (Specifically, a knitted skullcap in the case of men and a preference for skirts over slacks in the case of women.) Increasingly, however, observers have begun to remark on the salience of other distinguishing characteristics. For instance, research indicates that propensity for service, which in Israel is measured by a willingness to volunteer for conscript duty in combat units, is considerably higher overall among recruits who come from the national-religious sector than in any other population group. The results are easily observed. In many infantry brigades, the percentage of national-religious servicemen (estimated at 20 percent) is almost twice their proportion in the overall population (some 12 percent). In elite reconnaissance units (*sayarot*), the discrepancy in the ratio is often larger than three to one. Thus far, the influence of these trends on senior levels of command, although growing, has been only marginal. By contrast, their effect on the composition of the *junior* officer corps has been little short of revolutionary. Clearly, the national-religious community has now superseded the kibbutz movement as the single largest source for commanders at this critical level, which is where officers are closest to their troops. At a rough estimate, some 30 percent of all IDF lieutenants and captains now wear a knitted skullcap, the most obtrusive mark of male national-religious affiliation.

These figures attain especial significance when correlated with shifts of similar magnitude currently taking place in the nature of the military conflicts in which IDF troops find themselves engaged. Counterinsurgency missions, which were long relegated to a decidedly subsidiary position on the agenda of Israel's security concerns, have for several years now constituted its primary category of operational activity. Not since 1982, in fact, has the IDF deployed its formidable arsenal of armored and air power *en masse* against a "conventional" foe. Instead, in both Lebanon (until 2000) and in the occupied territories (especially since 2000) its operations have been principally targeted against motley collections of armed gangs, guerillas, terrorists, and—most of all—civilian insurgents, the vast majority of whom are drawn from the local Palestinian population.

As all the professional military literature now admits, the ethical challenges that counterinsurgency operations pose for regular armies are particularly acute. In part, the moral dilemmas involved stem from the difficulties of reconciling specific modes of violence with the general principles associated with correct military conduct.[47] More generally, however, problems arise because the frequently indistinct nature of the enemy with whom they come into contact tends to invalidate accepted distinctions between combatants and noncombatants. Under any circumstances, such conditions make rules of engagement difficult to formulate and implement. But the problems in doing so are compounded by the fact that the person charged with responsibility for making the decision is only very rarely an officer of senior rank. Because counterinsurgency operations are so often conducted by small and often isolated units, it is precisely the junior officers—among whom, as we have seen, national-religious troops are so heavily represented—who are most likely to have to decide whether or not to give the order to open fire.[48]

In an effort to help all its personnel to rise to that challenge, the IDF has recently followed the lead taken by other armies and published (and revised) its own code of ethics, entitled *The Spirit of the IDF*.[49] In what is widely interpreted to be a bow in the direction of national-religious sentiment, this document specifically refers to the "tradition of the Jewish people throughout the ages" as one of its four main sources of inspiration. But to judge from anecdotal evidence, literary as well as oral, national-religious troops seem to find that phraseology far too amorphous to be of any practical use. Instead, at a moment of crisis, they prefer to take counsel with their own conscience,[50] and while doing so to fall back on the teachings that they have imbibed in their homes and high schools.

Significantly, many have also been equipped to draw even more directly on the teachings developed during the course of Judaism's new *ius ad bellum* discourse. Indeed, they have both specifically studied the principal texts of that discourse and become acquainted with some of its principal protagonists. Some 13 percent of the male graduates of national-religious high schools now attend one of the dozen pre-military academies (*mekhinot kedam tzevaiyot*), whose students undergo a year of national and religious "fortification" before embarking on their military careers. A further 13–14 percent enrolls in one of the thirty *yeshivot hesder* ("'Arrangement' academies of higher Jewish learning"), where they pursue a five-year program in which periods of talmudic study and military service are interspersed.[51] Originally established in order to facilitate a combination of military service and religious instruction, institutions of both types have now become the prime laboratories for modern orthodox Jewish research into all aspects of the entire spectrum of topics encompassed by the junction of religion and warfare. This is particularly so since, as mentioned earlier in this essay, the majority of rabbinic participants in the new *ius ad bellum* discourse teach in one or another of these frameworks. As a consequence, the institutions are able to provide forums for dialogue between the new breed of spiritual mentor and the young soldiers who are most anxious to hear what their religion teaches about the specific military situations in which they now find themselves.

## Conclusions

At first glance, the subject of this essay might appear to be entirely *sui generis*. After all, it has focused on a unique set of religious beliefs, which are being explored within a similarly unique cultural and political context. Moreover, and as we have seen, the current *ius ad bellum* discourse in modern orthodox Judaism—although certainly revolutionary in content—is very much conservative in style and language. In many ways, it constitutes an intellectual exercise, which is fully intelligible only to a class of literati familiar with the introspective world of traditional Jewish scholarship. From that point of view, the discourse itself must be classified as an entirely domestic religious phenomenon, the influence of which can hardly be expected to go beyond the confines of its own arena.

At the same time, however, the implications of the processes described here do seem to have wider relevance. As has been pointed out, thanks to a confluence of sociological and strategic circumstances, the *ius ad bellum* discourse in modern orthodox Jewish thought has very definite practical implications. By virtue of their institutional affiliations and their own military backgrounds, many of the scholars most closely engaged in Judaism's new *ius ad bellum* discourse are uniquely placed to influence the behavior of the IDF's national-religious troops. Moreover, this latter segment now comprises a critical component of Israel's overall combat complement, and especially of its junior officer corps. Its behavior could shape the entire ethos of the IDF, especially in the morally ambiguous situations that are characteristic of the types of conflict in which the IDF is currently engaged.

Under those conditions, the ways in which the tenets of this particular discourse are transmitted and applied become topics of broader interest. How traditional Jewish teachings are today influencing Israeli troop behavior on the modern (and postmodern) battlefields can in fact serve as a case study of the degrees to which religion can altogether fulfill the functions of both a motivating factor and a legitimizing referent in situations of contemporary international conflict.

## Notes

1. Sovereign authority, just cause, and right intention were the prudential criteria prescribed as early as Aquinas. Subsequently, these were supplemented by the doctrines of proportionality, last resort, reasonable hope of success, and—most recently—the aim of peace as the purpose of the use of force. See Peter Ramsay, *The Just War* (New York: Charles Scribner's Sons, 1968); Michael Walzer, *Just and Unjust Wars*, 2nd. ed. (New York: Basic Books, 1992); James Turner Johnson, *The Holy War Idea in Western and Islamic Traditions* (Philadelphia: Penn State University Press, 1997).

2. David Biale, *Power and Powerlessness in Jewish History* (New York: Schocken, 1986). See especially chapter 2: "The Political Theory of the Diaspora," pages 34–57.

3. Richard G. Marks, *The Image of Bar Kochba in Traditional Jewish Literature: False Messiah and National Hero* (Philadelphia: Penn State University Press, 1994).

4. Eliezer Don-Yehiyah, "Religion and Political Terror: Religious Jewry and Retaliation During the 1936–1939 'Arab Revolt'" [In Hebrew] *Ha-Tziyonut*, no. 17 (1993): 155–90.

5. Efraim Inbar, "War in Jewish Tradition" *The Jerusalem Journal of International Relations* 9, no. 2 (1987): 63.

6. [In Hebrew] Menachem Friedman, *The Haredi (Ultra-Orthodox) Society—Sources, Trends, Processes* (Jerusalem: Jerusalem Institute for Israel Studies, 1991); Samuel C. Heilman and Menachem Friedman, "Religious Fundamentalism and Religious Jews: The Case of the Haredim," in *Fundamentalisms Observed*, ed. Marrin E. Martin and Roy Scott Appleby, (Chicago: University of Chicago Press, 1991): 197–264.

7. For an extended exposition of the argument that talmudic commentaries on the "three oaths" cited in the Song of Sol. (2:7; 3:5; 8:4) expressly forbid a resort to force for the purposes of returning to the Holy Land, see Yoel Teitelbaum, *Sefer Va-Yo'el Mosheh*, 3 vols., 2nd ed. (Jerusalem, 1974). This and other sources are analyzed in Aviezer Ravitzky, *Messianism, Zionism and Jewish Religious Radicalism* (Chicago: Chicago University Press, 1996), 40–78, 211–33.

8. Although in that case they have been supplemented by the argument that, in any case, Israel's supreme national need is now for Torah scholars rather than soldiers. See Stuart A. Cohen, *The Scroll or the Sword? Dilemmas of Religion and Military Service in Israel* (London: Harwood Academic Publishers, 1997), 94–101.

9. Charles S. Liebman, "Paradigms Sometimes Fit: The Haredi Response to the Yom Kippur War," *Israel Affairs* 1, no. 2 (1993): 171–84. "Wars, even one that ends as gloriously as the Six Day War and certainly the Yom Kippur War, are times of tears, trial and tragedy. They come as punishment for the sins of the Jews, the foremost being that of... excessive reliance on the state, the instruments of the state and human potential instead of belief and reliance on God" (178).

10. *Igrot Mosheh* ("Letters of Moses," Responsa: New York: Rappaport, 1974), Section "Choshen Mishpat," 78, 320.

11. Goren still awaits his Biographer. He collected his writings in "Responding to War,"

*Meishiv Milkhamah*, 4 vols., (Jerusalem: Idra Rabbah, 1983–93). On the IDF rabbinate, see Benny Michaelson, "The Military Rabbinate," [In Hebrew] in *The IDF and Its Arms*, vol. 16, ed. Ilan Kfir and Ya'akov Erez (Tel Aviv: Revivim, 1982), 83–132.

12. Examples of those which do retain this format are the following books: Nachum Eliezer Rabinovitch, *Melumedei Milkhamah* [Those Who Are Learned in War], 1994 Avi Ronetzki, *Ke-Chitzim be-Yad Gibor* [As Arrows in the Hands of a Hero], 2 vols. 1998; Mishal Rubin, *Ha-Morim ba-Keshet* [Those Who Draw the Bow], 1998 and Eyal Moshe Krim, *Kishrei Milkhamah Ties of War* [Those Who Are Learned In War], 1994; 2 vols. 1999.

13. Two of the most popular Web sites containing portals of an "Ask the Rabbi" genre are http://www.moreshet.co.il and http://www.kippah.co.il. Some of these respons are also published. See e.g., Yuval Sherlow, *Reshut Ha-Rabim* [The Public Domain] (Petach Tikva: Yeshivat Hesder of Petach Tikva, 2002), 94–104.

14. Detailed works of scholarship by a single hand were characteristic of the first generation of authors in this area. See Alter David Regensburg, *Mishpat Ha-Tzavah be-Yisrael* [The Law of the Army in Israel] (Jerusalem: Mosad Harav Kook, 1949); Shlomo Yosef Zevin, *Le'or ha-Halakhah* [By the Light of the Halakhah] (Tel Aviv: Tziyoni Press, 1957), 9–65; Shaul Yisraeli, *Amud Ha-Yemini* [The Right Pillar] (Tel Aviv: Moreshet, 1966). For examples of collaborative memorial volumes see Yeshayahu Gafni and Aviezer Ravitzky, ed., *Kedushat ha-Hayim ve-Hakravah Atzmit* [The Sanctity of Life and Self Sacrifice] (Jerusalem: Zalman Shazar Center, 1992); Eliezer H. Shenwald, ed., *Sefer Harel* [The Harel Memorial Book: Israeli Militarism through the Eyes of the Torah] (Chispin: Golan Yeshivah, 2002).

15. Four such publications warrant particular attention: (1) *Ha-Torah ve-ha-Medinah* [The Torah and the State], thirteen issues of which appeared between 1949 and 1962; (2) *Barkai* (six issues since 1983); (3) *Torah Shebe'al Peh* (proceedings of an annual conference on oral law, the first of which was held in 1959); and (4)—above all—*Tehumin*, a journal of contemporary halachal published annually since 1980.

16. For a magisterial overview of the text see Isadore Twersky, *Introduction to the Code of Maimonides (Mishneh Torah)* (New Haven: Yale University Press, 1980). The fact that Maimonides incorporates his discussion of warfare into his general analysis of the rights and duties of kings suggests that, like Clausewitz, he also regards the resort to organized violence as an essentially instrumental activity. Also see Inbar, "War in Jewish Tradition."

17. E.g., Zevin, *Le'or ha-Halakhah*, 57–65; Goren, *Meishiv Milkhamah*, 37–39; Yehudah Amital, "The Wars of Israel According to Maimonides" [In Hebrew] *Tehumin*, vol. 8(1987): 454–83; Avraham Sherman, "Israel's Wars—Their Halakhic Validity" idem. vol. 15 (1995): 23–30.

18. To tell the truth, matters are a little more complicated than that, since at least some of the primary talmudic texts also require that a "discretionary war" be sanctioned by the priestly oracular devices known as the "Urim and Thumim." To make matters worse, although Maimonides omitted this obligation from his code, he alluded to it in his *Book of Commandments* (at the end of "root" 14). For attempts to resolve these issues, see the sources cited in Natanel Aryeh, "The Initiation of Mandatory and Discretionary wars," [In Hebrew] in Shenwald, *Sefer Harel*, 96–100.

19. See, especially, Aviezer Ravitzky, "Prohibited Wars in the Jewish Tradition," *The Ethics of War and Peace*, ed. Terry Nardin, 115–127 (Princeton: Princeton University Press, 1996).

20. Whether or not the "court/*sanhedrin*" in fact ever existed (and even if it did, whether it fits the Maimonidean description) is of course hotly debated. See Elias Rivkin, "Beth Din, Boule, Sanhedrin: A Tragedy of Errors," *Hebrew Union College Annual*, vol. 46 (1975): 181–99.

21. The issue is fully discussed in Gerald Blidstein, *Political Concepts in Maimonidean Halakha* (Ramat Gan: Bar Ilan University Press, 1983), 58–61.

22. As could be signified, for instance, if 100 percent of all available manpower enlisted voluntarily for service in a discretionary war. See Eliezer Judah Waldenberg, *Sefer Hilkhot Medinah* [The Book of State Laws] (Jerusalem: Mosad Harav Kook, 1953), 112; Judah Gershuni, "Discretionary War and Mandatory War" [In Hebrew] *Torah she-be'al Peh*, vol. 13 (1973): 150–51.

23. Maurice Lamm, "After the War—Another Look at Pacifism and Selective Conscientious Objection (SCO)," in *Contemporary Jewish Ethics*, ed. Menachem Marc Kellner (New York: Sanhedrin Press, 1978), 221–38.

24. The sources have most recently been collated in Menasheh Shmerlovsky, "Discretionary War and Mandatory War," [In Hebrew] in Shenwald, *Sefer Harel*, 58–64.

25. Nachmanides addenda to Maimonides,' *Book of Commandments*, Negative Commandments, 17.

26. Abraham Isaac Kook, *Responsa Mishpat Kohen* [The Priestly Lan] (Jerusalem: Mosad Harav Kook, 1966). The relevant passage reads: "And besides, it appears that at a time when there is no king, since the laws of kingship also appertain to the general state of the nation, these rights of the laws revert to the people as a whole." For a subsequent analysis, see Shaul Yisraeli, "The Contemporary Jurisdiction of the Laws of Kingship," *Ha-Torah ve-ha-Medinah*, vol. 2 (1950): 76–88; Yehudah Shaviv, "The Prerogatives of Authority and the Obligation to Obey," *Tehumin*, vol. 15 (1995): 118–31.

27. *Responsa, Heikhal Yitzchak* [Chamber of Isaac] (Jerusalem: Mosad Harav Kook, 1972). For a subsequent analysis, see Yitzchak Kaufman, *Ha-Tzavah Ke-halakhah* [The Army as Halakhah] (Jerusalem: Kol Mevaser, 1994), 4.

28. The precise source for the third of Maimonides' illustrations is obscure, and has occasioned considerable learned comment. See the sources cited in Shmerlovsky, "Discretionary War," 76–77.

29. Rabinovitch, *Melumdie Milkhamah*, 22–25. Compare the more popular instances of the Palestinians = Amalakites equation cited in Amnon Rubinstein, *The Zionist Dream Revisited: From Herzl to Gush Emunim and Back* (New York: Schocken Books, 1984), 112.

30. Stuart Cohen and Efraim Inbar, "A Taxonomy of Israel's Use of Military Force," *Comparative Strategy* 10 no. 2 (1991): 121–38.

31. J. David Bleich, "Preemptive War in Jewish Law," *Tradition* 21, no. 1 (1983): 1–39.

32. On the distinction between "preemptive" and "preventative" wars, see Waltzer, *Just And Unjust Wars*.

33. The text and its commentaries are unraveled at length in Bleich, "PreemptiveWar," 4–5.

34. Aaron Eizental, "Deterrence—A Torah Perspective," [In Hebrew]. In Shenwald, *Sefer Harel*, 247–68. See also the distinctions between individual and communal threats made in Yisraeli, *Amud Ha-Yemini*, 147–54.

35. On this see Avner Yaniv, "Deterrence without Bombs: A Framework for the Analysis of Israeli Strategy" [In Hebrew] *State, Government and International Relations*, vol. 24 (1985): 63–85.

36. Yisraeli, *Amud Ha-Yemini*, 162–99; Goren, *Meishiv Milkhamah* vol. 4, 395–401. See also Moshe Ushpizai, "Preventative War—Discretionary or Mandatory?" [In Hebrew] *Tehumin* vol. 4 (1983): 90–96.

37. This was one of the arguments advanced by members of the right-wing Jewish Underground discovered in 1985. For background, see Ian S. Lustick, *For the Land and the Lord* (New York: Council on Foreign Relations Press, 1988) and David Weisburd, *Jewish Settler Violence: Deviance as Social Reaction* (Philadelphia: Pennsylvania State University Press, 1989).

38. For a comparatively early exposition on this theme see Shaul Yisraeli, "Military Action in Defense of the State," in *Amud Ha-Yemini*, ed. Shaul Yisraeli (Tel Aviv: Moreshet, 1966). This is a revised version of an article that first appeared in the wake of the Kibya raid of 1953. Considerably more explicit is Shlomo Aviner, "Mandatory War," [In Hebrew] in his book of essays *Mi-Hayyil El Hayyil* [From Strength to Strength] (Bet El: Havvah, 2000), 34–35, 37–38.

39. Altogether, Maimonides' attitude toward the land of Israel has become a subject of particularly intensive inquiry, especially when compared to that of Nachmanides (rabbi Moses ben Nahman, 1194–1270). Much of the argumentation is conveniently summarized in English in Rav Nachum Eliezer Rabinovitch, "Conquest of the Land of Israel—The View of the Ramban" and "Possession of the Land of Israel" *Crossroads*, vol. 2 (1988): 181–88, 197–206.

40. *The Code of Maimonides*, "Sabbath Laws;" 2:23. This ruling, in precisely the same language, is also found in the sixteenth-century code known as the *Shulkhan Arukh*, vol. *Orah Hayim*, Sabbath laws 329:6.

41. For examples of the latter see Ya'akov Ariel, "Self-Defense (the *Intifada* in the *Halakha*)" [In Hebrew] *Tehumin*, vol. 19 (1989): 62–75; and Hayim Druckman, "introduction" to *Ha-hayil ve-ha-Hosen* [Soldiering and Immunity] by Yehoshuah Hagar-Lau (Merkaz Shapira: Or Etzion, 1989), 9–11.

42. See, for instance, ibid., a surprisingly rich collation of scattered references to military matters in the Pentateuchal commentaries composed by rabbi Naftali Tzevi Judah Berlin of Volozhin (1817–93) and Rabbi Meir Simchah of Devinsk (1843–1926). See also Berlin's

commentary to chapter 4 of the Song of Sol. (which he interprets to be a depiction of an army camp) in Eliezer Shenwald, "Military Structure in Israel," [In Hebrew] in Shenwald, *Sefer Harel*, 269–99.

43. This dimension of the contemporary halachic enterprise is discussed at length by Eliezer Shenwald, "Until Its Destruction," [In Hebrew] in Shenwald, *Sefer Harel*, 119–83. See also Yisrael Meir Lau, *Responsa Yahel Yisrael*, vol. 3, no. 32 (Jerusalem, 2003), 262. For an outstanding example of the "creative" application of traditional sources to a concrete contemporary case, see Rabbi Ovadya Yosef, "The Entebbe Operation in Halakhah" [In Hebrew] *Torah she be'al peh*, vol. 19 (1977): 9–39.

44. See Aaron S. Klieman, *Israel & the World After 40 Years* (Washington DC: Pergamon-Brassey's, 1990), 41–63.

45. Yehuda Ben-Meir, *Civil-Military Relations in Israel* (New York: Columbia University Press, 1995).

46. For what follows, see Stuart A. Cohen, "Between the Transcendental and the Temporal: Security and the Jewish Religious Community" in *Security Concerns: Insights from the Israeli Experience*, ed. David Bar-Tal, Dan Jacobson, and Aharon Kleiman (JAI Press: Stamford, CT, 1998), 347–69.

47. This difficulty has been particularly pronounced in the case of the IDF's policy of "targeted killings." See the debate on this issue between Steven R. David and Yael Stein in *Ethics and International Affairs*, vol. 17, no. 1 (2003): 111–39.

48. This phenomenon is not, of course, limited to the Israeli context. See Michael Dewar, *The British Army in Northern Ireland* (London: Arms and Armor Press, 1985), 177–78. "The senior officer is more of a manager and co-ordinator than commander. Real operational 'command' in the sense of leading troops, has devolved downwards, through the battalion and company commanders to the NCO's. More often than not, it is these men who are confronted with the most difficult operational decisions." See also David Kellog, "Guerilla Warfare: When Taking Care of Your Men Leads to War Crimes," http://www.usafa.af.mil.jscope/JSCOPE97/Kellog97.htm

49. For a translation see http://www.us-israel.org/source/Society_&_Culture/IDF_ethics.html. For an amplification of the reasoning behind the document, published as a series of lectures by one of its principal authors, a professor of philosophy at Tel Aviv University, see Asa Kasher, *Military Ethics* [In Hebrew] (Tel Aviv: Ministry of Defense Publications, 1996). Partly in response to events after September 2000, the document was thoroughly revised in 2002.

50. Tamar Liebes and Shoshana Blum-Kulka, "Managing a Moral Dilemma: Israeli Soldiers and the Intifada" *Armed Forces & Society*, vol. 21, no. 1 (1994): 45–68.

51. These figures were kindly supplied by Drs. Abraham Laslow and Israel Rich of the Education Department at Bar Ilan University. For the origins and developments of these frameworks, see Cohen, *The Scroll or the Sword?*, 105–39.

# Religion, Postmodernization, and Israeli Approaches to the Conflict with the Palestinians

## JONATHAN RYNHOLD

### Introduction

On the memorial to Israeli prime minister Yitzhak Rabin in Tel Aviv the inscription states that "a religious Jew" assassinated him. The insertion of this phrase reflects the widespread sense in Israel that religion was to blame for this tragic crime. Indeed, many claim the assassin had rabbinical sanction for his act. Religious politicians sought to have the phrase "religious Jew" removed from the memorial. They argued that religion per se was not to blame. After all, the overwhelming majority of the religious public opposed such extremism, while some important rabbis endorsed the principle of "land for peace." Clearly, the relationship between religion and the peace process in Israel is far from simple. This article analyzes the relationship between religion and Israeli approaches to the conflict with the Palestinians. In particular, it seeks to explain why religion has become closely correlated with hawkishness since 1967.

While this question is clearly of importance in the Israeli context, it is also of relevance to the broader debate regarding the role of religion in international relations. In the international relations literature, religion tends to be dismissed as an epiphenomenon. In public discourse religious fundamentalism is often portrayed as part of a "clash of civilizations," which is declared to be the most important force in contemporary international politics. Recently Fox and others have begun to stake out an intermediate position, which has assessed the role of religion in conflict through its relationship to other ideational variables such as ethnicity.[1] This approach provides the basis for the following analysis.

In the context of the subject at hand, religion is narrowly defined in terms of the Orthodox Jewish tradition[2] and its system of belief, doctrine, norms, and practices—as well as the distinctive lifestyle of its adherents. The distinctive lifestyle of religious Jews is not only a function of the specific beliefs, norms, and practices of the religion, but is also a function of the way the religious community lives in order for it to survive and flourish. Correspondingly, religious norms, beliefs, doctrine, and practices do not exist in a vacuum, but are constantly being interpreted and reproduced within the social and cultural context in which they are embedded. In this vein, it is important to recognize the distinction made in Israeli society between two concepts that are often understood by outsiders as synonymous, *yahadut* (Judaism) and *dat* (religion). Judaism refers to the Jewish religious tradition, in general. As such, it is constitutive of the collective identity of religious and nonreligious Israeli Jews alike. Religion is differentiated from Judaism because it hinges on the observance of *halacha* (Jewish Law) as interpreted by Orthodox rabbis. Consequently, the analysis will focus on religion rather than Judaism.[3]

The first half of this article surveys the relationship between religion and Israeli approaches to the conflict with the Palestinians in three ways. First, the religious discourse is examined. This discourse consists of statements and writings made by political, religious, and intellectual leaders within the religious community who consciously attempt to extrapolate the meaning of religion with regard to the peace process. Most, though by no means all, of these figures are rabbis. Second, the attitudes of the self-identified religious public toward the peace process will be examined. In this case, the religiousness of the approach refers to a person's general level of religiosity, measured on a sliding scale in terms of their level of observance of *halacha* and their belief in core religious precepts. Third, the actual political behaviour of the self-identified religious community with regard to the peace process is examined. This enables one to gauge how far the leadership discourse and mass orientation of the religious sector influence their practical approaches to the peace process. In each case, religious approaches are compared with nonreligious approaches in order to ascertain how the religious approach differs. This multi-dimensional approach provides a comprehensive basis for the analysis undertaken in the second half of the article.

The second section begins by explaining the different approaches to the peace process within the different sections of the religious community. It is argued that messianic ideology and greater ethnocentricity inform the extreme hawkish approach among religious Jews, as distinct from the more moderate approaches within the community. The focus then turns to analysis of differences between religious and nonreligious approaches, and in particular why religion is so strongly correlated with hawkishness. This analysis centers on the effects of postmodernization on religion's changing relationship with three core elements of Israeli political culture: ethno-nationalism, liberalism, and republicanism. Postmodernization refers to a social and cultural process identified by Inglehart in over forty countries.[4] Postmodernization occurs among the middle class of the post–World War II generations in advanced industrial societies. It is reflected in the fact that their outlook differs from that of the older "modern" generations in its greater liberalism, individualism, multiculturalism, dovishness, and greater concern for "quality of life," coupled with a decreased affinity for collectivism, organized religion, nationalism and "security values."

In this context, a two-part argument is made. First, religion in Israel is strongly correlated with an orientation toward hawkishness primarily because religion encourages ethnocentricity. Second, the political prominence of the correlation between religion and hawkishness after 1967 has to do with the way religion interacted with changes in mainstream Israeli political culture, which were driven and facilitated by postmodernization. In this vein, religion served to shield its adherents from most of the cultural effects of postmodernization, while simultaneously encouraging counter-vailing trends. Consequently, whereas mainstream Israeli political culture has become less ethnocentric and more liberal (and thus more dovish), the religious community has moved in the opposite direction.

## The Religious Discourse Regarding the Conflict: Interpreting *Halacha*

The religious discourse has centered on the question of whether, according to *halacha* and the religious beliefs and values that inform it, it is permissible to give up parts of the land of Israel in order to save lives. Given the lack of a central authoritative halachic institution, many legitimate answers exist—particularly since this is a contemporary political issue related to war and peace. Because of the absence of a sovereign Jewish state for two thousand years there are few precedents for this case, and hence there is more room in which to interpretate *halacha*. This discourse is examined below from the vantage point of the three main Jewish religious subgroups in Israel: the ultra-Orthodox (*haredi*), the national-religious (*dati-leumi*), and Sephardi religious Jews associated with the *Shas* party.[5]

Ultra-Orthodoxy began in eastern Europe as a reaction to the threat of secularization posed by the Enlightenment and modernity. The ultra-Orthodox response to this threat was to closet themselves away from the modern world in communities that concentrated on the study of religion in academies known as yeshivas. Although the ultra-Orthodox are extremely factionalized, they are united by strict observance of *halacha* and by their negative stance toward modernity. In general, ultra-Orthodoxy is non-Zionist and it rejects the idea that the creation of the state of Israel is part of the messianic process of redemption.

The dominant ultra-Orthodox halachic approach to the question of "land for peace" is pragmatic. Thus the foremost ultra-Orthodox rabbi from the 1970s until the late 1990s, Rabbi Eliezer Menachem Shach, ruled that it is permissible to give up parts of the land of Israel in order to save lives. Since the state of Israel is of no intrinsic religious value to Shach, neither is its control over territory—even if that territory is holy. Shach argued that the study of religion, and not control over territory, is the key to the survival of the Jewish people.[6] Shach's approach was also influenced by the traditional quietistic political culture of ultra-Orthodoxy, according to which Jewish interests are best defended by not provoking non-Jews.[7] Within the ultra-Orthodox world two other minority approaches exist. First, there exists a tiny minority of extreme anti-Zionists known as the *Neturei Karta* sect. They are nominally represented within the Palestine Liberation Organization (PLO). Second, and more important, there is a hawkish wing of ultra-Orthodoxy represented by the *Habad* movement and *Hapoelei Agudat Yisrael*.[8] This camp attaches messianic significance to the Six Day War, fought in 1967, which brought many religiously significant sites under Jewish control. Whereas the secular state of Israel had always been difficult for ultra-Orthodox Jews to accept, the holiness of the land of Israel was a traditional value. In this vein the then head of *Habad*, the Lubavitcher Rebbe Menachem Mendel Schneerson, declared in 1992, "Better that the nations of the world rule in the Land of Israel than Jews surrender territory voluntarily."[9]

*Shas* is a religious party founded and supported by Sephardi Jews. Most of the leadership of *Shas*, which was set up in 1984, are Sephardi graduates of ultra-Orthodox yeshivas, though *Shas* is not ultra-Orthodox in the full sense of the term. While *Shas* is highly critical of Zionism for secularizing the Sephardi public, the basic Zionist idea is associated with continuity of Jewish tradition and not a rebellion against tradition, as it had been in Europe. Thus in contrast to the ultra-Orthodox, *Shas* was willing to join the Israeli government. On the other hand, the proto-Zionism of Sephardi Jewry is not characterized by the strong ideological overtones present within both the secular and religious variants of Zionism prominent within Ashkenazi Jewry. Unlike Ashkenazi Jewry, the Sephardim were not directly influenced by the rise of nationalist ideologies in nineteenth century Europe. This lack of ideological fervor contributed to a pragmatic approach to the peace process.[10] Thus, in the 1970s the acknowledged leader of Sephardi Jewry in Israel, Rabbi Ovadia Yosef, ruled that it was permissible to exchange part of the land of Israel in return for peace in principle, because the saving of life is more important than either the coming of the Messiah or holy territory.[11] This was a position he continued to support until the collapse of the Oslo Accords.

Religious Zionism views the creation of the state of Israel as being of great religious, and even messianic, significance. The movement was born in Europe and its leaders were thus primarily religious Ashkenazi Jews. Ideologically the movement was more open to modernity than the ultra-Orthodox, though it did not embrace it fully in the way that Reform Judaism did. After the Six Day War, the dominant approach among the national-religious was that of Rabbi Zvi Yehuda Kook, the head of the *Mercaz Harav* yeshiva and his disciples such as the former Ashkenazi Chief Rabbi, Avraham Shapira, and the former member of Knesse (MK), Rabbi Chaim Druckman. According to Kook, it is forbidden for Jews to transfer any part of the land of Israel to non-Jews. Kook also argued that the capture of the territories in 1967 was a crucial part of the messianic process and that the return of those territories had to be prevented in order to prevent a reversal of this process.[12] Aside from this messianic ideology, the national-religious leadership also supported the construction of settlements in the territories captured in 1967, which they viewed as the fulfilment of the classic pioneering values of Zionism. While the ultra-Orthodox were generally silent regarding Palestinian rights, the national-religious did discuss the matter. The thrust of the discourse was framed between one of two positions. Some argued that the Palestinians could receive autonomy and civil (not political) rights under the halachic category of *ger toshav* (resident alien), while others such as the former Ashkenazi Chief Rabbi Shlomo Goren argued that the Palestinians had no such rights.[13]

The minority position within religious Zionism was proposed by members of the religious peace movements *Oz Ve Shalom/Netivot Shalom* and by the religious political party *Meimad*. According to leading rabbinical figures within this school, such as Rabbi Yehuda Amital and Rabbi Aaron Lichtenstein, saving life takes precedence over that of the value of the land of Israel and consequently it is permissible to trade land for peace and dismantle settlements. Other ideological themes in this discourse echoed the moderate approach with secular Zionism. Thus, religious proponents of compromise spoke about the need for territorial compromise for demographic reasons, in order to maintain a Jewish majority within a democratic framework.[14] Religious doves also emphasized the need for withdrawal due to the high moral costs of continued occupation on Israeli society.[15]

Overall, the hawkish religious approaches to the peace process are infused with a messianic streak, according to which contemporary Jewish control over the Holy Land is seen as playing a central role in the messianic process. In contrast, the religious doves—especially the ultra-Orthodox ones—tend to downplay or ignore the messianic significance of Zionism.

### *Differentiating the Religious Discourse from the Nonreligious Discourse*

As noted above, there are similarities between the religious and nonreligious discourses on the peace process. This is particularly evident on the radical Right where both the religious and nonreligious discourse revolves around beliefs in messianism, the uniqueness of the Jewish people, and the eternity of anti-Semitism.[16] However, overall the religious discourse is more ethnocentric and hawkish than the nonreligious discourse. While religious language is highly prominent within Israel's radical Right[17] it is largely absent from the literature of the dovish movement, "Peace Now."[18]

In addition, the differences between the religious discourse and the nonreligious discourse are evident when comparing the thrust of the language used by religious and nonreligious doves. The nonreligious Left supports a Palestinian state in ideological terms, due to its commitment to the universal right of nations to self-determination and universal human rights. It views Palestinian rights as equal to Jewish rights in a fundamental sense. It is also totally opposed to settlements.[19] In contrast, the religious Left agrees with the religious Right that the fundamental Jewish right to the land is superior to that of the Palestinians because of the biblical promise made by God. Rather than being fundamentally opposed to settlements, two leading dovish rabbis, Amital and Lichtenstein, are actually the joint heads of a yeshiva situated in the West Bank. While they support compromise and withdrawal, their assessment is based on having to choose between *Conflicting Values* (the title of a *Meimad* pamphlet advocating compromise).[20] Instead of justifying compromise in terms of universal rights, religious doves emphasis the need for compromise in ethnocentric terms: because the lives of the "people of Israel" are more important than the "Land of Israel," or in order to preserve Jewish unity and prevent the moral deterioration of the Jewish people.[21]

In addition, while the nonreligious dovish discourse emphasizes its position in terms of idealism, religious doves tend to emphasize pragmatism and realism, which makes their discourse more akin to that of the nonreligious center than the left.[22] In this vein, Rabbi Shach wrote of the need to adopt a commonsense approach, not an approach based on an emotional attachment to territory. Ovadia Yosef declared that his opinion was expressedly based on consultations with military and political experts.[23] Rabbi Lichtenstein cautioned against an overly idealistic approach based on the idea that the key to political success is faith.[24] Indeed, in the early 1990s virtually all ultra-Orthodox MKs identified themselves as neither hawks nor doves but as pragmatists, and nearly all identified with centrist positions on the peace process.[25] In addition, it is worth noting that *Meimad*, the party of the dovish religious Zionists, is an acronym in Hebrew for "Religious Center Party." Furthermore, despite religious moderates' support for the principle of "land for peace," they are more cautious than the secular moderates in supporting this position. Rabbi Shach supported the 1991 Madrid Peace Conference, but in contrast to the nonreligious Israeli Left he was very skeptical of the Oslo Accords.[26] Whereas the Israeli Left reacted to the collapse of the peace process in 2000 by advocating renewed negotiations, international trusteeship, or unilateral withdrawal, Ovadia Yosef reacted by reversing his ruling on land for peace and making a number of extremely derogatory remarks about Arabs.[27]

## The Religious Public and the Peace Process

Public opinion surveys since the Six Day War have consistently demonstrated a very strong relationship between religiosity and hawkishness in Israel. The surveys usually place Jewish respondents into three or four categories according to self-identification, core beliefs, and the stated level of observance of religious practices and commandments. The first category relates to the secular, the second to the traditional, and the third to the religious. This last category is sometimes broken down into two subcategories: ultra-Orthodox and national-religious. Recent surveys[28] suggest that about 20 percent of the Israeli Jewish public is religious, just under half of whom are ultra-Orthodox. About a third of the public is traditional, the rest are secular.

Between 1972 and 1981 an average of 71 percent of religious people were unwilling to return any part of the West Bank, compared to 58 percent of traditional and 47 percent of secular people (Figure 1).[29]

Between 1984 and 1993 the mean score of the "very religious" regarding the return of the territories (5 = annexation, 1 = return) was 3.8, as compared to 3.4 for the religious, 2.9 for the traditional, and 2.4 for the secular (Figure 2).[30]

In the mid- to late-1990s research suggested that religiosity was the single most important determinant of hawkish attitudes among the Jewish public in Israel. These surveys showed that between 1994 and 1997, 4 to 12 percent of the ultra-Orthodox supported Oslo as compared to 16 to 24 percent of the religious, 28 to 31 percent of the traditional, and 44 to 67 percent of the secular (Figure 3).

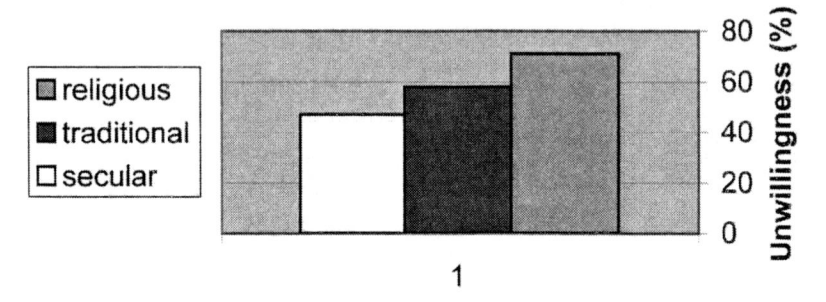

**Figure 1.** Average unwillingness to return all or most of the West Bank 1972–81. Data from Yael Yishai, *Land or Peace?* (Stanford: Hoover Institute, 1987) p. 185.

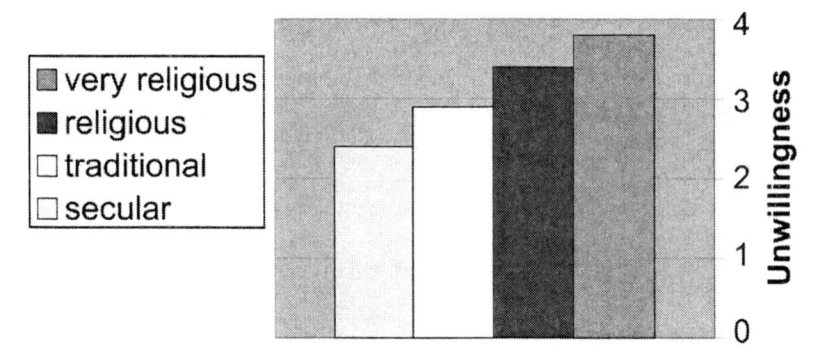

**Figure 2.** Mean unwillingness to return territory 1984–93. Data from Asher Arian, *Security Threatened* (Cambridge: Cambridge University Press, 1995) pp. 115–19.

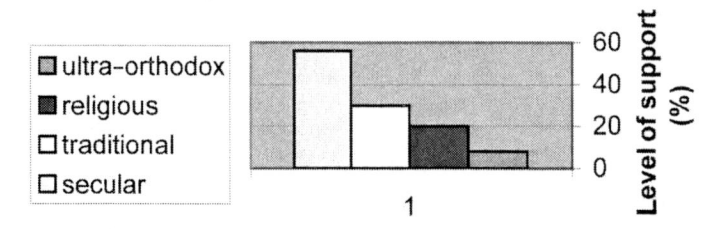

**Figure 3.** Levels of support for the Oslo process 1994–97. Data from Tamar Herman and Efraim Yaar, *Religious-Secular Relations in Israel* (Tel Aviv: Tami Steinmetz Centre for Peace, 1998) [Hebrew] pp. 62–67.

In 1997, 100 percent (!) of the ultra-Orthodox defined themselves as "Rightists" as compared to 81 percent of the national-religious, 55 percent of the traditional, and 22 percent of the secular. Also in 1997, 8 percent of the ultra-Orthodox believed that "the two peoples had national and civic rights in the Land of Israel" as compared to 13 percent of the religious, 17 percent of the traditional, and 36 percent of the secular.[31] Overall there is a clear progression in terms of hawkishness. The ultra-Orthodox are the most hawkish, followed by the national-religious, followed by the traditional, and lastly the secular who are the most dovish. Since the collapse of the peace process in September 2000, the general trend in Israeli public opinion has been in a hawkish direction, but nonetheless the religious public continues to be more hawkish than the public in general.[32]

## Religious Political Behavior Toward the Conflict

No religious party or politician has ever been primarily responsible for Israeli foreign policy. The lack of ultimate responsibility means that they can more easily afford to take a stance based either on pure principle or ulterior motives (say, as a bargaining chip to obtain more funds for religious institutions). This is particularly true for the ultra-Orthodox, who are especially dependent on state funding as over two-thirds of ultra-Orthodox men do not work, while their cost of living is high because of very large size of the average ultra-Orthodox family. Indeed, it is estimated that the total government assistance to an ultra-Orthodox yeshiva student and his family of ten children is about 11,000 New Israeli Shekels (NIS) a month net or 17,000 NIS gross (approximately $4,000). Financial support for small families also runs into thousands of shekels every month.[33] Thus, in judging the behavior of religious actors toward the peace process it is important to remember that their actions do not necessarily reflect what they would do if they were ultimately responsible for policy. With this caveat in mind, the section below assesses the behavior of religious actors toward the peace process.

### *Direct Action*

The religious settler movement *Gush Emunim* (Bloc of the Faithful) was responsible for founding the first illegal settlements in the territories in the 1970s, and they (and their various organizational offshoots) have led the way in setting up new settlements throughout the territories since then. Although many large settlements were subsequently set up by secular politicians such as Ariel Sharon and many secular people live in those settlements, there is no doubt that the religious community is disproportionally represented among the settlers and their political leadership.[34] Religious actors have also been especially prominent in terms of protests and demonstrations against the peace process. It was *Gush Emunim* that led the struggle against the withdrawal from the Sinai settlement of Yamit following the peace treaty with Egypt, and religious youth have struggled against the dismantling of illegal outposts in the West Bank recently.[35] The religious sector provided a large proportion of the people at demonstrations against the Oslo Accords.[36] Furthermore, extreme rightwing rabbis such as Chaim Druckman and two former Ashkenazi chief rabbis, Goren and Shapira, ruled that *halacha* requires religious soldiers to disobey any order to dismantle settlements.[37] Recently 500 Israeli rabbis signed a statement to this effect.[38] Finally, religious people committed the two major incidents of violence against the peace process perpetrated by civilian Israelis. In the mid-1980s the Jewish Underground, which grew out of *Gush Emunim*, attacked Arab mayors and plotted to blow up the Al-Aqsa Mosque on the Temple Mount. In 1995 a religious assailant, Yigal Amir, assassinated Prime Minister Rabin. He was apparently acting on the basis of a halachic ruling of extreme rabbis.[39] There have been rabbis and religious peace groups who have spoken out in favor of the peace process and against right-wing extremism. However, none of these have had anywhere near the amount of support among the religious public that *Gush Emunim* and other right-wing groups have enjoyed. The religious have not played an important role in left-wing direct action groups such as "Peace Now."[40] Nor were religious people involved in the "track 2" Israeli–Palestinian dialogue that led to the Oslo Accords.

### *Elections*

Prior to 1996, the elections were conducted on the basis of a single ballot for a political party. The ultra-Orthodox population voted for their parties, without regard to their stance on the peace process. National-religious voters paid greater attention to parties' stance on the peace process. In 1981 the National Religious Party (NRP) dropped from twelve to six seats due, in part, to a shift of support to the far Right *Techiya* party.[41] In 1984 the NRP dropped to four seats, losing support to a more hawkish religious party, *Morasha*. Indeed the NRP only recovered its electoral strength in 1992, when it took an unequivocally right-wing stance by refusing to join a governing coalition led by the Left for the first time. In 1988 a moderate religious party, *Meimad*, was set up. However, it failed to achieve a single seat in the Knesset. The party did obtain representation in the Knesset from 1999 to 2003, but only through reserved slots on a joint list with the Labour Party. One of the main reasons that *Meimad* ran with Labour was that it was concerned that it could not muster enough support to gain representation in the Knesset if it ran alone.

In 1996 and 1999 the elections were run on a dual ballot system, with one vote going for a party and another for prime minister. In 2001, there was a special election only for the prime minister. Unlike the vote for a party, which is based on a variety of considerations, the vote for prime minister is based more on attitudes toward the peace process. In 1996 and 1999 all the religious parties endorsed the right-wing candidate, Netanyahu, and the overwhelming majority of the religious public voted for him as well. In 1996, when the vote was extremely close, religiousness was the single most significant variable in differentiating Netanyahu from Peres supporters.[42] In 2001, the overwhelming majority of all voters backed the right-wing candidate, Ariel Sharon, though this time the ultra-Orthodox leadership called on their followers not to take part in the vote. In 2003, the single ballot system was reintroduced. Surveys showed that the national-religious voted in larger numbers than average for the center Right and far Right.[43]

### *Coalition Politics and Peace Agreements*

Since no party in Israel has ever received an absolute majority in a general election, the governing party is always dependent on smaller parties to form a stable coalition. Historically, religious parties have played a pivotal role in this process. In addition, religious politicians in the Knesset and the cabinet have helped determine policy. The behavior of the religious parties since the 1973 Yom Kippur War has generally oscillated between support for centrist and hawkish positions. With the rise of the "Young Guard" in the NRP in 1974, the party moved from a generally pragmatic to a relatively hawkish stance. Between 1974 and 1976 the party formed a kind of internal opposition within the government to Labour Prime Minister Rabin's policy through their support for the illegal settlements set up by *Gush Emunim*.[44] In 1977 the NRP clearly stated its preference for a government headed by the right-wing Likud, and was instrumental in helping Begin form a governing coalition.[45] In the 1980s, with the two main parties evenly balanced, the religious parties held the balance of power and their preference was generally for either a National Unity Government (NUG) or a narrow right-wing government. It was believed that the ultra-Orthodox would be prepared to join a left-wing coalition in return for massive financial support for their institutions. However, when Labour leader Shimon Peres tried to do just that in March 1990, he obtained the support of *Shas* but not that of the other ultra-Orthodox parties. Ultimately, Rabbi Shach preferred a right-wing government apparently because he believed that their more ethnocentric worldview was ultimately closer to religion than the more universalistic worldview of the Left. At the same time, other ultra-Orthodox MKs supported the Right based on the hawkish views of their leader, the Lubavitcher Rebbe.[46]

In the Knesset vote on the 1993 Oslo Accords, no religious party voted in favor, while all the religious parties voted against the 1995 Interim Agreement (Oslo II). In 1998, the NRP helped to bring down the right-wing Netanyahu government over the Wye Agreement, which mandated an Israeli withdrawal from a further 13 percent of the West Bank. Although the NRP joined the government led by Labour leader Ehud Barak in 1999, it led the internal opposition to Barak's peace policies. On the eve of the Camp David summit, the NRP and *Shas* left the government in protest at the concessions Barak was prepared to offer the Palestinians. Though *Shas* helped Barak to remain in power by supporting him from outside the government in November 2000, it ultimately abandoned Barak because of pressure from its hawkish supporters and activists. Finally, in the cabinet vote on the Clinton Framework for a Final Status Agreement between Israel and the Palestinians in December 2000, the only religious member of the most left-wing cabinet in Israeli history, *Meimad* leader Rabbi Michael Melchior, was one of only two members of the cabinet that voted against the agreement.[47]

Still, religious parties have not always acted to advance a hawkish agenda. On a number of occasions they have adopted a centrist stance. For example, they supported the Camp David Accords and the peace agreement with Egypt initiated by Menachem Begin's Likud-led government. They also supported the 1994 peace treaty with Jordan, which was also supported by the Likud, *Shas*, and the ultra-Orthodox *Yahadut HaTora* party, all of which also supported the 1998 Wye Agreement initiated by the Netanyahu government. On very rare occasions religious politicians did take an unequivocally dovish stance. For example, in 1982 the head of the NRP, Zevulun Hammer, pushed for a commission of inquiry into the massacre of Palestinians by Israel's Lebanese Christian allies in the Sabra and Shatila refugee camps, against the stance of Prime Minister Begin. Even in this instance other members of the NRP and the ultra-Orthodox parties opposed a commission of inquiry.[48] Only on one occasion has a religious party's behavior been crucial to the peace process, when in 1993 *Shas*'s abstention on the Oslo Accords allowed the measure to obtain a majority in the Knesset. Even here the fact that *Shas* could not bring itself to actually vote for the Oslo Accords demonstrates that religion was hardly in the vanguard of the peace camp. The only religious parliamentary grouping to be truly part of the peace camp is *Meimad*. As part of the Labour governments in 1995–96 and 1999–2001, *Meimad* did not play a direct role in policy formation, but its presence in the government helped to counter attempts to totally delegitimize the peace process among the religious public. Overall then, the practical approach of religious actors toward the peace process has generally ranged from hawkish to centrist, and as such reflects relatively faithfully the general orientations and outlook of both the religious leadership and the religious masses.

## Religion and Hawkishness: Understanding the Fundamental Correlation

The main question that emerges from the above survey of the relationship between religion and the peace process is why religion has become closely correlated with hawkishness since 1967. The answer has to do with the relationship between religion, Israeli political culture, and the historical process of postmodernization. According to Peled and Shafir,[49] Israeli political culture has always consisted of three citizenship discourses: republicanism, liberalism, and ethno-nationalism. The liberal discourse, with its emphasis on the individual and universal human rights, informs a dovish orientation to the peace process, the ethnonational discourse, which emphasizes collective Jewish ethno-national rights, is inclined toward hawkishness.[50] Though in tension, these discourses coexist within the consensual notion of Israel as a democratic Jewish state.[51] This synthesis was stabilized for many years by the third discourse, republicanism, which is theoretically compatible with the other two discourses. The republican discourse[52] relates to an ethos of active citizenship and voluntarism in service of the collective good. Since 1948, the main focus of republicanism has been service in the Israeli armed forces on the basis of the "nation in arms model." In terms of foreign relations and the peace process, republicanism emphasizes pragmatism and state security.[53]

The above analysis of the religious discourse regarding the conflict reveals that it is relatively more hawkish than the nonreligious discourse. Correspondingly, the religious discourse is also far more ethnocentric than the nonreligious discourse— even among religious doves—while giving little expression to universalistic values associated with liberalism.[54] This ethnocentric orientation explains why religious doves tend to be closer in their outlook to nonreligious centrists than to nonreligious doves. Even though religious doves support the principle of "land for peace," their ethnocentrism leads them to be relatively suspicious of Arab intensions, while their lack of commitment to national self-determination as a *universal value* means that Israeli concessions are measured primarily by their value in terms of saving Jewish lives and not in terms of fulfilling Palestinian national rights.[55] For example, even while justifying the principle of "land for peace," Rabbi Shach reaffirmed his fundamental belief in the intrinsically anti-Semitic nature of non-Jews by reference to myths rooted in the Jewish religious tradition, namely that "Esau (the Gentiles) hates Jacob (the Jews)" and that the Jews are "a people that dwells alone."[56]

These myths also became important in Israeli political culture in the 1970s and 1980s, and they have remained particularly potent among religious and traditional Israelis.[57] This, in turn, indicates the way in which ethnocentrism has been particularly strong in these sections of Israeli society. Thus, Arian has demonstrated that strong adherence to the ethnocentric "People Apart" syndrome is highly correlated to hawkishness and that correspondingly religious Jews in Israel are the most prone to strongly adhere to the "People Apart" syndrome.[58] In other words, it is because the mass of religious Jews are more ethnocentric than the nonreligious that they adopt a more hawkish approach to the peace process.

This finding reinforces the argument of both Shils and Smith that religion generally serves to encourage ethnocentricity.[59] Shils argues that religion generates a sense of an in-group and an out-group that serves to encourage an ethnocentric orientation, even in those religions with a very universalistic ideology. This religious basis for group differentiation gives ethnocentricity a reified quality that heightens its resonance. Smith argues that this is especially relevant to the Jewish religious tradition, which places God's covenantal relationship with the Jewish people (rather than with the individual) at its center.

Still, the relationship between religion, ethnocentricity, and hawkishness is not of the either/or variety. Opinion surveys consistently demonstrate a progression whereby the ultra-Orthodox are the most hawkish, followed by the national-religious, the traditional, and finally the secular. This progression is related to the degree of segregation from nonreligious culture and society. Social and cultural segregation widens the physical and psychological distance between "them" and "us." This, in turn, heightens a sense of ethnocentricity and thus hawkishness. The degree of segregation also signals the extent of group hostility to the liberal values and secular lifestyles of nonreligious society that are viewed as a threat to religion. Thus, the ultra-Orthodox who are the most segregated from nonreligious society are, correspondingly, the most hawkish, followed by the national-religious and then traditional Jews.[60]

The above argument explains the difference between the religious and the nonreligious on the attitudinal level. However, it does not account for the fact that the national-religious, who are less ethnocentric and more open to elements of liberalism than the ultra-Orthodox, are more hawkish in practice than the ultra-Orthodox. This is explained by their different ideologies. First, for most of the ultra-Orthodox leadership, the state of Israel is not of great religious significance and certainly not of messianic significance—thus maintaining control over all of *Eretz Yisrael* is not a core value. In contrast, for most of the national-religious leadership the state of Israel is of messianic significance and consequently maintaining control over all of *Eretz Yisrael* is a core value. Second, ultra-Orthodox ideology does not encourage republicanism, whereas national-religious ideology does. The fact that the ultra-Orthodox do not view the state of Israel as having intrinsic religious significance means that they tend to adopt a political approach focused on their narrow sectional interests; the conflict with the Palestinians is thus not a central concern. In contrast, the national-religious, who view the state of Israel as of great religious significance, are far more republican in their approach. Consequently, they not only seek to protect their sectional interests but also try to actively influence general state policy, especially regarding the peace process. Finally, the hierarchical nature of ultra-Orthodox society allows their pragmatic leadership to generally constrain their public's hawkish instincts. This is much more difficult for the national-religious leadership to achieve, given that they have developed more democratic political structures.

## Religion and Hawkishness: The Role of Historical Events and Processes

The question, however, remains as to why the strong correlation between religion and hawkishness only become apparent after 1967. If the correlation can be explained by the innate ethnocentric properties of religion or in terms of fundamental religious ideologies, then why did these factors apparently have no impact prior to the Six Day War? The answer to these questions requires analysis of the relationship of religion to changes in Israeli political culture.

In the 1930s, the leader of the hawkish Revisionist movement, Jabotinsky, recognized that his message was especially well received among religious Jews.[61] However, religious zionist leaders "reluctantly" accepted partition of the Holy Land and they also supported Labour's policy of restraint in response to Arab attacks.[62] The main hawkish groups prior to 1967 were not religious but rather secular nationalists inspired either by far Left or far Right ideologies. Thus in the 1950s, the main hawks hailed from *Herut*, the party of Revisionism, or from *Achdut Havoda*, the "activist" wing of the Labour movement. In contrast, prior to 1967 the religious parties did not focus on foreign policy. They felt threatened by secularism,[63] and consequently concentrated on nurturing religious institutions and protecting the role of religion in the state. This focus constrained the republicanism of the nationalreligious. As a result, the NRP generally deferred to *Mapai* on foreign policy. Still, when the NRP did express an opinion on foreign policy it was often moderate. Indeed, the leader of the NRP, Moshe Shapira, was actually one of the most dovish voices in Israeli cabinets from 1948 to 1967.[64] Prior to the Six Day War, although the religious public was apparently attracted to hawkishness, these sentiments were held in check by a moderate leadership that focused on sectional interests, which constrained their republicanism. Meanwhile, nonreligious ideologies promoted the most hawkish approach to the conflict.

## The Impact of the Six Day War

One reason often put forward for the growth of the association between religion and hawkishness is the impact of the Six Day War.[65] The capture by Israeli forces of many holy sites (including the holiest site in Judaism, the Temple Mount) clearly bore great religious resonance. It is one thing to be passive about the conquest of these areas, quite another to voluntarily agree to retreat from them. In addition, the experience of the war—in which the country went from the fear of a second Holocaust to an unprecedented military victory in less than a week—led many religious Jews to view matters in messianic terms. These feelings were evident not only among religious Zionists but also among some segments of the ultra-Orthodox community. The Six Day War made it easier for the ultra-Orthodox to identify with the agenda of the political Right as its main representatives, *Gush Emunim*, were religious—unlike their pre-1967 predecessors. Against this background, religious Jews tended to support retention of Israeli control over the areas captured in the war.

However, similar sentiments were also widespread throughout nonreligious Israeli society.[66] Secular Zionists such as Moshe Dayan also expressed euphoria at the return of the Jewish people to their "historic cradle."[67] As a result, immediately following the Six DayWar public opinion in general was very hawkish. Subsequently public opinion moved in a dovish direction in response to events such as the 1982 Lebanon War and particularly the 1987–92 intifada.[68] While this general trend affected both the religious and nonreligious public, the religious public has remained consistently more hawkish than the nonreligious public. Thus, while the Six Day War clearly triggered the rise of hawkishness, the real question is why this orientation has remained stronger among the religious community ever since then. The answer to this question is related to changes in nonreligious Israeli society as much as to changes in religious society.

## The Polarization of Israeli Political Culture and the Peace Process

Since at least the mid-1980s, within Israeli political culture there has been a general trend toward greater liberalism and individualism among the younger generation of secular Israelis.[69] Until the mid-1980s, the overall balance within Israeli political culture was weighed in favor of republicanism and ethno-nationalism, but since then republicanism has all but disappeared, ethno-nationalism has declined, and liberalism has gained significant strength. These trends have pushed Israel in a dovish direction. Thus, following the 1987–92 intifada, the decline of ethno-nationalism was apparent in the dramatic decrease in support for the territorial integrity of the land of Israel.[70] In addition, political and military leaders such as former Prime Ministers Rabin and Barak stated that part of the reason they felt it necessary to pursue a dovish policy was due to the erosion of the general public's fighting spirit, a reflection of the decline of the republican ethos.[71] The decline of the republican ethos was also brought on by the massive rise in the amount of ultra-Orthodox young men who received exemptions from army service, growing from a few hundred in the 1950s to around thirty thousand in the early 1990s.[72] Finally the growing liberal trend found expression in Israeli foreign policy through the rise of young, middle-class, liberal, dovish politicians in Meretz and the younger generation of Labour Party leaders.[73]

Yet within the national-religious community, from the 1960s onward the trend moved away from a moderate religious approach that was relatively liberal and valued elements of modernity on their own terms. This was accompanied by the rise of a more stringent extremist religious approach that was far more critical of modernity and nonreligious society as well as being ultra-nationalist in orientation. This approach was cultivated by the followers of Rabbi Zvi Yehuda Kook in religious boarding schools that were increasingly attended by the elite among nationalreligious youth. Both the ideology of the extremists and the social isolation of the boarding schools served to further heighten the sense of ethno-national particularism among the national-religious community. Meanwhile, the success of the religious community in stemming the tide of secularization led national religious youth to feel greater self-confidence. Subsequently they became critical of the NRP's narrow political agenda. Instead they wanted to adopt a more ambitious plan to influence the face of nonreligious Israeli society. The rise to the surface of this latent republican impulse, when fused with the religious ethno-nationalism described above, led to the creation of the voluntarist religious settler movement *Gush Emunim*.[74] In other words, the rise of *Gush Emunim* can be explained by the rise of the very orientations—republicanism and ethno-nationalism—that were on the wane in secular society.

The emergence of hawkishness as a factor in ultra-Orthodox politics is related to the increased role of the ultra-Orthodoxy masses in politics.[75] While this shift does not constitute full-blown republicanism, it is symptomatic of their increased sense of belonging. The rise of the Right to power in Israel in 1977 allowed the ultra-Orthodox to feel closer to the state because they perceived the right as more ethnocentric and more sympathetic to organized religion.[76] Subsequently, the ultra-Orthodox masses have become more interested in mainstream Israeli politics and this has had some impact on the peace process. For example, in 1996 the ultra-Orthodox leadership preferred to back Shimon Peres in the elections for prime minister, as his record on funding for ultra-Orthodox institutions was considered good, but pressure from below was a major factor that led them to adopt the opposite course of action.[77] Finally during the later stages of settlement construction, many ultra-Orthodox people moved to the territories in order to obtain cheap housing. This has given the community a certain interest in supporting the Right.[78]

To summarize, the reason religion has been so strongly correlated with hawkishness since 1967 is a function of changes in both religious and nonreligious society that found expression in the polarization of Israeli political culture. Whereas liberalism increased and ethno-nationalism and republicanism declined in secular society, the opposite processes occurred in religious society.

## Religion, Postmodernization, and Israeli Political Culture

Thus far the explanation of the relationship between cultural change and the development of the strong correlation between religion and hawkishness after 1967 has been based on domestic forces. However, in order to explain why the religion-hawkishness correlation became so prominent, it has been argued that one has to take into account changes in secular society at least as much as changes in religious society. This process of liberalization is best explained by reference to the global process of postmodernization. Postmodernization also served to facilitate the cultural changes that occurred among the religious public described above.

According to Inglehart,[79] just as the shift from traditional to modern society involved a move from traditional to modern values, so advanced industrial societies are engaged in a process of postmodernization evident in the shift from modern to postmodern values. Postmodern orientations are differentiated from modern orientations by a greater tendency toward liberalism, individualism, and self-expression; much greater support for democracy, minority rights, and multiculturalism; and much less affinity with collectivism, nationalism, and organized religion.

Postmodern values begin to develop in advanced industrial societies when the level of income reaches $6,000–$7,000 per year (in 1990 U.S. dollars). However, the relationship between economic development and cultural change is not one to one. Rather it depends on the relative level of economic and existential security a person feels during childhood and adolescence. This subjective experience determines the basic cultural orientation of different generations. Thus the generation acculturated during the 1930s and 1940s under conditions of economic depression and war demonstrates a tendency toward modern "security" values, while those acculturated during the relatively peaceful and prosperous 1950s and 1960s demonstrate a tendency toward postmodern values, as they take prosperity and physical security more for granted and are consequently more concerned with "quality of life" values. This cohort formed the core of the European peace movement in the 1970s and subsequently provided an important basis for left-wing politics in the advanced industrial world. However, not all of this cohort adopted a postmodern outlook to the same degree; the process has been constrained by the effects of local culture, and especially religion. The more the dominant institutionalized religious doctrine of a country is collectivist, and the more it tends to view all aspects of life as within the purview of religion, the less inclined such a country is toward postmodernism, and vice versa. Thus historically Protestant countries are more postmodern than historically Catholic countries, all other things being equal.[80]

A recent survey has demonstrated that Israel has also followed this trajectory; it has become a moderately postmodern country.[81] As in other countries, postmodern orientations are prevalent among the younger generation of the middle class, represented by the parties of the Left, and strongly correlated with a dovish approach to foreign policy. However, not all of the middle-class younger generation adhered to a postmodern outlook. One group in particular bucked this trend—the religious.[82]

This can be explained by the fact that Orthodox Judaism puts the emphasis more on the collective than the individual and because it tends to view all aspects of life and society as coming under the purview of *halacha*. This makes it closer in its cultural effects to Catholicism than Protestantism. This effect is reinforced by the institutional separation of religious and nonreligious pupils in the educational system and, to a lesser degree, in other walks of life. Consequently the religious have been sheltered from some of the direct effects of postmodernization. In this way the failure of postmodernization to penetrate deeply into the consciousness of the religious public has contributed to the polarization within Israeli political culture that has led to religion being so closely correlated with hawkishness since 1967.

Postmodernization also contributed to this polarization by helping to facilitate the rise of radicalism within the religious community in two ways. First, postmodern societies are marked by the fact that they give greater legitimacy to cultural pluralism. This puts less pressure on groups with alternative values to conform to the mainstream nonreligious society.[83] The decrease in the pressure to conform has strengthened the more extreme, separatist, and hawkish orientation in the Orthodox Jewish community not only in Israel, but worldwide.[84] Second, according to Flanagan the shift away from politics based on material interests associated with "modernism" is not only to be found on the political Left, but also on the political Right. Thus "new Right" parties are based not on class interests, but on the rise of a young generation seeking to promote traditional social and religious values, including nationalism and a hawkish approach to foreign policy.[85] This process seems to have found expression in Israel as well as the rise of the idealistic "Young Guard" in the NRP and *Gush Emunim* in the early 1970s, which put greater emphasis on "authenticity" and less emphasis on the material interests of the religious public.[86]

## Conclusion

The Jewish religion advocates no single definitive approach to the conflict with the Palestinians. Analysis of the different approaches to the conflict adopted by the Orthodox religious community in Israel reveals that the leadership discourse and political behaviour of the national-religious was generally more hawkish than that of the ultra-Orthodox. The main reason for this is the prominence of a messianic ideology among the national-religious, who attach great religious significance to the state of Israel and its control over the Holy Land. However, in terms of general public attitudes the ultra-Orthodox were more hawkish than the national-religious because of their greater ethnocentricity.

While one cannot speak in terms of a singular religious approach to the conflict, analysis of the discourse, public opinion, and political behaviour of religious and nonreligious Israeli Jews have demonstrated that the religious have been significantly more hawkish than the nonreligious since 1967. At the cultural level, this is because religion in Israel reinforces ethnocentricity among the Jewish public, which in turn is highly correlated with hawkishness. This relationship between religion and ethnocentrism is both an intrinsic property of religion per se and of the specific content of the Jewish religion. This relationship is reinforced by the segregated religious lifestyle pursued by contemporary religious Jews in Israel. In other words, it is not religion per se that is hawkish, but rather it is the way religion engenders ethnocentrism that makes it correlate so strongly with hawkishness.

On the political level, however, the general correlation between religion and ethnocentricity is not sufficient to explain why religion only becamemanifest as the main font of hawkishness in the Israeli political arena after 1967. This is a function of the way religion interacted with changes in Israeli political culture. Whereas mainstream Israeli political culture has becomemore liberal, less ethnocentric, and less republican, religious political culture has moved in the opposite direction. The rise of ethnocentrism and republicanismamong the religious hasmade their outlookmore hawkish, while making them simultaneously more active in pursuit of hawkish objectives in practice. Meanwhile, the rise of liberalism and the decline of republicanism among the nonreligious public has made them increasingly dovish both as a matter of liberal principle and because they have become less willing to pay the price of endemic conflict.

This process of cultural polarization was driven and facilitated by the process of postmodernization. In advanced industrial societies postmodernization generates a more liberal and more dovish middle-class, younger generation. The same process occurred among nonreligious Israelis. However, in Israel, religion shielded its adherents from most of the effects of postmodernization while simultaneously encouraging countervailing trends, which accounts for the polarization referred to above. In other words, the centrality of religion in promoting hawkishness since 1967 is not primarily a function of religion's discrete internal properties. Rather, it is the way religion has interacted with the process of postmodernization that has made it the most effective incubator for hawkishness in Israel since 1967.

In terms of the wider application of these findings to other conflicts, two hypotheses can be proposed. First, that the "inside-out" relationship between religion and ethnicity explains how religion generates ethnocentrism, which in turn generates hawkish orientations. Second, that the "outside-in" relationship between postmodernization and religion explains how and why religious orientations toward conflict increasingly diverge from nonreligious orientations, and why they become prominent in advanced industrial societies. It would make the most sense to test these hypotheses with regard to comparable international or ethno-religious conflicts occurring in advanced industrial societies—for example, Northern Ireland.

## Notes

1. On these issues see Jonathan Fox "Towards a Dynamic Theory of Ethno-Religious Conflict" *Nations and Nationalism* 5, no. 4 (1999): 431–63; Jonathan Fox, "Religion as an Overlooked Element in International Relations," *International Studies Review* 3, no. 3, (2001).

2. Nonorthodox variants of the Jewish religion are excluded from analysis because they attract only a very small number of adherents in Israel. It is also beyond the scope of this article to discuss the role of religion among the 20 percent of non-Jewish Israelis.

3. On the relationship between Judaism and Israeli national identity and orientations toward the peace process, see Anthony Smith, "Sacred Territories and National Conflict" *Israel Affairs* 5, no. 4 (1999): 13–31; Charles Liebman and Eliezer Don-Yehiya, *Civil Religion in Israel* (Berkeley: University of California Press, 1983).

4. Ronald Inglehart, *Modernisation and Postmodernisation* (Princeton: Princeton University Press, 1997), 53–74. Inglehart's earlier research referred to the shift from material values to postmaterial values, but recently he has framed this shift within the broader shift from modernity to postmodernity. For the purposes of clarity, the term postmodernization will be used consistently even when referring to Inglehart's earlier work.

5. In the context of Israeli society, the term Sephardi refers to Jews who immigrated to Israel from North Africa and Arab countries, while the term Ashkenazi refers to Jews who immigrated to Israel from Europe.

6. Rabbi Shach, "On Eretz Israel and Territories" in *The State of Israel and the land of Israel*, ed. Adam Doron (Bet Berl 1987–88): 504–505 [In Hebrew].

7. Avi Ravitsky, *Messianism, Zionism and Jewish Religious Radicalism* (Chicago: University of Chicago Press, 1996), 211.

8. Habad is a worldwide Hassidic sect, which is differentiated from other such sects by its extensive efforts to encourage nonreligious Jews to become religious. *Hapoelei Agudat Yisrael* refers to a section of the ultra-Orthodox political party *Agudat Yisrael* formed by ultra-Orthodox Jews who set up communal agricultural settlements in Israel in the twentieth century. For further details see ibid., 181–206.

9. *Jerusalem Report*, February 27, 1992, 7.

10. See Norman Stillman, *Sephardi Religious Responses to Modernity* (Amsterdam: Harwood Academic Press, 1995); Meir Roumani, "The Sephardi Factor in Israeli Politics," *Middle East Journal* 42, no. 3 (1988): 423–435.

11. Ovadia Yosef, "Mesirat Shtachim Me'Ertz Yisrael Bimkom Pikuah Nefesh," in *Lectures Given at the 31st Conference of Tora Sheba'al Pe'eh*, ed. Yitzhak Rafael (Jerusalem: Mossad HaRav Kook, 1990) [In Hebrew].

12. Zvi Yehuda Kook, *Or Le Netivati* (Jerusalem: Z. Y. Kook Institute, 1989).

13. Ehud Sprinzak, *The Ascendance of Israel's Radical Right* (Oxford: Oxford University Press, 1991), 122.

14. Rabbi Yehuda Amital, "The Trap of the Whole Land of Israel," [In Hebrew] in *The State of Israel and the Land of Israel*, 495–503 (Bet Berl, 1988), for a detailed exposition of this view see Amnon Bazak, ed., 4th ed. *That You Shall Live by Them: A Conflict of Values* (Jerusalem: Temurot, 2000).

15. Yeshiyahu Leibovitz, *Judaism, Human Values and the Jewish State* (Cambridge, MA: Harvard University Press, 1992), 223–51.

16. Jonathan Rynhold, "Re-Conceptualising Israeli Approaches to the Palestinian Question" *Israel Studies* 6, no. 2 (2001): 33–52.

17. Sprinsak, *Israel's Radical Right*.

18. David Cathala-Hall, *The Peace Movement in Israel 1967–87* (Basingstoke: Macmillan, 1989).

19. Ibid.; Rynhold "Re-Conceptualising Israeli Approaches."

20. Bazak, *That You Shall Live*.

21. Amital, "The Trap"; Ilan Grielsammer, "Campaign Strategies of the Religious Parties," in *The Elections in Israel 1984*, eds. Asher Arian and Michal Shamir (Tel Aviv: Ramot, 1986), 84.

22. Rynhold, "Re-Conceptualising Israeli Approaches."

23. Shach, *On Eretz Israel*; Yosef, "Mesirat Shtachim."

24. Bazak, *That You Shall Live*, 65–66.

25. Efriam Inbar, Gad Barzillai, and Giora Goldberg, "Positions on National Security of Israel's Ultra-Orthodox Political Leadership" *Journal of Developing Societies* 13, no, 2 (1997).

26. *Jerusalem Post* September 26, 1991; *Israeline*, December 29, 1995.

27. Gil Hoffman, "Shas Leader Reverses Land-for-Peace Ruling," *Jerusalem Post*, January 28, 2003.

28. Shlomit Levy, Hanna Levinsohn, and Elihu Katz, *A Portrait of Israeli Jews* (Jerusalem: Israeli Democracy Institute, 2002); Tamar Herman and Efraim Yaar, *Religious-Secular Relations in Israel* [In Hebrew] (Tel Aviv: Tami Steinmetz Center for Peace, 1998).

29. Yael Yishai, *Land or Peace?* (Stanford: Hoover Institute, 1987), 185.

30. Asher Arian, *Security Threatened* (Cambridge: Cambridge University Press, 1995), 115–19.

31. Herman and Yaar, *Religious-Secular*, 62–67.

32. Asher Arian, *Israeli Public Opinion on National Security 2002* (Tel Aviv: Jaffe Center for Strategic Studies, 2002).

33. http://www.haaretz.co.il/hasite/pages/QAHeb.jhtml?qaNo = 60. In terms of ultra-Orthodox institutions, 204 million NIS of the government budget was allotted for ultra-Orthodox boarding schools in 1999, while the overall budget for yeshivas jumped from 640 million NIS in 1996 to nearly 900 million in 1999 (approximately $220 million). See Shachar

Ilan, *Haredim Ba'am* (Jerusalem: Keter, 2000), 128–29. In 2001 the *Shas* educational system received more than 220 million NIS from the education budget, while a further 65 million NIS was spent on ultra-Orthodox cultural activities, see *Ministry of Education Annual Audit 2002*, [In Hebrew] http://207.232.9.131/hofesh/din_2002_7_8.htm.

34. David Newman, "Reflections on 25 Years of Settlement Activity in the West Bank" *Israel Affairs* 3, no. 1 (1996): 65–83.

35. Nadav Shragai, "Evacuations Proceed amid Clashes," *Ha'aretz*, June 27, 2003.

36. For example, Heidi Gleit, "Masses Turn Out against Summit," *Jerusalem Post*, July 17, 2000.

37. Stuart Cohen, *The Scroll or the Sword?* (Amsterdam: Harwood Academic Publishers, 1997), 27–31; Margot Dudkevitch, "Officer Jailed for Refusing to Dismantle Outpost," *Jerusalem Post*, June 29, 2003.

38. Nadav Shragai, "Rabbis: No Government Has the Right to Set up a Foreign State in the Land of Israel," *Ha'aretz*, June 24, 2003.

39. Samuel Peleg, "They Shoot Prime Ministers Too, Don't They? Religious Violence in Israel" *Studies in Conflict and Terrorism* 20, no. 1 (1997): 227–47.

40. Mordechai Bar-On, *In Pursuit of Peace* (Washington DC: U.S. Institute of Peace, 1996).

41. Shmuel Sandler, "The Religious Parties," in *Israel at the Polls 1981*, eds. Howard Penniman and Daniel Elazar (Bloomington: Indiana University Press, 1986), 105–27.

42. Asher Arian and Michal Shamir, "Candidates, Parties and Blocs," in *The Elections in Israel 1999*, eds. Asher Arian and Michal Shamir (Albany: State University of New York Press, 2000). The figures were generally over 95 percent in favour of Netanyahu in ultra-Orthodox districts see http://www.knesset.gov.il/elections/index.html.

43. Asher Cohen, "2003: Restless Youngsters" [In Hebrew] *Meimad Journal* 26 (2003): 2–6.

44. Charles Liebman and Eliezer Don-Yehiya, *Religion and Politics in Israel* (Bloomington: Indiana University Press, 1984), 107–111.

45. Sandler, "The Religious Parties," 118.

46. *Ha'aretz*, March 28, 1990; *Jerusalem Post*, April 6, 1990.

47. See Jonathan Rynhold and Gerald Steinberg, "The Peace Process and the Elections," in *Israel at the Polls 2003*, eds. Shmuel Sandler and Jonathan Rynhold (London: Frank Cass, 2004).

48. Grielsammer, "Campaign Strategies," 83.

49. Yoav Peled and Gershon Shafir, "The Roots of Peacemaking: The Dynamics of Citizenship in Israel," *International Journal of Middle East Studies* 28, no. 3 (1996): 391–413.

50. Shmuel Sandler, *Land of Israel, State of Israel: Ethnonationalism in Israeli Foreign Policy* (Westport, CT: Greenwood Press, 1993).

51. On these tensions, see Ruth Gavison, "Jewish and Democratic? A Rejoinder to the 'Ethnic Democracy' Debate," *Israel Studies* 4, no. 1 (1999): 44–72.

52. On republicanism, see Daniel Elazar, *Covenant and Civil Society: The Constitutional Matrix of Modern Democracy* (New Brunswick: Transaction, 1998).

53. Rynhold (note 18). Republicanism is also referred to in the literature as statism.

54. Especially since the Rabin assassination efforts have been made to remedy this, see the journal *Judaism and Democracy* [In Hebrew] (Ramat Gan: Bar Ilan University Press).

55. On the relative paucity of universal values within the halachic discourse on politics, see Gerald Blidstein, "Halacha and Democracy," *Tradition* 21, no. 1 (1997): 8–37.

56. Shach, *On Eretz Israel*.

57. Liebman and Don-Yehiya, *Civil Religion*.

58. Arian, *Security Threatened*, 178–186.

59. Edward Shils, "Nation, Nationality, Nationalism and Civil Society," *Nations and Nationalism* 1, no. 1 (1995): 93–112; Smith, "Sacred Territories."

60. The ultra-Orthodox maintain their own separate educational system and their own press. They do not watch television or mix socially with nonreligious Jews. A large proportion of the men are not part of the general workforce and almost none serve in the army.

61. Yonathan Shapria, *The Road to Power: Herut Party in Israel* (Albany: State University of New York Press, 1991), 19.

62. Cohen, *The Scroll*, 28.

63. Liebman and Don-Yehiya, *Religion and Politics*, chapter 2.

64. Michael Brecher, *The Foreign Policy System of Israel* (New Haven: Yale University Press, 1972), 169–74, 179–80.

65. Michael Rosenak, "Religious Reactions: Testimony and Theology," in *The Impact of the Six Day War*, ed. Stephen Roth (Basingstoke: MacMillan, 1988): 209–31.

66. Amnon Rubinstein, *The Zionist Dream Revisited* (New York: Shocken, 1981), chapter 6.

67. Moshe Dayan, *Mapa Hadasha* (Tel Aviv: Maariv, 1969), 173.

68. Yishai, *Land or Peace?*, chapter 6; Arian (note 31) chapter 4. The Lebanon War was the catalyst for the foundation of the religious peace movement *Netivot Shalom*. Its founder and leader, Rabbi Amital, was formerly identified with *Gush Emunim*.

69. Peled and Shafir, "Roots of Peacemaking."

70. Arian, *Security Threatened*, 30–31.

71. Jonathan Rynhold, "Barak, the Israeli Left and the Oslo Peace Process," *Israel Studies Forum* 19, no. 1, (2003): 9–33.

72. Ilan, *Haredim Ba'am*.

73. Peled and Shafir, "Roots of Peacemaking."

74. Liebman and Don-Yehiya, *Religion and Politics*, 102–37.

75. Yair Sheleg, *HaDati'im HeChadashim* (Jerusalem: Keter, 2000).

76. Nadav Shragai, "Religious, Right-Wing and Realistic," *Ha'aretz*, February 15, 2001; Aryeh Dayan, "A Haredi Home in the Likud," *Ha'aretz*, November 21, 2002.

77. Sheleg, *HaDati'im*, 164.

78. Shragai, "Religious, Right-Wing," Nadav Shragai, "Dizzying Growth in Haredi Betar Ilit in West Bank," *Ha'aretz*, July 13, 2003.

79. Inglehart, *Modernisation and Postmodernisation*.

80. Ibid, 80–107.

81. Ephraim Ya'ar, "Value Prioritisation in Israeli Society," *Comparative Sociology* 1, no. 3–4 (2002): 347–68.

82. Ibid.

83. Inglehart, *Modernisation and Postmedernisation*, 22–23.

84. Samuel Heilman and Steven Cohen, *Cosmopolitans and Parochials: Modern Orthodoxy in America* (Chicago: Chicago University Press, 1989).

85. Ronald Inglehart and Scott Flanagan, "Controversies: Value Change in Industrial Societies," *American Political Science Review* 81, no. 4 (1987): 306–08.

86. Liebman and Don-Yehiya, *Religion and Politics*, 102–106, 113–14, 127.

# Has the Israeli–Palestinian Conflict Become Islamic? Fatah, Islam, and the Al-Aqsa Martyrs' Brigades

## HILLEL FRISCH

Many indications in the latest round of conflict between Israel and the Palestinians suggest that the Israeli–Palestinian conflict reflects, if not a civilizational fault line between Jewish Zionism and Islam, at the very least the Islamization of the conflict from a Palestinian perspective. First, its Islamization is suggested by the very title or name Palestinians and other analysts have given the present outbreak of hostilities that began at the end of September 2000: "the al-Aqsa intifada."[1] Al-Aqsa is the name of the mosque situated on the Temple Mount in Jerusalem, holy both to Jews and Muslims, where the first acts of violence took place. Most Palestinians claim that the visit by then Israeli opposition leader Ariel Sharon to the Temple Mount (*al-Harm al-Sharif*) provoked the violence. However, Israel and some Palestinians, including some who were close to Arafat, claim that the violence was preplanned.[2] Second, in the negotiations between Israeli prime minister Ehud Barak and Palestinian chairman Yasser Arafat at the Camp David summit in July 2000, sovereignty over the Temple Mount issue was purportedly one of the key bones of contention between Israeli and Palestinian negotiators.[3] Third, the violence on the Temple Mount led to the most widespread demonstrations and riots among Israel's Arab citizens since the establishment of the state. In the course of four days of violence, twelve Arab citizens were killed.[4] Even the Arab Palestinian "nationalist" press within Israel, which usually downplays the religious overtones of the conflict, had to report that the chants heard during the riots and demonstrations were mostly religious in nature. One of the most popular slogans was: "*Haibar, Haibar, Ya Yahud, Jaish Muhammad sa Yaud*," ("Haibar, Haibar, oh Jews recall, the army of Muhammad will return").[5] The chant refers to a battle in 628 C.E. between Muhammad and the Jewish tribe of Haibar, in which the Muslim army utterly defeated the tribe. In addition, few can deny the importance of the suicide bombers in the current wave of violence and, initially at least, the religious sentiments motivating them.[6]

Never before has Fatah's political and military preeminence been so politically challenged as in the latest round of conflict by the Islamic movements. Polls conducted by Palestinian research centers in the past consistently showed a wide gap between support for Arafat and Ahmad Yassin, the assassinated leader of Hamas, and on the "party" level much wider support for Fatah than for Hamas and Islamic Jihad combined.[7] Before the conflict, 40 percent on average supported Fatah compared to 16–18 percent for Hamas. During the recent outbreak of violence, the gap in support between Fatah and Hamas has virtually closed (29 percent compared to 27 percent). Support for Arafat declined from 40 percent before the outbreak of violence to 24.5 percent in June 2002.[8] Finally, the very emergence of Fatah's major fighting arm, called the Al-Aqsa Martyrs' Brigades (*Kata'ib Shuhada al-Aqsa*), has suggested that not only has the arena as a whole been Islamized but the very organization that bore the banner of Palestinian nationalism itself is conforming to the winds of change.

The following article analyzes whether the emergence of the Al-Aqsa Martyrs' Brigades (henceforth the Al-Aqsa Brigades) as the major fighting arm of Fatah reflects a fundamental ideological change within Fatah. Another option could be that the change in name from the more neutral and opaque Fatah Tanzim (Organization) was a means of mobilizing larger numbers of Palestinians, who would be attracted to a more Islamic name, yet not at the expense of sacrificing the basically nationalist identity of Fatah. The article begins with a brief analysis of the importance of Islamic themes, symbols, and sentiments in the Israeli–Palestinian conflict; moves on to analyze Fatah's specific relationship to religion and religious trends within the wider Palestinian movement; explains briefly the origins of the movement; and finally analyzes the ideology and practices of Fatah and the Al-Aqsa Brigades in the present conflict within the context of a national movement seeking redress in an international system committed to a system of states and raison d'e·tat over religious considerations.

## Religious Themes and Symbols in the Israeli–Palestinian Conflict

When politicians, journalists, and commentators began characterizing the latest round of violence between Palestinians and Israel as the Al-Aqsa Intifada, thus wedding a uniquely religious term (al-Aqsa) with a political term (intifada), they were hardly being original in the context of the overall conflict. Many previous stages of this bi-communal struggle crystallized over religious sites, as well as on various religious occasions. In fact, the first Arab riots against the Jews in mandatory Palestine erupted in April 1920 as participants came back to Jerusalem from the burial site of al-Nabi Musa (Moses the Prophet), which according to Muslim tradition is situated on the road leading to Jericho.[9]

The next—far more intensive and persistent—wave of violence in the summer of 1929 focused on what Arabs perceived as Jewish attempts to change the traditional status quo along the Wailing Wall. This religious site covers part of one of the four walls surrounding the Temple Mount, upon which the Al-Aqsa Mosque is situated. Jewish worshippers, supported by the right-wing Zionist Betar movement (whose members bore flags with the Star of David), amassed along the length of the wall on the fast day commemorating the destruction of the Second Temple—bringing with them an ark for the Torah scrolls and seats for the worshippers. The Palestinian Arab community, led by Hajj Amin al-Husayni, the president of the Supreme Muslim Council, had for years been trying to mobilize the Arab population against what he perceived as Jewish attempts to wrest control of the Temple Mount. He used reports of the waving of nationalist flags and the bringing of furniture, to stir anti- Jewish sentiment.[10] Hostilities against both Zionists and anti-Zionist ultra-orthodox Jews resulted in 133 killed and 339 wounded in a community numbering approximately 200,000. There were 116 Arabs killed and 232 wounded, mostly in the course of British police and paramilitary efforts to quell the violence.[11] Because of the intensity, geographical distribution, and organized nature of the violence, many scholars view the Wailing Wall riots of 1928–29 as the first real major confrontation in the bi-communal struggle in Palestine between Jews and Arabs.

After the violence abated, Hajj Amin al-Husayni recast Jewish attempts to change the status quo as an attempt to destroy the Muslim sites on the Temple Mount and rebuild the temple. He then went on to try to rally the Muslim world, calling for it to save Al-Aqsa. In 1931 he succeeded in convening an international Islamic conference attended by representatives from twenty-two countries. The Jewish religious threat to places of worship was one of Hajj Amin's favorite themes in mobilizing Palestine's Arab population as well.[12]

The cry to save Al-Aqsa was heard once again when Israel took over the West Bank in 1967 and, with greater intensity yet, with the establishment of the Palestinian Authority (PA) after the signing of the Oslo Accords in 1993. Arab Palestinians viewed an attempt by an Australian citizen to set fire to the Al-Aqsa Mosque in August 1969 as yet another attempt to rebuild the temple even though the perpetrator was a Christian.[13] In September 1996, the security organs of the recently constituted PA and other Palestinian irregulars reacted violently in response to the opening of a sightseeing tunnel along the foundations of the western wall of the Temple Mount.[14] Palestinians, especially Hamas and Islamic Jihad but members of the PA as well, accused the Israelis of digging the tunnel with the aim of undermining the foundations on the Temple Mount in order to destroy the Islamic holy sites. Hamas and Islamic Jihad are the two major Palestinian fundamentalist movements in the territories. Hamas, by far the larger, is the acronym of the "Islamic Resistance Movement" in Arabic, which appropriately makes up the word "zeal."

Holy sites both under Israeli rule and in areas under jurisdiction of the PA continued to be arenas of intense inter-communal violence. In May 1980, Fatah members—who were also students of the Department of Religion in Hebron University (*Jami at al-Khalil*)—killed five yeshiva (religious seminar) students in Hebron (*al-Khalil*), an incident that reflected the homogeneous religious background of the settlers and the settlement drive in general.[15] On October 8, 1990, seventeen Arabs were killed on the Temple Mount during the holy month of Ramadan after throwing stones at hundreds of Jewish worshippers celebrating the Feast of the Tabernacles at the Wailing Wall sixty feet below.[16] Four years later, a Jewish physician, Baruch Goldstein, murdered twenty-nine Arab worshippers in the Cave of the Patriarchs in the now-partitioned city of Hebron, considered holy to both religions.[17]

The latter events reflected the fact that a number of burial sites in the West Bank have become contested territory since Israel occupied it in 1967. Israeli settlement buildings in the West Bank has been accompanied by claims on, and the "settling" of, burial sites. Kever Yosef, Joseph's assumed burial site and home to a yeshiva, became an Israeli enclave after Israeli withdrawal from the city of Nablus in 1996.

It was overwhelmed in October 2000 by Palestinian irregulars at the beginning of the present hostilities.[18] Contention over the holy site has not been settled since. Jewish worshippers have attempted repeatedly to pray at the site whenever Israeli troops reenter the city to conduct search-and-destroy missions.[19] The yeshiva, formerly based in the holy site, continues to function in a nearby Jewish settlement and vows to return at the first opportunity. A third burial site, Rachel's tomb, at the entrance of Bethlehem, has also been the scene of intense military and political rivalry between Israel and the PA as each claims jurisdiction over it. According to the Torah, these three burial sites formed the axis of the Jewish patriarchs' peregrinations in the land of Canaan. Thus, many Israelis regard them as the heart of sacred territory and ancient Jewish history. Despite the sacredness of Joseph's tomb, the Israel Defense Force (IDF) did not permit Jews to return when it reoccupied Nablus more or less permanently in June 2002.[20] This was the only area Israel was willing to relinquish during the last outbreak of violence, indicating that at least from the Israeli perspective, there was a tendency to minimize the religious overtones of the conflict.

## Nationalism and Religion in Fatah

In the Middle East, with the possible exception of modern Turkish nationalism, it is rare to find a republican form of nationalism that divorces itself entirely from religious sources. This was all the more true of the Fatah movement. To begin with, Fatah's very name is religiously inspired. The original acrynom for the *Harakat al-Tahrir al-Watani al-Filastini*, HATF, means in Arabic "death," hardly an appropriate logo for a movement that aspired to lead Palestinians to victory over the state of Israel. It was altered to Fatah, an acronym which means "conquest," used almost always in the context of the early conquests of Islam. The word also evokes a well-known chapter in the Koran.

Terms such as jihad, mujahideen, and fedayeen appeared regularly in Fatah manifestos and announcements. Fatah's relationship to Islam, even to political Islam, also runs through its leadership. Ziyad Abu Amer, a former scholar from Birzeit University and presently a member of the Palestinian legislative council, provides one possible reason. In a book on the sources of Palestinian nationalism in Gaza, from which most Fatah founding members emanated, he writes: "There is no doubt whatsoever that the founding elements emerged from the womb of the Muslim Brotherhood."[21] Especially active in that organization were Khalil al-Wazir (Abu Wazir) and Salah Khalaf (Abu Iyad). Several prominent Fatah members of the next generation—such as Munir Shafiq, Hamdi Tamimi, and Mohammad Hassan Bhais—have become religious and preach a synthesis between Islam and Palestinian nationalism.[22] Others, such as Ghzai al-Husayni and Bassam Sultan, aided the formation of the Jihad al-Islami.[23]

Nor was this a phenomenon limited to the command's middle and lower ranks. Arafat's speeches, especially in the last decade, are replete with quotes from the Koran, religious terms and symbols, and occasionally oral teachings imputed to Muhammad (the hadith). In the course of ten speeches he gave on principal commemorative days—the founding of Fatah on January 1 of each year, on al-Nakba Day on May 14, and Declaration of Independence Day in November between 1994 and 2001—Arafat quoted nineteen different verses.[24] Seven of the nineteen verses he quoted more than one time for a total of forty-two times, an average of nearly four verses over the course of one speech. The speeches are very short—between eight hundred and one thousand words delivered in the course of fifteen to twenty minutes. The impression given is of speeches infused with religious content. In almost all the speeches he begins with at least one verse and ends with a verse. The verses are thus strategically placed to provide the overall framework for the internal contents of the speech, with the dominant theme being a downtrodden people triumphing by liberating Jerusalem and the Haram al-Sharif as illustrious Islamic forebears did before them. The following is one typical illustration:

> Until we meet in Palestine, until we meet in Palestine, in Holy Jerusalem in Holy Jerusalem, the first of the directions of prayer and the third of the holy places, the [sight of the] nocturnal ascent of Muhammad the Prophet, May God Grant him peace, the abode of our Master the Messiah Peace be Upon Him, to the meeting place there, there there, together and in unison, until victory, until victory, until victory.[25]

Perhaps awkward to read, the oral cadence of this uninterrupted flow is emotionally powerful. Arafat often repeated key phrases two or three times, a common oratorical device in many cultural contexts. In as much as one can separate religious from nationalist messages, in this particular example the nationalist chants are nevertheless more marked. The repetition of "until victory" that concludes the speech echoes an older PLO slogan "revolution until victory" (*al-thawra hata al-nasr*). Both the religiously embedded and nationalist slogans reflect movement toward Jerusalem, one can even say a religiously inspired crusade, and a clear emphasis on victory that echoes a slogan from more militant times in the history of the PLO and Fatah.

Equally prominent are his opening and closing salutations. In the written versions of all his speeches as they appeared in the newspapers, the opening verse from the Koran is preceded by the traditional salutation "In the name of Allah, the Merciful and Compassionate" (*bismi allah al-rahman al-rahim*). At the end of each speech, following the last verse, he almost always cited the salutation, "Verily the great God speaks the Truth, peace and Allah's compassion be upon you as well as his blessings" (*sadaqa alahu al-adhim wal-salam alaikum warahmat allah wabarakatuhu*). Frequently, the phrase "Verily the great God speaks the Truth, peace" appears in the middle of the speech after a quotation from a verse.[26] This addendum both to the salutations and in the middle of the text is obviously meant to enhance the credibility of the message and its aura as absolute truth.[27]

Sensitivity to religion was also reflected in the organizational dynamics of Fatah's affiliated institutions. Fatah's *shabiba* (youth) movement in the West Bank and in the late 1970s that consisted of Gaza shabiba Committees for Social Action (*Lijan al-Shabib lil-Amal al-Ijtima i*) organized separate structures for boys and girls—in contrast to the frameworks set up by the communists, the PLFP, and the Popular Front for the Liberation of Palestine (PFDP), which were mixed.[28] Fatah's student movement acknowledged the importance of religion by organizing events on important commemoration dates in the Islamic calendar with traditional Islamic content.[29] Again, the contrast with the smaller movements of the Left was striking. At the same time, the Shabiba Student Movement (*Harakat al-Shabiba al-Tullabiyya*) did not segregrate between the sexes and in fact opposed attempts by the Islamic movements to impose segregation in universities in the West Bank.

Finally in the mid-1980s, partially in an attempt to meet the growing challenge of the Islamic opposition movements, Fatah helped set up a "nationalist" Islamic jihad movement called the *Saraya al-Jihad al-Islami*,[30] supported Shaykh Asad Bayyud al-Tamimi's *Harakat al-Jihad–Bayt al-Maqdis*, and later sponsored yet another organization called the *al-Jihad al-Islami-Kata'ib al-Aqsa*.[31] Though all three organizations enjoyed close relations with Fatah, they regarded themselves as independent organizations.

Ideologically, neither Fatah (nor its leadership within the PLO) employed the term "secular" (*almani*) in public discourse. This was especially striking during the debates held in the late 1960s and early 1970s that characterized the nature of the future Palestinian entity. The Democratic Front for the Liberation of Palestine employed the term to describe the future Palestinian state. Fatah skirted the issue by sticking to its position that delving into the nature of the relationship between state and society along any dimension (class, religion, political nature of the future regime) diverted energies away from the primary task—defeating the Zionist enemy. Arafat, for example, was reported to have stated on the Democratic Front for the Liberation of Palestine's (DFLP) idea of a "secular democratic state in Palestine" that "I am certain that this is a distortion of the democracy we proclaim."[32] Though ideologically Fatah has always concentrated on the struggle against Israel—and argued in its early debates with the various fronts for the liberation of Palestine to delay discussion over the internal characteristics of Palestinian society and its institutions until liberation—the symbols the movement has used are infused with religion.[33] Whereas the factions on the Left used a terminology almost exclusively taken from the European revolutionary tradition, Fatah borrowed from Islamic culture as well.

Yet with all its acknowledgement of Islam's importance, Fatah's basic conception of Islam and things Islamic was nationalist. Islam was part of the nationalist heritage both of Palestinian nationalism (*wataniyya*) and the way that nationalism was linked to the larger Arab nation (*qaumiyya*). Never in Fatah ideology was Islam construed as the normative and legal basis for Palestinian society in the way that Islamic movements such as Hamas perceived it in, for example, the covenant Hamas disseminated in the territories in the summer of 1988. The true litmus test between the two organizations relates to means and ends. Whereas for Fatah, Islam is basically a means, for Hamas the Islamic normative order and collective boundary is an end they aspire to realize.[34] As many of the terms Fatah employed were cultural, they appeared within the context of a secular, though by no means antireligious, nationalism that focused on national liberation of a territory, political institutions, and a common national belonging between Palestinian Christians and Muslims.

A comparative reading between Fatah's founding document with Hamas's makes this altogether clear, at least conceptually and formally. In the Basic Order, modified in 1989 and mistakenly translated in Fatah's official Web site as a constitution, only two brief references to religion appear. In article 9, liberating Palestine is regarded as "an Arab, religious and human obligation." Article 13 guarantees "protecting the citizens' legal and equal [sic] rights without any racial or religious discrimination".[35] In neither case, does the word Islamic appear but rather the generic *dini* (religious). The latter is a universal referent, which in the context of Palestinian society refers to Christians as well. In the Hamas constitution, by contrast, Islamic *fiqh* and sharia are the constitutive basis of the polity.[36]

The dichotomy should not, however, be overstated when it comes to real-life political positions and behavior. A forty-two-page document entitled *Strategic Moves*, written in late 1992 and which still appears on the main Fatah Web site, ends with several sentences which, if left unidentified, could easily have been identified as bearing the imprint of Hamas, both regarding its religious tenor and the political objectives:

> It is the will of the Palestinian people, the will of a nation of giants which will decide the level of stability in the area of the Middle East. It is capable of complete escalation, employing all the means of confrontation and struggle, in a situation in which the fixed rights will be ignored to a degree unacceptable to the Palestinian people. And it is also able to interact in complete unison with the will of the peoples of the area, with the Arab nation, in dictating the state of the Palestinian peace and the Arab peace. The peace of al-Quds, the peace of the brave which they were able throughout history to fuse into the civilization of the Arab and Islamic nation all the transient attackers and to protect the ancient human legacy in this area, the area of the first direction of prayer and the third of the noble holy places (al-haramain al-sharifain), which Allah blessed around it. He blessed all of Palestine from the river to the sea, from the sea to victory.[37] (In Arabic the last clause rhymes—"*min al-nahr ila'l-bahr, min al-bahr ila'l-nasr*").

Not only did this document construe the liberation of all of Palestine as the most fundamental goal of the movement, it perceived the source of legitimacy for attaining this objective as being rooted in the Koran, Islam's sacred text. The "Palestine that God blessed" in the closing sentence of the document refers to a verse in the Koran located in what is sometimes called the Chapter of the Children of Israel or the Nocturnal Ascent. The verse reads as follows:

> Glory be to him, who carried His servant by night from the Holy Mosque to the Further Mosque the precincts of which We have blessed that We might show him some of Our signs.[38]

The mosque in both classical and popular exegesis is identified with the nocturnal ascent of Muhammad from the precincts of the Mecca "Holy Mosque" to the "further mosque" long identified with the Al-Aqsa Mosque on the Haram al-Sharif.[39] The night of the nocturnal ascent is an official holiday in the Islamic calendar. In the 1920s and 1930s, Hajj Amin al-Husayni, the Arab Palestinian leader, frequently quoted the opening of this verse and extended its meaning to include all of Palestine. He then claimed that all of Palestine was an Islamic endowment, inalienable and therefore unamenable to territorial compromise.[40] The Islamic Resistance Movement (Hamas) later picked up on the theme and formalized it in its constitution that it disseminated in the West Bank and Gaza in the summer of 1988 when the first intifada was at its height.[41] Arafat quoted this verse once in a speech he made in Ramallah on December 31, 1995, to commemorate the Fatah takeoff when he extolled the Palestinian people, especially those in Jerusalem, to participate in the coming elections for the Palestinian Legislative Council in order to defend the "holy land" (*al-ard al-muqaddasa*).[42] This document indicates that the idea that the holyness of Palestine made it inalienable had been accepted by Fatah as well.

Essentially, Fatah's attitudes and uses of religion place it at a midpoint on the spectrum between left-wing factions such as the DFLP (which seeks a secular Palestinian state based on the Turkish model) and Hamas, which is dedicated (albeit in low-key fashion) to establishing a theocracy. On the instrumental level, Fatah uses religious belief and emotion as a mobilizing tool on behalf of Palestinian nationalist goals. In the realm of ideas, Fatah recognizes the importance of Islam as an important component of the collective identity and culture of Palestinians, most of whom are either traditional or devout Muslims. Fatah's instrumental use of Islam was best reflected in the creation of two fighting arms during the latest round of conflict between Israel and the Palestinians. By far the more important organization to emerge was the Al-Aqsa Martyrs' Brigades. Yet there were also the Brigades of the Return (*Kata'ib al-Awda*), established under the leadership of Husayn al-Sheikh. The right of return refers to the insistence that Palestinian refugees living both in diaspora and in the territories be allowed to return to their original places of residence within the borders of mandatory Palestine. The basis for this claim is a clause in UN Resolution 194 from December 1948.[43]

## The Al-Aqsa Martyrs' Brigades—Islamic or Nationalist?

In March 2002, two reports on the Al-Aqsa Martyrs' Brigades appeared in the American media. In the first, reporter Matthew Kalman wrote that "unlike two other major Palestinian militant groups, the Islamic fundamentalist Hamas and Islamic Jihad, the brigade is secular."[44] In the second, Khaled Abu Toameh and Larry

Derfner described how 'in downtown Ramallah Manara Sqaure, dozens of al-Aqsa men shouted 'Allahu Akbar' ('God is Great') as they took turns firing AK-47 and M-16 rifles at Israeli tanks about 200 yards away."[45] In the organization's training camp in Gaza recruits told the reporters "we are all sacrificing our lives for al-Aqsa." The Al-Aqsa Brigades first became known to the public when their "anti-corruption" unit, they claimed, gunned down Hisham Miki, the head of the Palestinian Authority Television Authority in Gaza on January 18, 2001.[46] The organization differed from the Islamic Jihad formations Fatah supported in the past in that it is emerged within Fatah itself. Then which of the two reports is correct?

On the one hand, there can be little doubt that the name "Al-Aqsa Martyrs' Brigades" is infused with Islamic meaning. More Islamic still is its logo, a relief of the Temple Mount (in actual fact Umar's Mosque rather than the visually inferior Al-Aqsa) framed partially by two AK-47 rifles, above which appears a complete verse from the Koran. Below the relief is found the name of the organization. Nor can there be any doubt that Fatah was responding to widespread feelings that Palestinian political life should be more Islamic. A poll conducted in March 2000, six months before the outburst of violence surrounding the Al-Aqsa Mosque, showed that an overwhelming percentage of the respondents (85.8 percent) felt that the PA should be more religious than it was.[47]

Certainly, religious content is richer and more prominent in the preamble and announcements of the Al-Aqsa Brigades than in the commentaries and documents brought out by the various branches of the Fatah movement, just as the name is so strikingly different from previous Fatah armed groups. Stylistically, the preamble is embellished with religious trappings similar to material produced by Hamas. For example, below the title appears the prelude *Bismi Allah al-Rahman al-Rahim*, followed by a verse from the Koran. Three more verses appear in the subsequent 3,000-word essay, each at the end of a subchapter. During the first intifada, the names of the various fighting arms that operated under the Fatah umbrella reflected a borrowing from Western and third world revolutionary and nationalist legacies. The inspiration for the name "Black Panther" might conceivably be linked to the Black Panthers of the United States, though it also might (as with the Hawks) be due simply to figures that denote power and ferociousness. Similarly, "Red Eagle" might have been borrowed from the Marxist revolutionary tradition. Regarding the term "Popular Army," which incidentally continued to appear in the sign-off of Al-Aqsa announcements, there can be little doubt where its origins lie.

On the other hand, the instrumental nature of the use of religion is no less pronounced, as the preamble that appears on the organization's Web site makes clear:

> It is altogether natural that the (Fatah) movement should reproduce itself in a new cloth and in a new framework that interacts with the changes that have occurred... as an organization that has always interacted pragmatically under changing circumstances yet at the same time remaining loyal to the Palestinian problem, national liberation and "long-term popular war."[48]

Under the heading entitled "from al-Asifa to the al-Aqsa Martyrs' Brigades" (*Min al-Asifa ila Kata'ib Shuhada al-Aqsa*), it then goes on to claim that this reproduction under new names dates back to the beginning of Fatah. The *Al-Asifa* (Storm) forces were Fatah's first fighting organization, which initiated Palestinian guerrilla action against Israel in January 1965:

The Fatah movement took off and renewed itself continuously. First it was the al-Asifa Movement under the leadership of Yasir Arafat. Abu Yusuf al-Najjar... and their colleagues.... In the first intifada, the Shabiba Committees for Social Action, were a Fatah creation. Groups [committed to] local military resistance action appeared like the Black Panther, the Hawks, the Red Eagle and the Popular Army. A large segment of the leaders and heroes... met martyrdom. These and the likes of them represent the legions that imbibed and partook from the water of the holy revolution and the fragrance of heaven until the creative horizon burst forth to produce the al-Aqsa Martyrs' Brigade, to announce, renew and continue the procession.[49]

According to the preamble, Fatah constantly reproduces itself to go along with the changing times, but its essence remains unchanged.

## Analyzing the Obituary Notices of the Martyrs

The element of mobilizing the masses is not only reflected in the specific Islamization of the fighting arm rather than the parent organization, but also in the material disseminated to mobilize men and women to resist the Israelis. Not all the military announcements expressed the same amount of religious conviction or prejudice. Thus, for example, apart from a secondary heading with the phrase "Allah is Great" repeated three times, the press release invoking the martyrdom of Abd al-Salam Sadiq Mari Hasuna from Bayt Amrin near Nablus on November 17, 2002, is almost bereft of anything specifically Islamic.[50] The enemy is referred to as "the Zionist entity."

Only slightly more Islamic in tone is the announcement commemorating the martyrdom of Wafa Ali Idris from al-Amari refugee camp, the first successful female suicide bomber.[51] It begins with the prelude "In the name of God the Compassionate and Merciful," followed by the first part of the verse "Say: Work; and God will surely see your work and His Messenger, and the believers..."(9:106). Otherwise, the body of the text is free of Islamic allusions. Instead, the Al-Aqsa Brigades introduced for the first time the motto that subsequently appeared at the end of most of the announcements: "The Martyrs of al-Aqsa Brigades, who do what they say and fulfill what they promised." (In Arabic it rhymes—*ithan qalat, faalat, waithan wa adat, awfat*). This is certainly a modern secular slogan.

Both contrast sharply with the Al-Aqsa Brigades subsequent legacy (*wasiya*) left by Said Ibrahim Said Ramadan, the son of "steadfast al-Tell," a village near Nablus, who was killed in a shooting attack in Jerusalem after killing two and wounding thirty. Written in the first person, possibly by the assailant himself, the statement condemned "the enemies of God, the Jews, the pigs Sharon and his government and gang of murderous gangsters—who with the support of the apex of apostasy, America, carry out the most heinous of crimes." Its author was also obviously motivated by deep religious conviction: "I have donated my spirit to God Almighty to fight the enemies of God, beseeching God to accept me and to merit me a martyr in Heaven, God willing." He signed off "the living martyr (Said Ramadan), the son of the al-Aqsa Martyrs Brigades."[52] Barring one mention of the Palestinian people (and even that reference is qualified by the distinctively Islamic adjective *al-murabit*— tied to God), there is nothing particularly nationalist about the departing message.

The statement could have easily been made by a suicide bomber belonging to Hamas's Izz al-Din Brigades that are in *Filastin al-Muslima*, the Hamas monthly published in London and disseminated in the territories. The Al-Aqsa Brigades' "military announcement" the following day announcing Ramadan's death played down the religious elements considerably. There were no verses from the Koran and the enemies of Allah were no longer the Jews writ large but "pigs Sharon, Mofaz [the Israeli Army's chief of staff] and his government."[53] The very fact that the Islamic content of the announcements changes from incident to incident, from one suicide bomber to the other, reflects a pragmatic rather than substantive use of Islam. Where the suicide bomber (and most probably his immediate environment) is motivated by Islamic conviction, the Al-Aqsa Brigades reciprocate accordingly. Where the family in question is less devout, the emphasis (in as much one can divorce the two) is more nationalist.

Variation between the announcements could also be found regarding the final political objectives of the violence. The military announcement from the end of May 2002 began with a statement "Oh Zionists depart from our land because we will not stop as long as there is a rapacious Occupier on our land," leaving the possibility that it might be referring exclusively to the West Bank and Gaza.[54] The announcement a week later (June 6) announcing the attack on an Israeli bus killing nine justified it on the grounds of the "aggression reflected by the occupation of Palestine."[55] A month later, a similar military announcement was even more explicit stating that the attack "emphasizes how impossible it was to smother the intifada until the decimation of the occupation and the elimination of this entity from the land of Palestine."[56]

## Between the Islamization of the Brigades and Secular Fatah

There can be little doubt that the emergence of the Al-Aqsa Brigades is part of a deliberate attempt to respond to the religious convictions so prevalent in Palestinian society and the growing yet limited popularity of the Islamic movements. I stress limited because as much as polls show a more balanced support between Fatah and the Islamic movements, the largest single group polled still favor "independents"— politicians that are not affiliated with Fatah, other PLO factions, or the Islamic movements. In other words, these polls demonstrate growing disillusionment with all institutionalized Palestinian political organizations.

Perhaps partially for this reason, the "parent" organization Fatah—represented by a variety of institutions such as the Central Committee, the Central Council, and the Higher Committees of the West Bank and Gaza—continues through formal announcements from these institutions or through member interviews to represent a broader, if not more secular and nationalist, narrative.

A summary of an interview with Hani al-Hasan, a member of Fatah's Central Committee, in *Al-Quds* is typical of many interviews with Fatah personalities such Marwan Barghuthi, Amin Maqbul, and others. The interview with Hasan, like interviews with the others, is notable for its omission of anything specifically Islamic:

> Hani al-Hasan was addressing a meeting of members of the Palestine National Council [PNC] in Amman yesterday. He said that the Palestinian leadership is very proud of the intifadah and that it will reap the fruits of the intifadah. He added that the Palestinian leadership has been aware of

the fact that the intifadah will produce fruits. Therefore, the Palestinian leadership enhanced its political demands.

Al-Hasan asserted that the intifadah will not stop unless real gains are achieved, such as the Israeli withdrawal from all the territories Israel occupied in 1967, fixing a date for the declaration of the Palestinian state with Jerusalem as its capital, removal of the Israeli settlements and fulfilling other demands.[57]

This omission of anything specifically Islamic is equally true of the copious material presented on the general Fatah Web site and that produced by the Higher Movement Committee for Gaza. The contrast with the announcements of the Al-Aqsa Brigades is all the more glaring if one takes into account these organizations' serial publications as well, such as *Al-Nashra al-Markaziyya*, Fatah's newsletter or Fatah announcements that often correspond to events that form the basis for the Al-Aqsa Brigades announcements.[58] Just as the latter are infused with Islamic content, the Fatah general announcements are bereft of them.[59]

## Explaining the Paradox

There are two main reasons accounting for the gap between infusion of Islamic symbols on the operative and tactical level and their conspicuous absence in either internal policy forums or pronouncements of Fatah personalities relating to Palestinian foreign relations, the peace process, demands on the Europeans, and the relationship to the United States.

Islamic symbols and references are important as tools of mobilization. At the same time, Fatah wants to clearly demonstrate that its basic message and vision of the state is nationalist rather than religious and as such clearly distinguishable from Hamas and Islamic Jihad not only in terms of political objectives on matters relating to Israel and statehood, but also in characterizing the nature of the future Palestinian state.

Its recourse to nationalist secular discourse is even more striking in foreign and international affairs—for good reason. Since the nineteenth century, if not since Westphalia, the international system has been dominated by states which, for all the variation they have shown in the relationship between religion and the public weal within their domestic structures, are adamantly opposed to the creation of theocratic states.[60] By theocratic states, one means those in which religious law is constitutionally supreme. Such states propagate the faith in a way that might potentially undermine existing nation-states. If some tolerance toward theocracy and fundamentalism was countenanced in the early part of the twentieth century (in the creation of Saudi Arabia, for example) it has attenuated considerably since then.

The norms these core states have created and propagated are not only territorially centered, but man-made and secular. From Wilson's fourteen principles to the United Nations (UN) Charter, the ideas and values expressed in these documents relate to republican and liberal ideas, which for the most part clash with the basic propositions articulated by Islamic, Jewish, and perhaps Christian political fundamentalists. Consider the following: whereas in the international system, territorial sovereignty of the state was considered (until recently at least) exclusive and all religions equal and to be tolerated, in theocratic thought the religious identity of the state is seen as exclusive and dominant. Other religions must, by definition, be discriminated against. A people living on a certain piece of land may make a claim to self-determination on the basis of being ethnically or nationally different, but not on the basis of religious differences. Religious sects can demand tolerance, but not political satisfaction.

Nor is the issue only a matter of who wields power in the system and structures its norms. The secular nature of the international system is also reflected in the values propagated by the international organizations and the types of projects and institutions they foster. Even in a day and age when the diaspora of vast numbers of Muslims and other members of non-European-centered religions foster the growth of international religious nongovernmental organizations (NGOs), the overwhelming bulk of financial resources are still in the hands of liberally minded organizations. Because these core states and NGOs, motivated by liberal or republican values, are ultimately responsible in most instances for bequeathing the territorial state, movements aspiring to create states must play according to *their* rules. This is also true for most states in the system. Even an oil-rich state such as Iran bears the brunt of its theocratic claims and constitution.

This is all the more true for the Palestinians, who were in any case latecomers to state building and must play by the secular norms international actors impose upon them. No state actor, with the possible exception of Iran, will support the Palestinian cause in the international arena based on the claim that Palestine was ruled by Muslim rulers in the past, and has therefore become an Islamic endowment that is inalienable and not negotiable. By contrast, a Palestinian claim to self-determination on the basis that Palestinians form the majority of the inhabitants of the West Bank and Gaza, and that their claim from this perspective had been recognized by the UN in the past, does carry political weight. This is especially true when the normative territorial claim is backed by a certain degree of political power. The Palestinians argue, with some degree of credibility, that even if they cannot force Israel to withdraw, they can continue to punish it and place the larger region in a state of tension that makes it worthwhile for the international community to explore ways to meet their national aspirations. And if this were true before the Al Qaeda attacks on September 11, it is more the case now that the international system will respond more affirmatively to nationalist rather than to religious movements. In other words, Fatah realizes that it has a considerable advantage over its rivals in Hamas and al-Jihad al-Islami by remaining secular.

## Conclusion

Circumscribing Islamic symbols and Koranic verses to its fighting arm, the Al-Aqsa Brigades demonstrate that Fatah, particularly its policy-making structures such as the Central Committee, perceives the change as a means of mobilization and recruitment rather than a reflection of an essential change in the character of the movement. In any event, none of the Islamic quotes from verses in the Koran and the hadith that appear in the logo, posters, and announcements of the Al-Aqsa Brigades have much bearing on the legal norms and institutions of the actual Palestinian political system. The Islamic symbols and allusions are affective rather than programmatic, designed to mobilize the public against Israel and thwart the expansion of the Islamic movements internally rather than to impact on the character of the larger Palestinian political entity. The creation of the Al-Aqsa Brigades, then, reflects on the growing societal salience of political Islam but it hardly softens the great divide between the two competing movements, the nationalist and the Islamic, over the character of the future entity. Fatah continues to leave open the question whether that entity will be a sharia state or a nation-state that combines the universal with the particularistic. Its continued silence on the matter indicates that it remains loyal to the nationalist rather than sharia-theocratic model.

Fatah's relationship to religion in many ways conforms to the experiences of many Arab states such as Syria, Egypt, and Jordan. In the face of growing salience of Islam, General Hafiz al-Asad was portrayed in the official Syrian armed forces journal as a devout Muslim; in Egypt, it led to a revision in 1980 in the constitution that proclaimed Islamic jurisprudential principles no longer merely *a* source of legislation but *the major* source. Meanwhile the Hashemite rulers of Jordan proclaim prominently their descent to the Prophet but keep their distance from making sharia state law. As in the case of Fatah, Islamization should be perceived more as a means of cushioning fundamentalist blows rather than a true change of heart.

Avoiding linking theocratic content to overarching goals or making it the basis of legitimacy for governmental institutions makes even more sense regarding a nationalist movement that has yet to achieve statehood. Wedding theocracy with nationalism in international forums hardly makes sense in a unipolar world dominated by a state that is waging a war mainly on Islamic terrorism. To the contrary, maintaining a secular discourse in regional and international forums serves as an asset in the arsenal of Fatah and the PLO in its internal struggle with Hamas and al-Jihad al-Islami.

## Notes

1. Ghassan Khatib, "One Way to Make Things Worse," http://www.bitterlemons.org (2002). Khatib is presently the minister of labor in the Palestinian Authority.

2. Mamduh Nufal, a prominent Palestinian commentator and advisor, emphasized the Palestinian Authority's role in the outbreak of the intifada in a roundtable on the subject: "This current movement is distinguishable from the first intifada and is perhaps unique altogether. From the beginning, this movement was led and accompanied by the forces of the PA. It is not a mass movement divorced from the Authority nor did it burst in isolation from it, but to the contrary, took off as a result of a central decision taken by the authority before it became a popular movement. It occurred directly during Sharon's visit to al-Aqsa, when the organs of the political and security organs of the PA decided to defend al-Aqsa. Yasser Arafat regarded the visit to al-Aqsa a volatile point sufficient not only to ignite the fire on Palestinian soil but to inflame the situation outside the borders of Palestine. Decisions were taken regarding operational preparations, meetings were held for the participating forces of the Authority and it was decided to mobilize them towards al-Aqsa on Friday.... Directives were made to the security organs to enter it and defend it." "Nadwa: Wujhat Nazar fi Tatawwurat al-Intifada wa-Ahdafiha," *Majallat al-Dirasat al-Filastiniyya*, no. 47 (2001): 44. Nabil Amru (Amer), the former minister of parliamentary affairs in the Palestinian Authority and a close confidant of Arafat, was even blunter: "The intifada, all of it, is the making of the Authority, even if one ought not, out of sheer political wisdom, to adopt or say it.... but it is known, and those that know it thoroughly are the Israelis. This is why they know where to strike. The essential foe for them is the Authority.... The question is can we as the Authority adopt this within the political margin of maneuver offered. I think the answer is no." "Hawar Sakhin Bayna Nabil Amru wa Islah Jad," *Majallat al-Dirasat al-Filastiniyya*, no. 50 (2002): 13.

3. Robert Mali and Hussein Agha, "Camp David: The Tragedy of Errors," *Journal of Palestine Studies* 33 (2001): 163–75.

4. This series of events eclipsed by far the violent events of Land Day on March 30, 1976, in which six of Israel's Arab citizens were killed in demonstrations that lasted a single day.

5. *Kull al-Arab* (October 3, 2000).

6. Gal Luft, "The Palestinian H-Bomb," *Foreign Affairs* 81, no. 4 (2002): 2.

7. Khalil Shikaki, "Palestine Divided," *Foreign Affairs* 81, no. 1 (2002): 91.

8. JMCC Poll, *Jerusalem: Jerusalem Media and Communications Center*, no. 45 (May 29–31, June 1–3, 2002).

9. Yehoshua Porath, *The Emergence of the Palestinian Arab National Movement 1918–1929* (London: Frank Cass, 1974), 41.

10. Ibid., 269.

11. Christopher Sykes, *Cross Roads to Israel* (London: New English Library, 1967), 116.

12. Hillel Frisch, "The Evaluation of Palestinian Nationalist Islamic Doctrine: Territorializing a Universal Religion," *Canadian Review in Nationalism* 21 (1994): 57.

13. Nissim Mishal, *Those Were the Years* (Tel Aviv: Yedihot Ahronot Press, 1998), 155. On this incident's continuing impact, see the report on a recent rally in Gaza sponsored by the PA's ministry of endowments and religious affairs that commemorated thirty-three years since the burning in *Al-Hayat al-Jadida* (July 22, 2002).

14. Rima Hammami and Salim Tamari, "The Second Uprising or New Beginning," *Journal of Palestine Studies* 30, no. 2 (2001): 13.

15. Eli Rekhess, "The West Bank and Gaza Strip," *Middle East Contemporary Survey* 5 (1981): 324–48.

16. Wendy Kristianasen, "Challenge and Counterchallenge: Hamas's Response to Oslo," *Journal of Palestine Studies* 28, no. 3 (1999): 34.

17. Ibid.

18. Hammami and Tamari, "The Second Uprising," 8–9.

19. *Haaretz*, July 11, 2002.

20. Israel Radio, July 13, 2002.

21. Ziad Abu Amer, *Usul al-Harakat al-Siyasiya al-Filastiniyya fi Quta Ghazza* (Accre: Dar al-Aswar, 1989), 83.

22. Khaled Khroub, review of *Islam and Salvation in Palestine: The Islamic Jihad Movement*, by Meir Hatina, *Journal of Palestine Studies* 31 (2001): 109.

23. Hatina, *Islam and Salvation in Palestine: The Islamic Jihad Movement*, 33.

24. The following table lists the speeches by day of commemoration and the date the speeches were published in *al-Ayyam*, a Palestinian newspaper published in Ramallah near Jerusalem.

| Fatah commemoration day | Nakba (Disaster) day | Declaration of Independence |
|---|---|---|
| 12/31/1995 (Ramallah) | 5/15/1998 | 11/16/1996 |
| 1/1/1996 (Tulqarem) | 5/16/2001 | 11/15/1998 |
| 1/1/1996 (Qalquilya) |  | 11/15/1999 |
| 1/1/1999 |  | 11/16/2001 |
| 1/1/2002 |  |  |

25. *Al-Ayyam*, May 16, 2001.

26. *Al-Ayyam*, May 15, 1998; November 11, 1998.

27. A textual analysis of speeches given by other Arab leaders demonstrates to what extent religious sentiment pervades their speeches. President Mubarak cited three verses nine times in eleven public speeches he gave between 1999–2001. His speeches are also substantially longer; 3,000 words on average compared to 750 to 1,000 words. In none of Mubarak's speeches, moreover, did the verses appear at the beginning or the end, nor were they necessarily followed by religious salutations.

28. On the nonsegregated nature of the (Communist) Committees of Voluntary Action, see *Al-Talia*, July 17, 1982.

29. On the religious activities of the Shabiba, see for example a write-up on the Shabiba Committee for Social Action in the old city in *Al-Bayadir al-Siyasi*, no. 110 (July 14, 1984): 37. The report recounts how after cleaning the Temple Mount they attended as a group the al-Fajr prayers in the Al-Aqsa Mosque.

30. Hatina, *Islam and Salvation in Palestine*, 33–34.

31. Interview with Dr. Fa'iz al-Aswar (Abu Abdallah) from Jihad al-Islami-Kata'ib al-Aqsa. *Al-Hayat al-Jadida*, January 23, 1996.

32. Alain Gresh, *The Struggle Within* (London: Zed, 1985), 34.

33. Nels Johnston, *Islam and the Politics of Meaning in Palestinian Nationalism* (London: Kegan and Paul, 1982), 71–72.

34. Muhammd Zahhar, one of the leaders of the Hamas movement in Gaza, spoke in an interview of waiting for the PLO and nationalism to self-destruct, of establishing the universal Islamic state, and of fighting the West. Muhammd Zahhar, "Hamas: Waiting for Secular Nationalism to Self-Destruct," *Journal of Palestine Studies* 24, no. 1 (1995): 83.

35. Fatah, "The Constitution," http://www.fateh.net/e public/constitution.htm (accessed 5 March 2004). In the text in Arabic it is called "al-Nizam al-Asasi," that should be more accurately translated as the Basic Order.

36. *Covenant of the Islamic Resistance Movement—18 August, 1988*. (n.p.: n.d.).

37. Fatah, "Al-Intilaqa-Istratijiyyat al-Thawra Hata al-Nasr," http://www.fateh.net/public/alintilaka/index.htm (accessed 5 March 2004).

38. Arthur J. Arberry, *The Koran Interpreted* (Oxford: Oxford University Press, 1991).

39. *Encyclopedia of Islam* (Leiden: Brill, 1993), S. V. "Al-Miradj."

40. *Kitab al-Sayyid Muhammad Amin al-Husayni fi'l-Ijtimaal-Islamial-Kabir li-Wufud al-Qura* (Jerusalem, 1935), 1–2.

41. *The Covenant of the Islamic Resistance Movement*, Article 11.

42. *Al-Ayyam*, December 31, 1995.

43. John Moore, *The Arab-Israel Conflict*, vol. 3 (Princeton: Princeton University Press, 1974), 37.

44. Matthew Kalman, "Terrorist Says Orders Come from Arafat, Al-Aqsa Martyrs Brigade Leader," *USA Today*, March 14, 2002.

45. Khaled Abu Toameh and Larry Derfner, "Yasser Arafat's 'Martyrs'" *U.S. News and World Report* 132, no. 9 (2002): 16.

46. Lamia Lahoud, "Palestinian Group Claims Killing of TV Chief in Gaza," *Jerusalem Post*, January 19, 2001.

47. JMCC Poll, *Jerusalem Media and Communications Center*, no. 36 (2000).

48. Fatah, "Katai'ib Shuhada al-Aqsa," http://www.fateh.tv/aboutus.htm

49. Ibid.

50. http://www.fateh.tv/17-01-2002.htm

51. http://www.fateh.tv/19-01-2002.htm

52. http://www.fateh.tv/21-01-2002.htm

53. http://www.fateh.tv/22-01-2002.htm

54. http://www.fateh.tv/27-05-01-2002.htm

55. http://www.fateh.tv/03-06-2002.htm

56. http://www.fateh.tv/06-07-2002.htm

57. "Report on Statements by Fatah's Hani Al-Hasan: Intifadah Is Reply to Israeli Aggression," *Al-Quds*, November 28, 2000.

58. A textual analysis of the third issue of *Al-Nashra al-Markaziyya* (February 15, 2002), the official bulletin of Fatah, which covers approximately fifty pages of text revealed no specific reference to a verse, hadith, or to a specifically Islamic theme. The issues can be found in at http://www.fateh.net/public/newsletter/index.htm.

59. All of the sample of thirty-three announcements issued by the Al-Aqsa Brigades contained at least the Islamic salutation "in the name of Allah the Merciful and the Compassionate" or "Allah is Great" and twenty-two verses from the Koran appeared in them. The eighty-nine Fatah announcements analyzed included no such prelude or salutation and quoted only two verses from the Koran.

60. For a more extended discussion on why the international system favors national movements over religious, see Hillel Frisch and Shmuel Sandler, "Religion, State, and the International System in the Israeli–Palestinian Conflict," *International Political Science Review* 25, no. 1 (2004): 77–96.

# Conflict over Israel: The Role of Religion, Race, Party and Ideology in the U.S. House of Representatives, 1997–2002

ELIZABETH A. OLDMIXON, BETH ROSENSON, AND
KENNETH D. WALD

**Introduction**

In April 2003, George W. Bush traveled to Dearborn, Michigan, to address the community's large Arab American population. The president hoped the trip would mollify Arab American voters, part of his electoral coalition in 2000 and a voting bloc that was now wavering in response to the harsh words uttered against Islam by neoconservatives and evangelical Christian leaders close to the president.[1] Bush reassured the Dearborn audience that he did not share the hard-line views toward Islam expressed by his close allies, ministers such as the Reverends Franklin Graham, Pat Robertson, and Jerry Falwell, and by Daniel Pipes, the president's appointee to the board of the U.S. Institute of Peace. Nonetheless, the backlash against the president led to the emergence of a new organization, "Arab American Republicans against Bush," with the goal of diverting votes and money away from the incumbent.[2]

A month later, hundreds gathered in Washington's Omni Shoreham Hotel for "The Interfaith Zionist Leadership Summit." Sponsored by, among others, the Christian Broadcasting Network, Christian Friends of Israel, and the International Christian Embassy, the summit featured speeches by such prominent Protestant evangelicals as Gary Bauer (former director of the Family Research Council), Roberta Combs of the Christian Coalition, and Ed McAteer of the Religious Roundtable.[3] These organizations were instrumental in turning out conservative voters for George W. Bush in 2000. The program also included some of the neoconservative critics of Islam whose influence on the White House worried many of the Arab Americans in Dearborn. Scheduled to close after the singing of "America the Beautiful" and "Hatikvah," which is Israel's national anthem, the task of the assembly was "to solidify and chart future strategy for the emerging alliance of Jewish and Christian Zionists."[4]

The conjunction of these two events suggests that Henry Kissinger's famous complaint about the lack of a "real" foreign policy in Israel may also apply to the United States. That is, the making of American foreign policy, which is often portrayed by scholars as an elite-driven search for the national interest, is heavily marked by domestic political considerations in general and the agendas of ethno-religious groups in particular.[5] Do these forces register in the more cloistered environment of the U.S. Congress? Is this a case of what the volume editors describe as "crossing borders," the application to global politics of what are essentially domestic religious forces? Those are the underlying questions of this study.

The extent to which Congress influences U.S. foreign policy is a matter of debate among scholars. While some argue that presidential powers eclipse Congress in this area, others suggest that the legislative branch has reasserted itself in the post-Vietnam era.[6] Both the interest and activism of Congress are apparent with regard to U.S.–Israeli relations, and have been for many years.[7] Since the establishment of the state of Israel in 1948, both chambers of Congress have generally expressed solid support for Israel. While certainly not unequivocal, backing for Israel from both the executive and legislative branch today is still strong, mirroring a broader American commitment that exists at the mass level.[8]

The basis of that support, diverse and varied, includes a sense of religious duty that resonates strongly with much of the American public. The cause of the Jewish people has drawn on a durable tradition of Christian Zionism that predates the birth of political Zionism as a mass movement among Jews.[9] Rooted in apocalyptic visions that became central to evangelical Protestantism in the nineteenth century, this movement perceives Jewish control of the Holy Land as a prerequisite to the dawning of the messianic era. Hardly a marginal phenomenon, this perspective animated many American presidents throughout the twentieth century. It has also animated many legislators in Congress. Not simply passive observers of presidential action on Israel, during certain periods legislators have played a key role in initiating, increasing, and encouraging financial aid to Israel, and in issuing statements of support designed to influence presidential action.[10] Congress's proactivity or independence on Israel should not be overdrawn, however. Members have been responsive to heavy lobbying by pro-Israel groups such as the American Israel Public Affairs Committee.[11] The efforts of such groups to press their cause on Capitol Hill have only increased over the years.[12]

The last decade has seen a great deal of both violence and negotiation between Israelis and Palestinians, with the United States often acting as facilitator of the negotiations in this ongoing conflict. Against this backdrop, congressional sympathy toward Israel appears to have increased among Republican conservatives, particularly among powerful legislators such as House Majority Leader Tom DeLay. At the same time, anecdotal evidence suggests that support among Democrats, while still strong, is perhaps slightly more muted. The reasons behind the varying intensity of members' commitment to Israel have not been clearly identified, although recently both journalistic accounts and the occasional scholarly study point to a potential role of religion, specifically evangelical Protestantism, in influencing members' attitudes toward the Jewish state.[13] This factor was not considered to be important in earlier accounts of congressional attitudes toward Israel. For example, Feuerweger places the religious beliefs of members last in his account of member beliefs that influence voting on Israel, after beliefs about the importance of democracy, support for the country's proven friends and allies, and ideology.[14]

This paper explores the contours of support for Israel in the U.S. House of Representatives from 1997 to 2002, with the goal of documenting and explaining the changing dynamics of support. In an analysis of votes and cosponsorship decisions, we tap the intensity of legislators' support for the state of Israel. Ultimately, the analysis suggests that in a very short period of time, congressional support for Israel became more conflictual, more partisan, more ideological, and more religiously driven.[15] Moreover, we find that there is an element of racial tension inherent in this issue. In the arena of domestic politics the consequences of this are striking, since African Americans and Jews have provided the Democrats with such loyal support at the mass level. Indeed, this issue may potentially divide Democrats, while unifying Republicans. In the arena of foreign policy, the consequences of this are striking because they demonstrate the influence of domestic ethno-religious forces on policy making. Rather than simply an assessment of national interests in the Middle East—though we do not reject the importance of that—legislator decision making on Israel seems heavily influenced by group-based loyalties that become salient in response to exogenous events.

## Explaining Congressional Support for Israel

Congressional support for Israel takes several forms: military, economic, and symbolic. Symbolic support is manifested in the numerous resolutions that Congress passes periodically, generally by large margins. Over the past decade, for example, such resolutions have condemned terrorist acts by Palestinians; urged the Arab League to end its boycott of Israel; and expressed the "sense of Congress" that the United States should promote an end to Israel's exclusion from any United Nations (UN) blocs. Other resolutions have called upon the president and the secretary of state to affirm that Jerusalem must remain the undivided capital of Israel and have congratulated Israelis on the thirtieth anniversary of the reunification of Jerusalem.

Even though such resolutions are widely supported by both houses of Congress, legislators nevertheless vary in the levels of support they exhibit. Roll call votes, sponsorship of bills and resolutions, and speechmaking on the floor show that some members are clearly more committed to Israel than others. In today's Congress, for example, House Majority Leader Tom DeLay (R-TX), and Rep. Tom Lantos (D-CA) are two of Israel's most vocal advocates. These two legislators joined across party lines to cosponsor a pro-Israeli resolution in May 2002 right before President Bush met with Israeli prime minister Ariel Sharon. On the other hand, Rep. Bob Ney (R-OH) and Rep. John Dingell (D-MI), among others, have been outspoken critics of Israel and defenders of the Palestinian cause.

A substantial and well-developed literature exists which explores congressional behavior as it relates to both domestic and foreign policy issues. However, the work on foreign policy tends to focus on interbranch conflict rather than support for internationalism more generally. The existing research on congressional attitudes toward Israel is sparse, with less than a handful of empirical studies.[16] The limited scholarly literature and also the popular media have focused on several factors that may influence attitudes toward Israel: Jewish population in legislator districts, partisanship, liberal-conservative ideology, and more recently (as mentioned above) the religious affiliations of legislators themselves.

The electoral connection makes it likely that constituency preferences will play an important role in explaining legislative behavior.[17] Citizens tend to have less-developed preferences on foreign policy issues compared to domestic policy issues, and therefore elected representatives may be less constrained in how they vote on foreign affairs issues.[18] But with regard to Israel, at least one sub-constituency has strong preferences and is relatively attentive. These are American Jews, who not surprisingly tend to hold a pro-Israel position. Trice[19] found that the size of the Jewish population in a senator's state was the most important factor in determining how U.S. senators voted on Israel issues in the early 1970s. Garnham also found a moderately strong positive relationship between the size of a member's Jewish constituency and House members' support for Israel in the Ninety-third Congress.[20]

Conversely, we might expect members from districts with a relatively large Arab American population to be less supportive of Israel; John Dingell of Michigan, whose district includes Dearborn and has more Arabs and Muslims than any other in the country, fits this profile.[21]

Past work suggests a less consistent role for partisanship and ideology than for constituent religious affiliation. During the limited time frame he examined, Trice found that partisan differences explained little variation in members' support for Israel, with some evidence that Democrats were marginally more supportive.[22] Feuerweger points out that both party platforms since 1944 had included pro-Zionist statements and that both parties' leaders were supportive of Israel, suggesting that there were no real party differences in support through the mid-1970s.[23] Some recent journalistic accounts, however, suggest that Republicans have become more supportive than Democrats.[24] With regard to ideology, Trice also found that liberal senators were more likely to support Israel than conservatives, and Garnham similarly argues that liberalism was correlated with greater support in the House during the Ninety-third Congress.[25]

However, their data are three decades old, and patterns of ideological support may have changed since the 1970s. It has been argued that liberals are more likely to support Israel than conservatives because liberals tend to identify with vulnerable groups and perceive Israel as the "underdog" in the Israeli–Palestinian conflict.[26] Even if this were once true, it may no longer be the case. Some of today's prominent leftists, of whom Noam Chomsky is one of the most outspoken, argue that the Palestinians are the true underdog in the conflict. As the conflict between Israelis and the Palestinians has heated up in recent years and Israel has engaged in a perceived repression of the Palestinians in various ways, some liberal members may have switched sides.

Indeed, we might instead expect conservatives, not liberals, to be more pro-Israel to the extent that conservatism is associated with greater support for democracies abroad and Israel is considered the "outpost" of democracy in the Middle East.[27] Although the Middle East is no longer viewed primarily through a cold war lens, and thus Israel no longer merits special status there for its role in the battle against communism, conservatives may still be strongly supportive of Israel because they see it as representing pro-democratic, pro-Western values. Rhetorically at least, this makes it valuable in the war on terrorism. Even without the Soviet threat, the United States still has clear national interests at stake in the Middle East such as protecting oil exports from the Persian Gulf and reducing nuclear proliferation.[28] Conservatives may be more likely to support Israel as part of a broader effort to protect such national interests.

While it has not been explored in the literature, race might also influence legislator support for Israel. African Americans and American Jews were political allies during the civil rights movement, but the relationship between these two groups has been strained in recent years. Freedman notes that the "black-Jewish era, in many ways, is over.... For reasons of demography and politics and the mere passage of time, it should be retired to the realm of history or mythology."[29] Among Whites, American Jews had been the strongest supporters of the civil rights movement, but this was at a time when the movement focused on removing institutionalized barriers to political equality in the South. When the movement "moved to Northern cities and came to focus on de facto expressions of racism" Jews and African Americans came into direct competition over employment, business ownership, school board positions, and more generally, control of community life. With that, the special kinship between these two groups deteriorated.[30] Of course, to the extent that the special kinship was instrumental, we might have expected this kind of deterioration. Ginsburg suggests that Jews supported the civil rights movement because it benefited them, not because they were particularly altruistic. Forty years after the freedom rides, Jewish social acceptance and mobility are not clearly tied to African American empowerment. At the same time, anti-Semitism has become a useful tool among a new generation of African American elites, who are trying to delegitimize the old leadership and establish themselves as leaders in the community.[31]

It is possible that some African Americans came to see Jews as an enemy, not an ally. Prominent African American leaders such as Al Sharpton, Jesse Jackson, and Louis Farrakhan have all been accused of using anti-Semitic rhetoric. In the 2002 congressional elections, incumbent Democrat Cynthia McKinney, an African American, and her father both made not-so-veiled anti-Semitic remarks suggesting that New York Jews were actively engaged in efforts to unseat her (McKinney lost in the Democratic primary). Although African American legislators, like Caucasian legislators, generally show strong support for Israel, to the extent that relations between African Americans and Jews are strained, African American citizens and members of Congress might identify with and be more sympathetic to the Palestinians. The Israeli–Palestinian conflict itself may also be a factor driving apart American Jews and African Americans. Some African Americans have begun to identify with groups that they regard as victimized by American power abroad, including the Palestinians. In two incidents from the pre-Oslo era, Andrew Young lost his position as U.S. ambassador to the UN for unauthorized talks with the Palestinian Liberation Organization (PLO) in 1979 and Jesse Jackson's campaign for the Democratic presidential nomination languished among Jewish Democrats offended by Jackson's photographed embrace of Yasir Arafat. Moreover, those African Americans who identify with various Islamic movements may develop a Pan-Islamic sensitivity that encourages them to see the Palestinians as brothers and sisters in the same cause.

A final factor that has been emphasized in recent treatments of U.S.–Israeli relations is the role of religion in explaining both elite and mass support for Israel. The impact of elite religious beliefs on public policy making has been emphasized with regard to "morality" policies that tap conflicts over "first principles."[32] Religion has been shown to influence political opinions, both on domestic policy issues[33] and foreign policy issues.[34]

The distinction between Catholics and non-Catholics has been stressed with regard to abortion, living wills, and other domestic morality policies, as well as with regard to the cold war and other foreign policy debates.[35] However, we suspect that this is not the most salient religious cleavage with regard to Israel. As noted, we expect the distinction between Jews and non-Jews to be significant. In addition, whether or not one subscribes to the popular prophetic system of premillennial dispensationalism, promulgated by radio and television evangelists and fundamentalist and Pentecostal pastors such as Jerry Falwell and John Hagee, may affect legislator behavior. Dispensationalists oppose policies such as shared control of Israel and support Jewish settlements in the West Bank on biblical grounds.[36] They see events such as Israel's founding in 1948 and the recapture of Jerusalem's Old City in 1967 as a "series of last day signs... as steps in God's unfolding plan."[37]

Evangelical leaders, some of whom are politically oriented, have promoted support for Israel as the correct biblical position, particularly since the 1980s.[38] Hence we see Janet Parshall, former spokesperson for the evangelically oriented Family Research Council, addressing a pro-Israel rally in Washington DC, and the Anti-Defamation League publishing columns by Christian Right leader and Israel supporter Ralph Reed.[39] The Interfaith Zionist Leadership Summit mentioned at the beginning of this article also emphasizes the biblical roots of contemporary support for Israel. That said, some evangelical leaders deny the eschatological and biblical connection to their support for Israel. When recently speaking at Temple Beth Shalom in Framingham, Massachusetts, Pat Robertson denied the connection but stated that "there's a visceral, heartfelt love in the hearts of evangelicals for Israel and the Jewish people."[40]

Regardless, the support for Israel of born-again Christian politicians such as Tom DeLay and President Bush is increasingly explained in the media by reference to their "devout religious beliefs."[41] Yet one might expect evangelicals to be relatively less supportive of Israel because of survey data finding that they hold negative opinions about Jews.[42] Wald et al. found that evangelicalism did not necessarily predict greater support for Israel among members of Congress.[43] Looking at voting in the House on the 1994 and 1995 appropriations bills, they found evangelical representatives to be *less* supportive than fellow House Republicans of the foreign aid bill which included over $2 billion annually for Israel.[44] Social liberals, many of whom are mainline Protestants, were more sympathetic than the evangelicals. However, they did find a positive correlation between evangelicalism and expressions of support for Israel among clergy, religious activists, and the mass public. Among these groups, born-again Christians were more supportive of Israel than mainline Protestants and Roman Catholics. Thus their evidence is mixed with regard to the influence of evangelicalism on attitudes toward Israel. Since there is a dearth of other attempts to test for this influence, the impact of religion on members' support for Israel is an open question and one that requires additional study.

## Hypotheses and Methods

This analysis explores the effects of religion, partisanship, ideology, and race on support for Israel in the U.S. House of Representatives in the 105th, 106th, and 107th Congresses (1997–2002). We expect that identification with different religious and racial groups, plus broad normative orientations captured by ideology, will affect legislator attitudes on this issue.

### Dependent Variable

The dependent variable is the level of support expressed for Israel by representatives in the aforementioned Congresses. Important legislation was identified by searching the *Congressional Record*. (See the appendix for a list of the legislation included in the analysis.) A few Israel-related votes were excluded from the analysis because they were essentially consensual. For votes that offered some variance, legislators were given 1 point if they voted pro-Israel and a 0 if they did not vote pro-Israel. Legislators were given 0 points if they voted "present" or did not vote at all. It is difficult to be certain what a "present" vote means; one cannot know a legislator's true preference if it is not revealed. However, we wish to capture intensity of support. By voting "present" or not voting at all, legislators may not be voting against Israel (maybe they were sick or preferred to vote on a competing resolution), but it is also clear that they did not take the opportunity to register support for Israel. For whatever reason, they opted not to go on record in the affirmative. With the goal of measuring the intensity of support, it makes sense to consider a "present" vote or no vote at all as less supportive than a "yes" vote.

In the case of bills that did not come to a vote, legislators could still register support for Israel by cosponsoring legislation. Legislators were given 1 point if they decided to cosponsor pro-Israel legislation and 0 points if they did not. The decision to cosponsor legislation is qualitatively different than the decision to vote on a roll call. Even so, we include voting and cosponsorship in a combined measure because in theory we expect high scores to indicate intensity.[45] The decisions on the votes and cosponsorship items are then taken together and summed, generating an index of support for Israel. A score of 0 indicates no support for Israel and higher numbers indicate higher levels of legislator support for Israel. Ordered probit was used to analyze these data.

Even though these votes deal with Israel, we make no claim that they reflect the priorities of the various Israeli governments in whose name the bills and resolutions were sometimes offered. During the time that Yitzhak Rabin was prime minister, he informed pro-Israel groups that his principal concern was the status of Israel's allocation in the foreign aid bill—an item that does not appear in our data because it was part of an omnibus bill that dealt with a myriad of subjects. The bills and resolutions we examine are important nonetheless because they give members of Congress an opportunity to publicly endorse or reject the state of Israel. In this sense, they may say more about Israel as a "domestic" issue in American politics than about American policy in the Middle East.

## Independent Variables

With regard to religion, we expect that legislators who are religious conservatives—that is, fundamentalist and evangelical Protestants—and legislators with greater proportions of religious conservatives in their districts will express higher levels of support for Israel than nonreligious conservatives and legislators with lower proportions of religious conservatives in their districts. We also expect that Jewish legislators and legislators with higher proportions of Jews in their districts will express higher levels of support for Israel than non-Jewish legislators and legislators with lower proportions of Jews in their districts. Dummy variables for member religion are used for Jewish (Jewish = 1, non-Jewish = 0), Catholic (Catholic = 1, non-Catholic = 0), and religious conservative (religious conservative = 1, not conservative = 0).[46] Percentages of each congressional district classified as Catholic, Jewish, and religiously conservative are used to measure district level religion. While we would have liked to include the number of Arab Americans in members' districts, such data were not available.[47]

Legislators' partisanship is coded as a dummy variable (Democrat = 1, Republican = 0). District level partisanship is operationalized as the percentage of the vote given to the Democratic presidential candidate in the most recent election. We expect to find that Democratic partisanship is associated with lower levels of support for Israel. Ideology is measured using Poole and Rosenthal's[48] DW-Nominate scores. These scores range from −1 to 1, with 1 indicating the highest level of conservatism. Borrowing from Haider-Markel and Wattier and Tatalovich, we reduced the collinearity between ideology and legislator partisanship by regressing elite ideology on party and using the residuals from that equation in place of the DW-Nominate scores.[49] This new indicator reflects the proportion of ideology not explained by partisanship. We expect that, particularly in recent years, ideological conservatism will produce greater support for Israel. To capture the effects of race, we use a dummy variable for each legislator (African American = 1, others = 0). At the district level, the proportion of each district classified as African American by the U.S. Census Bureau is used. We expect that African American legislators and legislators with larger African American populations in their districts will express lower levels of support for Israel.

## Analysis

In the 105th Congress, the distribution across the three possible categories indicates strong support for Israel among legislators. Only 5.98 percent of legislators expressed no support for Israel. Overall, more than 80 percent of all legislators expressed some support for Israel. In the 106th Congress, the categories were 0–8, and 42 percent of members fell into the modal category of 4. Just over 31 percent of legislators expressed higher levels of support for Israel, and about 26 percent of legislators expressed lower levels of support for Israel. In the 107th Congress, the mode moves to the lower half of the index. The modal category is 2 (range 0–6), with 28.94 percent of legislators falling there. About 21 percent of legislators score 0 or 1, and about 55 percent of legislators score 3 or above. The intensity of support thus varies, but in each Congress more members express moderate to high support than low support for Israel.

As an initial exploration of our research question, we calculated the mean levels of support for Israel in each Congress for key groups of legislators and ran difference of mean tests. Table 2 provides these data. In all three Congresses, the mean levels of support for Jewish legislators are higher than for non-Jewish legislators and the difference is statistically significant. Mean levels of support among African American

**Table 1.** Support for Israel in the 105th, 106th, and 107th Congresses

| Index category | | Proportion of Representatives | | |
| --- | --- | --- | --- | --- |
| | | 105th | 106th | 107th |
| Low Support | 0 | 5.98% | 0.92% | 4.94% |
| | 1 | 69.66 | 3.91 | 11.06 |
| | 2 | 24.37 | 5.29 | 28.94 |
| | 3 | — | 16.55 | 22.82 |
| | 4 | — | 41.61 | 15.29 |
| | 5 | — | 18.39 | 10.12 |
| | 6 | — | 10.34 | 6.82 |
| | 7 | — | 2.07 | — |
| High Support | 8 | — | 0.92 | — |
| Total | | 100.1% | 100% | 99.9% |
| N | | 435 | 435 | 425 |

*Note*: Due to rounding, columns do not add up to 100%.

**Table 2.** Mean support by key groups of legislators, 105th–107th Congress

|  | 105th Congress | 106th Congress | 107th Congress |
|---|---|---|---|
| Overall Mean | 1.18 | 4.06 | 2.90 |
|  | (0.520) | (1.34) | 1.53 |
| Jewish | 1.64** | 5.26** | 4.72** |
|  | (0.638) | (1.14) | (1.34) |
| Not Jewish | 1.16 | 3.99 | 2.78 |
|  | (0.497) | (1.35) | (1.47) |
| Democrat | 1.20 | 3.98 | 2.77* |
|  | (0.560) | (1.47) | (1.60) |
| Republican | 1.17 | 4.15 | 3.04 |
|  | (0.482) | (1.21) | (1.44) |
| African American | 1.11 | 3.14** | 1.83** |
|  | (0.567) | (1.64) | (1.46) |
| Not Af. American | 1.19 | 4.15 | 3.00 |
|  | (0.515) | (1.28) | (1.50) |
| Rel. Conservative | 1.16 | 3.81 | 3.24* |
|  | (0.505) | (1.41) | (1.53) |
| Not Rel. Conservative | 1.19 | 4.09 | 2.86 |
|  | (0.520) | (1.35) | (1.52) |
| Range | 0–2 | 0–8 | 0–6 |

Significance tests using One Way ANOVA
Standard deviations in parentheses
*Difference significant at .10
**Difference significant at .001

legislators are lower than for non–African American legislators in all three Congresses. The difference is statistically significant in the latter two Congresses. The aggregate patterns of support by party and religious conservatism evolve in the years under consideration. Democrats exhibit higher mean levels of support than Republicans in the 105th Congress, but lower mean levels of support in the 106th and 107th Congresses. Religious conservatives exhibit lower mean levels of support than nonreligious conservatives in the 105th and 106th Congresses, but higher mean levels of support in the 107th Congress. These data are largely consistent with our expectations. Moreover, our anecdotal impressions, which suggested that the patterns of support for Israel have changed in recent years, seem to be confirmed by the data. The multivariate analysis allows us to explore these initial findings in a more rigorous manner.

Table 3 provides the results of the ordered probit models for each Congress. The coefficients point to some interesting results. As expected, Jewish legislators are more likely to express higher levels of support for Israel than non-Jewish legislators. The presence of large Jewish constituencies has a similar effect. The coefficients for both these variables are strongly significant and positive in each Congress. As stated earlier, Congress is very pro-Israel. It appropriates billions of dollars in aid to Israel each year, and in relevant floor votes the vast majority of legislators take the pro-Israel position. That said, the models indicate that personal or electoral identification

**Table 3.** Ordered probit analysis of support for Israel

|  | 105th Congress | 106th Congress | 107th Congress |
|---|---|---|---|
| **Legislator Variables** | | | |
| Jewish | 0.856*** | 0.845**** | 1.315**** |
| Fundamentalist | .125 | −.068 | .354** |
| Catholic | −.164 | −.080 | −.107 |
| Democrat | .334* | −.206 | −.603**** |
| Ideology | −1.066** | −0.082 | 0.992*** |
| African American | −0.118 | −0.777** | −1.003**** |
| **District Characteristics** | | | |
| % Jewish | .065*** | .047*** | .058**** |
| % Fundamentalist | −.0002 | .003 | −.001 |
| % Catholic | .010 | .011** | .006 |
| Democratic Partisanship | −.021** | .002 | .005 |
| % African American | .007 | .005 | .009* |
| Cut 1 | −2.117017 | −2.144607 | −1.567574 |
| Cut 2 | 0.2613383 | −1.391234 | −0.7817882 |
| Cut 3 | | −.9823093 | .16979 |
| Cut 4 | | −.2911744 | .842581 |
| Cut 5 | | 0.8828481 | 1.401088 |
| Cut 6 | | 1.567001 | 2.039741 |
| Cut 7 | | 2.478805 | |
| Cut 8 | | 3.116895 | |
| $X^2$ | 47.15 | 64.84 | 100.61 |
| Pseudo R2 | .0721 | .0461 | .0679 |
| N | 429 | 423 | 415 |

****Difference significant at the .001 level
***Difference significant at the .01 level
**Difference significant at the .05 level
*Difference significant at the .10 level

with the Jewish community produces higher levels of support for Israel among representatives.

The other religious variables do not perform as well across Congresses. The Catholic coefficients suggest a negative but statistically insignificant relationship between legislator Catholicism and intensity of support for Israel. However, the presence of large district level Catholic populations produces the opposite result. The models indicate that legislators from strongly Catholic districts will support Israel at higher levels. The coefficient for this variable is significant only in the 106th Congress, but it just barely misses significance in the 105th Congress.

The presence of fundamentalist and evangelical Protestants at the district level has an inconsistent and insignificant relationship with support for Israel. Personal legislator identification as a religious conservative also performs inconsistently. In the 105th Congress the coefficient is positive and in the 106th it is negative. But in both Congresses the relationship is insignificant. However, in the 107th Congress this variable emerges as significant. The coefficient indicates a positive relationship between members' religious conservative identification and support for Israel.

Over the three Congresses the relationship between legislator partisanship and support for Israel changes. In the 105th Congress, the coefficient is weakly significant and indicates that Democratic partisanship is associated with higher levels of support for Israel. In the 106th Congress, the coefficient is negative and loses significance. In the 107th Congress, the coefficient reemerges as significant and indicates that Democratic partisanship produces *lower* levels of support for Israel. The coefficient for district level partisanship is only significant in the 105th Congress. It indicates that higher levels of district level Democratic partisanship produce lower levels of support for Israel. The effects of both elite and district level partisanship come as a surprise, given that Jews have traditionally been such strong supporters of the Democratic Party.

The effects of legislator ideology nicely mirror the effects of legislator partisanship. In the 105th Congress, ideological conservatism seems to produce lower levels of support for Israel. Rather, it is liberalism that produces support for Israel. The variable loses significance in the 106th Congress. But in the 107th Congress, it reemerges as significant. What is more, the substantive effect of ideology changes. Then, it is conservatives—not liberals—who expressed the highest levels of support for Israel.

Finally, the race variable produces interesting results. The district level coefficient indicates a positive relationship between presence of African Americans in the district and support for Israel, but it is only (weakly) significant in the 107th Congress. The legislator dummy variable indicates that African American legislators supported Israel at lower levels than their non–African American colleagues. The coefficient is negative across all three Congresses and statistically significant in the 106th and 107th Congresses.

## Discussion

The analysis indicates that Jewish legislators and legislators with large Jewish constituencies are some of Israel's strongest supporters. The relationship between elite and district level Jewishness is significant and consistently positive. Beyond that, the effects of the other independent variables change over time. Along with Jews, liberals were Israel's strongest supporters in the 105th Congress. It is intuitively obvious why the fate of Israel would be important to American Jews. Perhaps liberals expressed such strong support for Israel because they viewed Israel as the more vulnerable group in the larger geopolitical context of the region. In any case, the resolutions considered by the 105th Congress did not appear to elicit an alternative framework for viewing the Israeli–Palestinian conflict. One item congratulates Israel on the anniversary of Jerusalem's reunification, and the other is designed to promote Israel's equality at the UN. The chief sponsors of both were Democrats.

In the 106th Congress, the issue appears to be nonpartisan and nonideological. At the same time, the decision-making items in the 106th Congress are qualitatively different than the ones in the 105th Congress. There are more of them, and they directly engage the Palestinian issue. For example, H.Con.Res.24 expresses congressional opposition to the unilateral declaration of a Palestinian state and urges the president to assert similar opposition. H.R.5272 also opposes a unilaterally declared Palestinian state and goes further to say that certain measures should be applied in the case of such a declaration, for example withholding U.S. contributions to international organizations that recognize the state. H.Con.Res.426 clearly takes sides in the conflict by "expressing solidarity with the Israeli state and its people at this time of crisis" and "condemning the Palestinian leadership for encouraging violence." Whereas the main sponsors of the two resolutions in the 105th Congress were Democrats, the main sponsors of these three resolutions were Republicans. Indeed, Republicans were the key sponsors of five of the eight resolutions in the 106th Congress.

This change in the nature of the resolutions between the 105th and 106th Congresses may have evoked a new racial cleavage among legislators. African Americans and Jews are longtime Democratic Party allies, but on this issue African Americans may be more likely to identify with what they perceive to be a landless, oppressed group. The pattern of decreased support for Israel among African American legislators continued in the 107th Congress, as the political context surrounding the conflict continued to evolve. The level of violence between Israelis and Palestinians escalated after September 2000, with suicide bombings that crisscrossed the entire country and Israeli reprisals and military strikes.[50] Also, September 11 may have changed perceptions of Israel. Some Americans may have become more sensitive to the domestic terror threats faced by Israelis, while others may have grown concerned that the deprivation on the Arab street was breeding terrorists in the first place.

In the 107th Congress, the House moved further in the direction of pro-Israel, anti-Palestinian resolutions. Most of the items in the 107th Congress directly addressed Arafat and the Palestinian question. For example, a resolution sponsored by Rep. Henry Hyde (R-IL) expresses "solidarity with Israel in the fight against terrorism." Another, sponsored by Tom DeLay (R-TX), expresses similar solidarity and states that the United States and Israel "are now engaged in a common struggle against terrorism and are on the front-lines of a conflict thrust upon them against their will."

Two other resolutions, sponsored by Rep. Eric Cantor (R-VA) and Rep. Roy Blunt (R-MO), take direct aim at the PLO, the Palestinian Authority (PA), and Arafat himself. The first prohibits assistance to either organization. The second is a lengthy condemnation of Arafat. It states, for example, that Arafat has "failed to exercise his authority and responsibility to maintain law and order," which has "resulted in ongoing acts of terrorism against Israeli and American civilians in Israel" and holds Arafat "responsible for the murder of hundreds of innocent Israelis and the wounding of thousands more since October 2000" (see appendix for more details). The key sponsors of four of the six resolutions in the 107th were Republicans.

In this new environment, with clear battle lines being drawn by the sponsors of these resolutions, it is not Jews, Democrats, and liberals who are carrying Israel's banner in the House. Rather, it is Jews, evangelical and fundamentalist Protestants, Republicans, and ideological conservatives. The effects of party and ideology in the model shift rather dramatically, and a racial cleavage emerges. The growing salience of the Palestinian question seems to have reframed this issue for many legislators and crosscut existing coalitions. That exogenous factor may have set the stage for a coalition shift that took place in a remarkably short period of time.

Beginning in the 106th Congress, legislators were not just supporting Israel, they were taking sides in a conflict. Seen through this lens, the cleavage was no longer friendly democratic Israel versus the Arab world. For some the conflict may have been transformed into oppressor Israel versus the oppressed Palestinians. For others it may have been transformed into the divinely ordained state of Israel versus hostile Islamic groups that would threaten its security. It thus appears that the patterns of legislator decision making changed as the context changed. In addition to the emergence of the Palestinian issue and the escalation of violence, the domestic political context in this country may have influenced the politics of this issue. Perhaps the presence of an unabashed Christian conservative in the White House starting in the 107th Congress contributed to an environment in which fundamentalists and evangelicals on Capitol Hill felt more encouraged to take a strong pro-Israel stand.

## Conclusion

The cultural (or morality) policy literature characterizes certain political conflicts as representative of larger values and norms. In these conflicts, antagonists battle over their respective ways of life. The dividing line is between us and them, between those who do and do not embrace traditional values. We suggest that identification with certain social groups, ethno-religious groups in particular, affects the extent to which legislators identify with and support Israel. Contrary to the realist paradigm in international relations, this research suggests that domestic socioreligious and racial groups respond to international events, and that policy makers in the House, in turn, respond to the influence of these domestic groups. While it is possible that a two-level game is taking place,[51] purely instrumental-rational arguments about making foreign policy seem to be undermined. That is, legislator decision making seems to be influenced by phenomena outside the realm of the realist paradigm as conventionally understood, but very much consistent with Weber's classic argument about value rationality.[52]

In the 107th Congress, the Israeli issue became more religiously driven, more partisan, more ideological, and more racial. With the escalation of tension between Israel and the Palestinians, different cleavages became salient to legislators. With that, group allegiances switched. Liberals and African Americans started to identify with the Palestinians—not Israel—as the oppressed group in this conflict. At the same time, religious and ideological conservatives and Republicans started to identify with Israel as a just state under attack from individuals considered to be outside their larger religious tradition. These findings undermine the key contentions of modernization and secularization theories, discussed in the introduction to this volume. These approaches, which predicted the privatization of religious faith and its withdrawal from active engagement with the state, are not supported by this study. Rather, in the case of congressional support for Israel, religious beliefs are becoming more rather than less important in explaining variation in members' positions. Doctrinal beliefs seem to have shaped how at least some members have responded to changing events in the Middle East.

Such findings may shock observers who assume that constitutional restrictions on the role of religion in government preclude such influence in policy making. However, an impressive collection of scholarship over the past quarter century has documented convincingly that religious factors remain a potent source of political change in even an avowedly secular state such as the United States.[53] Moreover, scholars have argued that such religious influence is compatible with liberal democracy, providing it respects what Barbara A. McGraw has described as America's two-tiered public forum.[54] Religious forces are appropriate contenders in the *conscientious* public forum, the arena for persuasion and voluntary action on matters of morality free from government coercion, but have a very limited role in the *civic* public forum, the arena for law and its enforcement, i.e., where government coercion is permitted. Because one would be hard-pressed to argue that the influence of religious values on legislator decision making about foreign policy could be construed as coercive, the activity seems to fall within the protected zone. Protected or not, it flourishes.

It is important to not overstate the results with regard to variation in support for Israel. Even in the 107th Congress, support for Israel was overwhelming, with many more Democrats and African Americans supporting than not supporting Israel. Thus we are talking about marginal increments in group tendencies rather than binary support patterns. Still, the Israel issue did change. As it is currently framed, the issue of support for Israel may present Democrats with a problem since it has the potential to divide their coalition. Jews, African Americans, and liberals have been the heart of the Democratic Party for decades. Jews may align with the other elements of the party base on other issues, but they apparently are now out of step on this highly salient issue. In the long run, the question is whether Jews will remain loyal to the Democratic Party, defect, or realign.

The increased role played by evangelical and fundamentalist Protestant representatives in carrying the torch for Israel on Capitol Hill also has important implications for American Jews.[55] It is problematic for Jews to count on evangelicals as an unwavering source of support for Israel. As a recent article in the *New Republic* notes, the problem is that this support is rooted in interpretation of the Bible rather than in recognition of Israel's importance as a democratic state, or in recognition of Israel's significance to the Jewish people in the light of the Holocaust, or in any other secularly based rationale for supporting Israel. Indeed, evangelical attitudes toward Jews and Israel should be characterized as "complex and ambivalent," not unconditionally supportive. While messianism may produce respect for Jews as the heirs of biblical Israel and the critical actor in the restoration of the Davidic kingdom, sectarianism imbues evangelicals with the sense that Jews are morally depraved.[56]

Thus, evangelicals may support Jews and the state of Israel in the foreign policy arena, but express antipathy for Jews in other areas. But even this begs the question, what would happen if Israel decided to withdraw from part or all of the West Bank? Would evangelicals then withdraw their support for the Jewish state? James Inhofe, an evangelical senator from Oklahoma, said in a speech entitled "An Absolute Victory": "God appeared to Abram and said, 'I am giving you this land'—the West Bank. This is not a political battle at all. It is a contest over whether or not the word of God is true."[57] If Israel takes actions that are perceived by religious conservatives as going against the word of God, it may lose its legitimacy in their eyes and be seen as less deserving of favorable treatment.

As the introduction to this volume suggests, religiously rooted positions can act as both a source of support and as a constraint on U.S. foreign policy. This appears to be the case with American policy toward the Jewish state, where doctrinal beliefs clearly limit the range of defensible behavior in the eyes of adherents. The evangelical pro-Israel position is therefore a double-edged sword: "There is no secular moral rationale for the Christian Right's support for Israel because, for the Christian Right, Israel's claims are moral only insofar as they are biblical."[58] Thus secular Jews, and other secular Americans who care deeply about Israel, must be cautious about relying too heavily on evangelical support.

## Appendix: Votes and Cosponsorship Decisions[59]

*105th Congress (1997–98)*

Support scores range from 0 to 2.

1. H.CON.RES.60 – VOTE (Y = 1, N = 0): Congratulating the residents of Jerusalem and the people of Israel on the thirtieth anniversary of the reunification of that historic city (Schumer, D-NY). 185 cosponsors.
2. H.R.3236 – COSPONSORSHIP (Y = 1, N = 0): To promote full equality for Israel at the UN (Rothman, D-NJ). 113 cosponsors.

*106th Congress (1999–2000)*

Scores range from 0 to 8.

1. H.CON.RES.24 – VOTE (Y = 1, N = 0): Expressing congressional opposition to the unilateral declaration of a Palestinian state and urging the president to assert clearly U.S. opposition to such a unilateral declaration (Salmon, R-AZ). 280 cosponsors.
2. H.CON.RES.109 – COSPONSORSHIP (Y = 1, N = 0): Commending the people of Israel for reaffirming through elections their dedication to democratic ideals (Capps, D-CA). 101 cosponsors.
3. H.CON.RES.117 – VOTE (Y = 1, N = 0): Opposing the UN resolution condemning Israeli occupation and convening a conference to address Israeli violations of the Fourth Geneva Convention and unfairly placing full blame for deterioration of the peace process on Israel; commending the State Department for the U.S. vote against this resolution, and urging the member states and secretary of the UN to oppose this politicization of the Fourth Geneva Convention (Rothman, D-NJ). 30 cosponsors.
4. H.CON.RES.426 – VOTE (Y = 1, N = 0): Urging that the Israeli–Palestinian conflict be resolved by peaceful negotiation; expressing solidarity with the Israeli state and its people at this time of crisis; condemning the Palestinian leadership for encouraging violence and urging it to stop all violence and settle all grievances through negotiations (Gilman, R-NY). 163 cosponsors.
5. H.R.2529 – COSPONSORSHIP (Y = 1, N = 0): To take certain steps toward recognition by the United States of Jerusalem as the capital of Israel, i.e., appropriating money for construction of a U.S. embassy in Israel, identification of Jerusalem as the capital in official government documents and recording the place of birth as Israel if a U.S. citizen is born in Jerusalem (Reynolds, R-NY). 58 cosponsors.
6. H.R.2785 – COSPONSORSHIP (Y = 1, N = 0): To take certain steps toward recognition by the United States of Jerusalem as the capital of Israel (same steps as H.R.2529 except for appropriating money for construction of an embassy) (Reynolds, R-NY). 52 cosponsors.
7. H.R.3405 – COSPONSORSHIP (Y = 1, N = 0): To promote full equality for Israel at the UN (Rothman, D-NY). 63 cosponsors.
8. H.R.5272 – VOTE (Y = 1, N = 0): Opposing the unilateral declaration of a Palestinian state, withholding diplomatic recognition of any state that is unilaterally declared, and applying certain measures if such a state is declared (e.g., prohibiting nonhumanitarian assistance from the United States to the West Bank

and Gaza, withholding U.S. contributions to international organizations that recognize a unilaterally declared Palestinian state, and opposing membership of this state in international financial institutions and loans to the state by such institutions) (Gilman, R-NY). 8 cosponsors.

*107th Congress (2001–2002)*

Scores range from 0 to 6.

1. H.CON.RES.280 – VOTE (Y = 1, N = 0): Expressing solidarity with Israel in the fight against terrorism (Hyde, R-IL). 65 cosponsors.
2. H. CON.RES.392 – VOTE (Y = 1, N = 0): Expressing solidarity with Israel in its fight against terrorism "whereas the United States and Israel are now engaged in a common struggle against terrorism and are on the front-lines of a conflict thrust upon them against their will" (DeLay, R-TX). 112 cosponsors.
3. H.R.1795 – COSPONSORSHIP (Y = 1, N = 0): To require the imposition of sanctions with respect to the PLO or the PA if the president determines that these entities have not complied with certain commitments made by the entities (Ackerman, D-NY). 157 cosponsors.
4. H.R.3624 – COSPONSORSHIP (Y = 1, N = 0): To prohibit assistance to the PA and any instrumentality of the PA (Cantor, R-VA). 71 cosponsors.
5. H.R.4693 – COSPONSORSHIP (Y = 1, N = 0): To hold accountable the PLO and the PA; finding that the PLO under Arafat has failed to abide by its promises enumerated in the Oslo Accords; that Arafat has failed to exercise his authority and responsibility to maintain law and order in the West Bank and Gaza, which has resulted in ongoing acts of terrorism against Israeli and American civilians in Israel; that Arafat and the forces under his control are responsible for the murder of hundreds of innocent Israelis and the wounding of thousands more since October 2000, that Arafat has been directly implicated in funding and supporting terrorists, and that Arafat's failure to end the homicide bombings further complicates the prospects for resolution of the conflict in that region; that the United States should continue to urge an immediate and unconditional cessation of all terrorist activities; that the PLO and PA should immediately surrender to Israel those Palestinian extremists wanted for the assassination of the Israeli minister of tourism; that Arafat must publicly condemn all acts of terrorism, including and especially homicide bombings, and confiscate and destroy the infrastructures of terrorism; denial of U.S. visas to any member of the PLO and freezing assets of the PLO and PA (Blunt, R-MO). 79 cosponsors.
6. H.AMDT.39 (H.R.1646) – VOTE (Y = 1, N = 0): Prohibiting international military education and training funding to Lebanon unless the president certifies that the Lebanese Army has deployed to the internationally recognized border between Lebanon and Israel and the government of Lebanon is effectively asserting its authority (Lantos, D-CA).

**Notes**

1. R. W. Stevenson, "For Muslims, a Mixture of White House Signals," *New York Times*, April 27, 2003.
2. K. Turaani, "Arab-American Republicans against Bush Press Release," http://www.aarab.org/.

3. We use the term "evangelical," to refer to a family of Protestant Christians distinguished by belief in Jesus as a personal source of salvation, the inerrancy of the Bible, and a commitment to converting others. This style of religious commitment dominates such major denominations as the Southern Baptist Convention and the Assemblies of God and is a potent factor among many Methodists, Presbyterians, and other traditions. Although most black Protestants share this theology, they have traditionally drawn very different political inspiration from it and are not a component of the Christian Right movement. For a useful overview, see J. Christopher Soper, *Evangelical Christianity in the United States and Great Britain: Religious Beliefs, Political Choices* (London: Macmillan, 1994).

4. See http://www.cc.org/events/interfaithzionist.htm.

5. Tony Smith, *Foreign Attachments: The Power of Ethnic Groups in the Making of U.S. Foreign Policy* (Cambridge, MA: Harvard University Press, 2000).

6. For an extended scholarly debate, see Holbert N. Carrol, "The Congress and National Security Policy," in *The Congress and America's Future*, ed. David Truman (Englewood Cliffs, NJ: Prentice-Hall, 1973); Robert Dahl, *Congress and Foreign Policy* (New York: Harcourt Brace, 1950); Louis Fisher, *Congressional Abdication on War and Spending* (College Station: Texas A&M University Press, 2000); Thomas M. Franck and Edward Weisband, *Foreign Policy by Congress* (New York: Oxford University Press, 1979); Roger Hilsman, *The Politics of Policy-Making in Defense and Foreign Affairs* (New York: Harper Row, 1971); Barbara Hinckley, *Less than Meets the Eye: Congress, the President, and Foreign Policy* (Chicago: University of Chicago Press, 1994); Bert Rockman, "Presidents, Opinion, and Institutional Leadership," in *The New Politics of American Foreign Policy*, ed. David Deese (New York: St. Martin's Press, 1994); Aaron Wildavsky, "The Two Presidencies," *Trans-Action* 4, no. 2 (1966): 7–14.

7. Marvin C. Feuerweger, Congress and Israel: *Foreign Aid Decision-Making in the House of Representatives, 1969–1976* (Westport, CT: Greenwood Press, 1979).

8. Charles Lipson, "American Support for Israel: History, Sources and Limits," in *U.S.–Israeli Relations at the Crossroads*, ed. Gabriel Sheffer (London: Frank Cass, 1997); S. Telhami and J. Krosnick, "U.S. Public Attitudes Toward Israel: A Study of the Attentive and Issue Publics," in *U.S.–Israeli Relations at the Crossroads*, ed. Gabriel Sheffer (London: Frank Cass, 1997). Public opinion polls have consistently shown high and widespread support for Israel since the Jewish state was established in 1948. Sympathy for Israel is considerably greater than sympathy for the Palestinians among both political elites and the general public. For example, a Gallup poll conducted in April 2002 showed that 47 percent of those surveyed sided with Israel in the Israeli–Palestinian conflict, while only 13 percent backed the Palestinians. See Miles A. Pomper, K. Foerstel, and J. Broder, "DeLay Flexes Muscles on Middle East Issue," *CQ Weekly*, May 4, 2002, 1139.

9. Yaakov S. Ariel, *On Behalf of Israel: American Fundamentalist Attitudes Toward Jews, Judaism, and Zionism, 1865–1945* (Brooklyn, NY: Carlson Publishing, 1991); Paul Charles Merkley, *The Politics of Christian Zionism, 1891–1948* (London: Frank Cass, 1998).

10. Feuerweger, *Congress and Israel*. However, this is not to say support for Israel has been constant over time. Presidents and members of Congress have sometimes shown ambivalence and even vocal opposition to Israel. See Lipson, "American Support for Israel."

11. David Howard Goldberg, *Foreign Policy and Ethnic Interest Groups: American and Canadian Jews Lobby for Israel* (New York: Greenwood Press, 1990); Robert J. Lieber, "Domestic Politics and Foreign Policy: Making Sense of America's Role in the Middle East Peace Process," *World Affairs* 161, no. 1 (1998): 3–9; Vernon W. Ruttan, *United States Development Assistance Policy: The Domestic Politics of Foreign Economic Aid* (Baltimore: Johns Hopkins University Press, 1996); Paula Stern, *Water's Edge: Domestic Politics and the Making of American Foreign Policy* (Westport, CT: Greenwood Press, 1979).

12. Pomper, Foerstel, and Broder, "Delay Flexes Muscles on Middle East Issue," *CQ Weekly*, May 4, 2002, 1139.

13. For a rare scholarly study that addresses the role of religion in explaining congressional attitudes toward Israel, see Kenneth D. Wald et al., "Reclaiming Zion: How American Religious Groups View the Middle East," in *U.S.–Israeli Relations at the Crossroads*, ed. Gabriel Sheffer (London: Frank Cass, 1997). For journalistic accounts, see for example P. Beinart, "Bad Move," *New Republic*, May 20, 2002; Miles A. Pomper, Karen Foerstal, Jonathan Broder, "Delay Flexes Muscles on Middle East Issue," *CQ Weekly*, May 4, 2002, 1139.

14. Feuerweger, *Congress and Israel*.

15. We measure legislator religion categorically, classifying legislators as Roman Catholic,

Jewish, mainline Protestant, or religious conservative based on the denominational affiliation reported in various editions of *CQ's Politics in America*. At the district level, religion is operationalized as the proportion of constituents belonging in each of these classifications.

16. Feuerweger, *Congress and Israel*; Robert H. Trice, "Congress and the Arab-Israeli Conflict: Support for Israel in the U.S. Senate, 1970–1973," *Political Science Quarterly* 92, no. 3 (1977): 443–63; Kenneth D. Wald et al., "Reclaiming Zion."

17. R. Douglas Arnold, *The Logic of Congressional Action* (New Haven: Yale University Press, 1990); Benjamin G. Bishin, "Constituency Influence in Congress: Does Subconstituency Matter?" *Legislative Studies Quarterly* 24, no. 3 (2000): 389–415; Charles F. Cnudde and Donald J. McCrone, "The Linkage between Constituency Attitudes and Congressional Voting Behavior: A Causal Model," *American Political Science Review* 60, no. 1 (1966): 66–72; David Mayhew, *Congress: The Electoral Connection* (New Haven: Yale University Press, 1974); D. Miller and D. E. Stokes, "Constituency Influence in Congress," *American Political Science Review* 57, no. 1 (1963): 45–56.

18. Gabriel A. Almond, *The American People and Foreign Policy* (New York: Harcourt Brace, 1950); Barry B. Hughes, *The Domestic Context of American Foreign Policy* (San Francisco: W. H. Freeman, 1978); Paul C. Light and Celina Lake, "The Election: Candidates, Strategies and Decisions," in *The Elections of 1984*, ed. Michael Nelson (Washington: Congressional Quarterly, 1985); James N. Rosenau, *Public Opinion and Foreign Policy* (New York: Random House, 1961); but see also John H. Aldrich, John L. Sullivan, and Eugene Borgida, "Foreign Affairs and Issue Voting: Do Presidential Candidates 'Waltz Before a Blind Audience?'" *American Political Science Review* 83, no. 1 (1990): 23–41.

19. Trice, "Congress and the Arab-Israeli Conflict."

20. David Garnham, "Factors Influencing Congressional Support for Israel during the 93rd Congress," *Jerusalem Journal of International Relations* 2, no. 3 (1977): 23–45.

21. Tom Squitieri, "Israel Finds Support in Congress," *USA Today*, April 10, 2002.

22. Trice, "Congress and the Arab-Israeli Conflict."

23. Feuerweger, *Congress and Israel*.

24. Beinart, "Bad Move," Pomper, Foerstel, and Broder, "Delay Flexes Muscles on Middle East Issues," *CQ Weekly*, May 4, 2002, 1139.

25. Garnham, "Factors Influencing."

26. Gil C. Alroy, "Patterns in Hostility," in *Attitudes Toward Jewish Statehood in the Arab World*, ed. Gil Carl Alroy (New York: American Academic Association for Peace in the Middle East, 1971).

27. Mary Barberis, "The Arab-Israeli Battle on Capitol Hill," *Virginia Quarterly Review* 52, no. 3 (1976): 203–223.

28. Lipson, "American Support for Israel."

29. Samuel G. Freedman, "A Relationship That's Past Its Prime," *New York Times*, May 17, 2003.

30. Kenneth Wald, *Religion and Politics in the United States* (Lanham, MD: Rowman and Littlefield, 2003), 286–87.

31. Benjamin Ginsberg, *Fatal Embrace: Jews and the State* (Chicago: University of Chicago Press, 1993).

32. Peter L. Benson and Dorothy L. Williams, *Religion on Capitol Hill: Myths and Realities* (San Francisco: Harper and Row, 1982); Christine L. Day, "State Legislative Voting Patterns on Abortion Restrictions in Louisiana," *Women and Politics* 14, no. 2 (1995): 45–63; S. F. Gohmann and R. L. Ohsfeldt, "Predicting State Abortion Legislation from U.S. Senate Votes: The Effects of Apparent Ideological Shirking," *Policy Studies Review* 9 (1990): 749–64; John C. Green and J. L. Guth, "Religion, Representatives and Roll Calls," *Legislative Studies Quarterly* 16 (1991): 571–84; Kenneth Meier, *The Politics of Sin* (Armonk, NY: M. E. Sharpe, 1994); Christopher Z. Mooney and Mei-Hsien Lee, "Legislating Morality in the American States: The Case of Pre-Roe Abortion Reform," *American Journal of Political Science* 39 (1995): 599–627; Christopher Z. Mooney, *The Public Clash of Private Values: The Politics of Morality Policy* (New York: Chatham House, 2001).

33. James W. Button, Barbara A. Rienzo, and Kenneth D. Wald, *Private Lives, Public Controversies: Battles over Gay Rights in American Communities* (Washington DC: CQ Press, 1997); Donald Haider-Markel and K. Meier, "The Politics of Gay and Lesbian Rights: Expanding the Scope of the Conflict," *Journal of Politics* 58 (1996): 332–50; Donald Haider-Markel, "Morality in Congress? Legislative Voting on Gay Issues," in *The Public Clash of*

*Private Values: The Politics of Morality Policy*, ed. Christopher Z. Mooney (New York: Chatham House, 2001); Elizabeth Oldmixon, "Culture Wars in the Congressional Theater: How the U.S. House of Representatives Legislates Morality, 1993–1998," *Social Science Quarterly* 83, no. 3 (2002): 775–88.

34. Alfred O. Hero Jr., *American Religious Groups View Foreign Policy: Trends in Rank-and-File Opinion, 1937–1969* (Durham, NC: Duke University Press, 1973); David Leege, Joel Lieske, and Kenneth Wald, "Toward Cultural Theories of American Political Behavior: Religion, Ethnicity and Race, and Class Outlook," in *Political Science: Looking to the Future*, ed. William Crotty (Evanston, IL: Northwestern University Press, 1991); David Leege and Lyman A. Kellstedt, *Rediscovering the Religious Factor in American Politics* (Armonk, NY: M. E. Sharpe, 1993); Milton Rokeach, "Religious Values and Social Compassion," *Review of Religious Research* 11, no. 1 (1969): 24–39; Milton Rosenberg, "Attitude Change and Foreign Policy in the Cold War Era," in *Domestic Sources of Foreign Policy*, ed. James N. Rosenau (New York: Free Press, 1967).

35. P. Fabrizio, "Evolving intoMorality Politics:U.S. Catholic Bishops' Statements on U.S. Politics from 1792 to the Present," in *The Public Clash of Private Values: The Politics of Morality Policy*, ed. Christopher Z. Mooney (New York: Chatham House, 2001); S. Hays and H. Glick, "The Role of Agenda Setting in Policy Innovation: An Event History Analysis of Living Will Laws," *American Politics Quarterly* 25, no. 4 (1997): 497–516; Kenneth D. Wald, *Religion and Politics in the United States* (Washington, DC: Congressional Quarterly Press, 1992).

36. Paul S. Boyer, "John Darby Meets Saddam Hussein: Foreign Policy and Bible Prophecy," *Chronicle of Higher Education*, February 14, 2003, B10.

37. Ibid.

38. Kenneth Wald and Lee Sigelman, "Romancing the Jews: The Christian Right in Search of Strange Bedfellows," in *Sojourners in the Wilderness: The Religious Right in Comparative Perspective*, ed. James Penning and Corwin Smidt (Lanham, MD: Rowman and Littlefield, 1997).

39. Beinart, "Bad Move."

40. Jeff Jacoby, "Israel's Unshakable Allies," *Boston Globe*, May 15, 2003.

41. Pomper, Foerstel, and Broder, "Delay Flexes Muscles on Middle East Issues," *CQ Weekly*, May 4, 2002, 1139.

42. Charles Y. Glock and Rodney Stark, *Christian Beliefs and Anti-Semitism* (New York: Harper and Row, 1966); Gregory Martire and Ruth Clark, *Anti-Semitism in the United States: A Study of Prejudice in the 1980s* (New York: Praeger, 1982); Harold Quinley and Charles Y. Glock, *Anti-Semitism in America* (New York: Free Press, 1979); Gertrude Selznick and Stephen Steinberg, *The Tenacity of Prejudice: Anti-Semitism in Contemporary America* (New York: Harper and Row, 1969); Rodney Stark, et al., *Wayward Shepherds: Prejudice and the Protestant Clergy* (New York: Harper and Row, 1971).

43. Wald et al., "Reclaiming Zion."

44. They note, however, that this lack of support may be attributable not so much to members' attitudes toward Israel, but possibly to attitudes toward foreign aid spending in general or other factors.

45. We ran separate analyses of votes, cosponsorship decisions, and the combined measure for every Congress. For the most part, the coefficients are very stable, though some lose significance when we disaggregate the dependent variable.

46. The following denominations are classified as fundamentalist or evangelical: Brethren in Christ, Seven Day Adventist, Apostolic Christian (Nazarene), Church of God, Evangelical, Christian Missionary Alliance, Baptist, Southern Baptist, Independent Baptist, and Assemblies of God. This is based on the Green and Guth, "Religion" classification.

47. These data were graciously provided by John Green and are based on data collected by the Glenmary Research Center.

48. Keith Poole and Howard Rosenthal, "Patterns of Congressional Voting," *American Journal of Political Science* 35, no. 1 (1991): 228–78.

49. Haider-Markel, "Morality in Congress?"; Mark Wattier and Raymond Tatalovich, "Senate Voting on Abortion Legislation over Two Decades: Testing a Reconstructed Partisanship Variable," *American Review of Politics* 16, Summer (1995): 167–83.

50. "Carnage as Israel Violence Escalates," *Guardian*, March 5, 2002.

51. R. Putnam, "Diplomacy and Domestic Politics: The Logic of Two-Level Games," *International Organization* 42 (1988): 427–460.

52. For the distinction between instrumental and value rationality see Max Weber, *The Protestant Ethic and the Spirit of Capitalism*, trans. Talcott Parsons (New York: Scribner's, 1958).

53. This literature is summarized in Kenneth D. Wald, *Religion and Politics*, (2003).

54. Barbara A. McGraw, *Rediscovering America's Sacred Ground: Public Religion and Pursuit of the Good in a Pluralistic America* (New York: SUNY Press, 2003).

55. Because evangelical Protestants and American Jews are generally on opposite ends of the political spectrum (see Wald and Sigelman, "Romancing the Jews"), cooperation on the Middle East runs up against their traditional differences.

56. Yaakov Ariel, "Philosemites or Antisemites? Evangelical Christian Attitudes toward Jews and the State of Israel," in *Analysis of Current trends in Antisemitism*, no. 20 (Jerusalem: Hebrew University of Jerusalem, 2002).

57. Beinart, "Bad Move."

58. Ibid.

59. Descriptions taken from THOMAS.loc.gov.

# Third-Party Intervention in Ethno-Religious Conflict: Role Theory, Pakistan, and War in Kashmir, 1965

## GAURAV GHOSE AND PATRICK JAMES

### Introduction: Third-Party Intervention in Ethno-Religious Conflict

Third-party intervention in ethno-religious conflict is an old phenomenon, although scholarly attention with a general range of application is relatively new and uncommon.[1] This study will attempt, through a systematic review of religion and other factors that can impact upon foreign policy role performance, to explain Pakistan's intervention in Kashmir, which led to full-scale war in 1965.

Religion, as will become apparent through the case at hand, is a key element of ethnic identity and can play a significant role in interventionism in particular and foreign policy action in general. The position of religion within theorizing about international politics, however, is marginal.[2] While few, if any, important political events are produced purely by religion, its influence on foreign policy is threefold. Foreign policy can be influenced by "religious views and beliefs of policymakers and their constituents." Religion also can serve as a source of legitimacy for foreign policy actions recommended by both government and critics. Furthermore, religious issues can spread across borders.[3]

Empirical evidence suggests that the preceding assertions about religion and foreign policy are on target.[4] Moreover, findings from aggregate data suggest some specific connections to be pursued in this study. From research on interventions in ethnic conflicts from 1990 to 1995, Fox finds that religious affiliation makes a difference in terms of intervention by states in ongoing conflicts.[5] Religion is coded as a trichotomy: Christian, Muslim, and other. Among the 275 cases, 69.8 percent and 22.9 percent attracted political and military intervention, respectively. Two findings from this study are especially interesting. First, ethnic conflict involving groups of different religions is more likely to produce political but not military intervention.[6] Second, military intervention is much more likely to occur on behalf of Christians or Muslims. Elsewhere, analysis of the same data set reveals that religious affiliation is a statistically significant predictor of intervention by foreign governments.[7]

This study focuses on foreign policy decisions about intervention as related to religion, ethnicity, and other factors. The analysis is divided into five additional sections. The second section introduces *systemism*, a framework that brings together unit- and system-level factors. The theory of role analysis in foreign policy and its usefulness in explaining third-party, ethno-religious intervention is covered in the third section. Section four brings together systemism and role theory and elaborates linkages, with an emphasis on religion and other salient factors from the literature on foreign policy and international conflict. The fifth section presents the case study of Pakistan's intervention in India in 1965. Section six sums up the findings from the case study and offers a few observations about the contemporary situation in Kashmir.

## Systemism: A Framework for Analysis

How can factors at multiple levels be connected to create an overall framework for analysis? *Systemism* provides the answer through a commitment to understanding a system in terms of a comprehensive set of functional relationships. In international relations, the set of relationships reveals the connections between and among international (system-level) and domestic (unit-level) factors.[8]

Figure 1 presents Bunge's framework of systemism; specifically, it shows the functional relations in a social system.[9] The figure traces the full range of effects that might be encountered in any such system, which includes both micro- and macro-factors. (Uppercase and lowercase letters in the figure refer to macro- and micro-level factors, respectively.) The logically possible connections are micro-micro, micro-macro, macro-macro, and macro-micro.

Macro entities may impact upon each other, as in the case of X affecting Y, with the functional form represented by F. For example, if the system is defined as South Asia, X might refer to the balance of power between India and Pakistan, with Y as their propensity to go to war.[10] Connections also are found at the micro-level, as in the case of x impacting upon y through function f. In this instance, x could represent the level of repression by the Indian government against the Muslim minority in Kashmir, with y as the amount of protest or rebellion in the region (and this linkage, of course, also could be from y to x). Systemism therefore allows for *both* micro-micro and macro-macro connections. Furthermore, systemism recognizes that effects also can move *across* levels. Thus the macro-micro linkage of X to x through function g also appears in the figure, as does the micro-macro connection from y to Y on the basis of function h. To continue with the example, X to x might focus on how the balance of power affects India's level of repression in Kashmir, with y to Y referring to the impact of protest and rebellion in Kashmir on the likelihood of war between India and Pakistan. To complete the stylized example, the external environment might come into play with outside powers becoming involved in the Indo-Pakistani conflict as a result of one or more of the preceding connections.

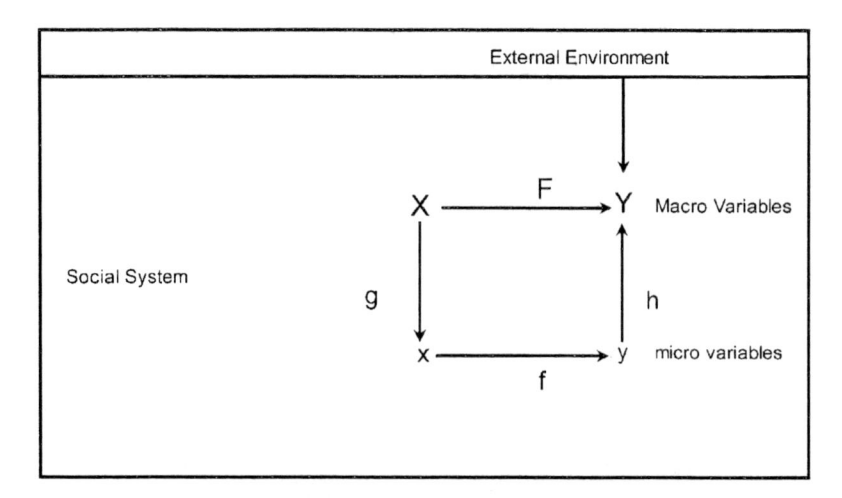

**Figure 1.** Systemism's functional relations in a social system. Source: Mario Bunge, *Finding Philosophy in Social Science* (New Haven: Yale University Press, 1996), 149.

Systemism, in short, demands that a theory tell the "full tale" of units and systems, which includes the four kinds of linkages, along with the effects of the external system. Thus, by utilizing systemism, this study seeks to unify unit- and system-level factors with those at the external level to account for third-party ethno-religious interventionism as a foreign policy decision.

## The Value of Role Theory in Explaining Ethno-Religious Interventionism

Role theory can be used to explain foreign policy decisions and outcomes by connecting different levels and units and, in the process, providing a unified analysis. Such movement across levels and units consists of a

> judicious mix of three elements: first, a richly multidimensional delineation of *role*...; second, self-conscious flexibility in assigning alternating functions to independent, dependent and intervening variables...; and third, key determinants of decision making... that are so defined so as to generate linkages between familiar abstract categories of factors—for example, personal, organizational, social, cultural traits;... the nature of the political system; and the external environment.[11]

Walker identifies three reasons for utilizing role analysis in understanding foreign policy: descriptive, organizational, and explanatory.[12] Descriptively, role theory provides varied images of foreign policy behavior that depend on the focus of analysis: systemic, national, or individual. Besides this multilevel advantage, role theory extends the scope of analysis by moving beyond the narrow confines of looking at a "continuum of cooperative and conflictual behavior."[13] Organizationally, it can help explain behavior either in terms of structure or process. Finally, the explanatory value of role analysis depends on whether "its concepts are theoretically informed (a) by an appropriate set of self-contained propositions and methods, or (b) by the specification of an appropriate set of auxiliary limiting conditions and rules linking these conditions with the role concepts."[14]

This study of ethno-religious interventionism as a foreign policy decision is informed by role theory, which offers a wide range of advantages.[15] *The goal is to account for the decision by one state to intervene in an ongoing ethno-religious conflict of another state.* A part of Holsti's concept of "role performance"—which encompasses the attitudes, decisions, and actions the national government takes to implement its self-defined "national role conceptions" or "role prescriptions" that emanate from the external environment—can be used to explain foreign policy decisions and actions. Thus, instead of defining role performance as a way to implement role conception or role prescription[16] we utilize Rosenau's concept of "role expectation," which can encompass factors from both domestic and external levels.[17] Role expectation, which can emanate in a contradictory way from respective levels, is a concept that helps to bridge the gap between national role conception and role prescription.

Conflicting role expectations have domestic and international sources that produce role performance. Rosenau refers specifically to the number of roles in the range of systems that decision makers occupy.[18] These leaders thereby become subject to conflicting role expectations:

> those that derive from the private systems in which they are or previously were members, from the government institutions in which their policy

making is located, from the society in which they make policy, and from the international systems in which their society is a sub-system *as well as* the expectations to which they are exposed in their top-level, face to face decision making unit. (emphasis in original)

Thus, in the context of role theory, an effective foreign policy "is one that not only protects or achieves its goals but also meets the expectations and demands of others in the situation. Although this set of criteria is *ipso facto* more difficult to satisfy, it is our contention that these norms are precisely what participants in foreign policy essentially strive to meet."[19] It almost goes without saying that the anticipated range of expectations for different levels is consistent with the frame of reference put forward via systemism in the preceding section.

National decision makers are faced with multiple role expectations that come simultaneously from the international (i.e., regional subsystem and external system) and domestic levels. Depending on the nature of domestic politics and influence from subsystem-level factors, either ordering or merging of role expectations can be expected to take place.[20] Thus role performance with regard to involvement as a third party in an ethno-religious or ethnic conflict will reflect the interaction of factors from the external, regional, and domestic levels.

Given the nature of international politics, with interactions between and among factors at different levels influencing foreign policy decisions and actions, the role performance of an intervener in a situation such as Pakistan's 1965 intervention inKashmir should be judged in terms of resolving role differences arising out of conflicting role expectations, which refer to the cues that emerge from various levels enumerated by systemism.

## Systemism and Role Theory

While many factors might be introduced in an explanation of foreign policy role performance, several emerge as salient for a comparative analysis with religion. Sustained research findings about the balance of power, international organizations, religious affiliations, domestic institutional constraints, ethnic diversity and domination, national leadership, and historical analogies in relation to foreign policy decision making and international conflict make these the priorities for inclusion.[21]

Systemism in application begins with the effects of the external environment. Both instrumental factors (such as the balance of power and international organizations) and affective factors (like religious affiliations) must be considered in accounting for foreign policy role performance. These same factors also need to be addressed at the regional level. Finally, domestic sources of a state's role expectation are most elaborate and also include both affective and instrumental factors. While institutional constraints[22] are instrumental, ethnic domination and diversity, as well as religious affiliations, are affective. Two other factors are hybrids that contain both instrumental and effective elements: national leadership[23] and historical analogies.[24] These domestic factors influence the national government's forming of role expectations, which in turn impact upon its role performance.

The international balance of power is the traditional starting point for the explanation of foreign policy. Relations between and among major powers and their effective presence generate expectations for other states.[25] Attributes of the external system and alterations in them are important in accounting for changes in role expectations of states at the regional level. This becomes evident if we compare the cold war and post-cold war periods. With the Soviet Union gone as the balancer, role expectations of states have undergone a dramatic change vis-à-vis the United States and other powers, including Russia.

The external environment also includes international organizations, which can generate a different kind of role expectation for a state. Russett and Oneal argue that international organizations can contribute to cycles of peace and reduce the likelihood of conflict.[26] The importance of international organizations and institutions lies in their "teaching" a set of norms and thereby helping to revise states' conceptions of power. In particular, Russett and Oneal argue that a multilateral rather than unilateral approach to global issues on the part of the United States would be more beneficial and better for world peace.[27] In this case, where the virtues of multilateralism are being emphasized, we can cite the example of the United Nations (UN), whose members are expected to adhere to the charter and principles therein. Thus, in cases of conflict, the UN could call for restraint and even vote against third-party intervention, leading to a different role expectation for the intervening state. The cues sent by the UN can be expected to influence smaller states more than larger ones and its presence provides at least some hope for peaceful management and resolution of conflict.

Linkages within the external environment also are worth noting. The most salient link, immediately following our discussion of the role expectations generated by an international organization like the UN, is the one between the balance of power and the functioning of international organizations. Cooperation with, or opposition to, a UN resolution is affected by power "equations" and the existing structure of the international system, which consists of the great powers with, again, a notable difference between the cold war and post-cold war periods. Thus we should not consider the influence of an international organization on a state's role expectation in isolation from the existing balance of power.

Religious affiliations from the external environment can be anticipated to shape the national government's role expectations. If one or more external actors should happen to share the religion of the presumed target of intervention, that might cause the potential intervening state from within the region to give pause for one of two reasons. First, if the possible intervention by a great power from outside the region is expected to be in a preferred direction (i.e., in favor of ethnic brethren), it could cause a "free rider" effect.[28] Action by the great power would be preferred because of greater resources and a higher probability of success, along with removing the need by the present state to absorb any costs from involvement. If, by contrast, the outside intervener would be coming in against ethnic brethren, that also could serve to discourage intervention because then the conflict would include a high-capability (and possibly overwhelming) adversary. Either way, indifference from the external environment would tend, all other things being equal, to encourage role expectations that entail intervention.

With regard to the regional subsystem, the factors parallel those from the external environment—but with a regional rather than global/international dimension. The regional balance of power[29] is expected to elicit one kind of role expectation that would assume significance in an emerging scenario of third-party ethnic intervention. In fact, a dominant state at the top of a regional hierarchy can assume much more importance than interactions among great powers in the external environment.[30] Lemke's "multiple hierarchy model" entails multiple, smaller "pyramids" within the international hierarchy of power: "They are local/regional systems or subhierarchies. ...These local hierarchies are often geographically small. They encapsulate local relations between geographically proximate states."[31] In addition, "structure in a subsystem would...be defined by the distribution of power between its parts and the relations that subsist between them."[32] The structure of the regional subsystem and interaction of its units will influence role expectations of states within that structure.[33]

Next come regional organizations. Regional organizations are formed with a view toward cooperation in the interests (mostly toward economic and cultural integration, but in some cases strategic) of the participating states of the region concerned while respecting the sovereignty of the member countries. On issues of conflict and intervention, strategies and tactics of regional organizations like the North Atlantic Treaty Organization (NATO) (during the cold war) have reflected superpower rivalry. NATO's involvement and continuous dialogue and negotiation with Turkey on the issue of Cyprus throughout the 1960s represents a significant instance of a regional organization's role in preventing overt intervention.

As pointed out at the level of the external environment (i.e., the case of the UN), here also the effectiveness of the regional grouping is constrained by the regional balance of power. The region's dominant power would seem to have leeway on many of the controversial decisions, such as intervention. India in South Asia is acknowledged as a hegemonic power for its sheer size and economic and military power; it dwarfs the other countries that comprise the regional grouping. So when India decides to intervene, a regional organization such as South Asian Association of Regional Cooperation (SAARC) generally will have to watch as a bystander.[34]

Religious affiliations within South Asia would be anticipated to follow the same logic as they do at the external level with respect to other states that are friendly to religious brethren, but with a reversal of effect otherwise. If another state in the region might intervene on behalf of religious brethren, the above-noted idea of the free rider once again becomes relevant. In other words, why make the effort if another government might do so instead? Possible intervention against religious brethren, however, does not automatically discourage action by the national government because interveners from within the region are not necessarily great powers. Instead, power balancing might be anticipated to take place, with the national government responding to—or possibly even seeking to head off—an intervention against those who share its religion.

Institutional constraints refer to the underlying patterns of domestic institutions, namely, the political and constitutional structure of the state, which are major determinants of elite policy making. Thus institutionalization can be considered in terms of low constraints whereby the power of the elites does not depend on support from the population at large. States in which elite decision making is unconstrained by popular opinion or constituent interests include military dictatorships, one-party totalitarian and authoritarian regimes, and revolutionary republics and monarchies. By contrast, high constraint states are those where leaders are directly accountable to the people and their fate depends on regular elections. Legislative and electoral politics are the arenas in a federal system that form the basis of a relationship between elites and masses and constrain elites.[35] Role expectations will vary with the degree of institutional constraint imposed on the leadership.

Historical analogies refer to the policy makers' developing role expectations based on understanding the present by looking at the past. Analogies with the past

"(1) help define the nature of the situation confronting the policy maker, (2) help assess the stakes, and (3) provide prescriptions. They help evaluate alternative options by (4) predicting their chances of success, (5) evaluating their moral rightness, and (6) warning about dangers associated with the options."[36] Analogies, of course, also can be used poorly, resulting in harmful role expectations.

National leadership refers to the personal characteristics of political leaders and a few other high-level policy makers who affect foreign policy. It is possible that, depending on the quality of the national leadership, conflicting role expectations can be reconciled favorably. Decisiveness and aggressive style can result in a more interventionist policy. The cultural background of policy makers can influence resolution in favor of one over others. Similarly, relations among the top leaders are crucial in decision making—one domineering individual can set the tone and others can simply follow.

Ethnic composition in terms of whether the state is dominated by a single ethnic group or diverse ethnic groups is a crucial source in generating one kind of role expectation. Whether a single ethnic group enjoys political control over the state or various ethnic groups are equally important will affect how elites behave in framing policies. In the former case, elites appeal to their ethnic constituency and virtually all policies are made in favor of the dominant ethnic group, even when the issues are of marginal interest to them. In ethnically diverse states, leaders appeal to more than one ethnic group and see support from multiple ethnic identities. Policies, in this case, reflect interethnic compromise.[37]

Finally, religious affiliations within a state can be expected to influence its propensity toward intervention. If a conflict includes religious differences, and there is an affiliation with one or more of the groups involved, intervention becomes more likely. Furthermore, the specific religions involved become important as well. If the intervening state is Muslim or Christian, and either of those groups is involved in the conflict elsewhere within the region, then that is the most likely scenario for intervention.[38] In a more general sense, the content of a religion as an *ideology* is worth attention, as well, because it may affect foreign policy choices in specific ways. Religion, for example, may be used as source of legitimacy for one course of action or another.[39] Free rider effects, as noted above, are less relevant because pressure to act comes from within society and cannot be satisfied in the same way by actions from another state. In other words, ethno-religious mobilization in favor of interventionism concentrates on what the national government itself is doing—it must be seen as acting in some way and cannot risk inaction when the pressure becomes intense.

## Ethno-Religious Intervention in South Asia: The Case of Kashmir

Like the first war over Kashmir in 1947–48, the second, in August and September of 1965 (code-named Operation Gibraltar) involved a fully armed and militarily trained force of infiltrators that, according to the plan, would enter clandestinely into the valley in small groups, cross the border in the first week of August, and stir up a popular uprising among the presumably disaffected Kashmiri people.[40] Pakistan's planning reflected confidence derived from a relatively successful show of strength against Indian forces during a clash in April 1965 in the Rann of Kutch, a barren area bordering the western state of Gujarat. This led Pakistani policy makers and military strategists to conclude that the time was ripe to strike Kashmir and resolve the dispute once and for all—a calculation based on Pakistan's "fundamentally flawed inference"[41] that India, still believed to be reeling under the disastrous impact of the 1962 Indo-China clash, would be unprepared and therefore unable to fight a full-fledged war.

Pakistan's leaders also believed that Kashmiris were clamoring for an end to their subjugation under Indian rule. Several developments supported that belief: (a) continuous unrest in the valley, which broke out for various reasons (including the arrest of their ruler, Sheikh Abdullah); (b) theft of a sacred relic, the hair of the Prophet, from the Hazaratbal shrine in Srinagar; and (c) attempts by the central government of India to erode the autonomy of Kashmir, which had been granted earlier by a special provision under the constitution, by integrating it within the Indian union (like any other Indian state) through certain constitutional measures. Anti-India demonstrations by the Kashmiris because of the preceding reasons caused Pakistan's leaders to infer, again incorrectly, that these events showed support for Pakistan and even Pakistani intervention.[42] Finally, Pakistan did not see anything coming out of attempts by the United States and United Kingdom to pressure India to resolve the dispute. Karachi saw the Indian leadership as adamant because it steadfastly resisted suggestions coming from the Western powers. Pakistan also looked upon the UN as ineffective. The world body had hoped to use a plebiscite to force India into a settlement at the end of the hostilities that broke out immediately after independence and partition in 1947–48. This did not succeed.

Things did not turn out as Pakistan had hoped. The military conflict ended inconclusively, only to be followed by a UN call for an end to hostilities. By September 22, both sides accepted a cease-fire and the war came to an end. The United States showed no interest in helping the two adversaries reach an amicable postwar settlement, but the Soviet Union stepped in and—on January 10, 1966, in Tashkent—Pakistan and India agreed to withdraw their forces to the *status quo ante*, i.e, to positions held prior to August 5, 1965. Both sides also agreed to abstain from using force in settling outstanding disputes. Finally, India gave up certain strategic areas—Haji Pir and Tithwal significant among them—and Pakistan did the same, giving up some of the territories it had gained in the conflict.[43]

We now move on to an analysis of Pakistan's intervention in Kashmir from a systemist point of view informed by role theory. All three types of factors—from the external system, regional subsystem, and domestic level—are useful in generating Pakistan's role expectations and subsequent involvement in Kashmir for a second time. Moreover, religion is significant, both alone and in combination, with factors at the latter two levels. Analysis begins at the highest level of aggregation and moves downward to completion.

Changing behavior of the major powers in the international system affected Pakistan's attitude and, in turn, the course of the intervention. U.S. policy toward India in the 1950 s and early 1960 s affected Pakistan's foreign policy behavior. In the immediate context of the regional subsystem, great powers like India and China also influenced the role expectations and role performance of Pakistan.

The international balance of power moved in a favorable direction for Pakistan when Ayub Khan came to power. He immediately assured Western allies, the United States and United Kingdom in particular, that Pakistan remained committed to the Southeast Asian Treaty Organization (SEATO) and Central Treaty Organization (CENTO) or Baghdad pact regional pacts. In March 1959, Pakistan and the United States signed an agreement of cooperation for security and defense.

Things began to change in the 1960s, as Ziring points out:

Pakistan's relevance to United States policy began to erode in the sixties due to a number of developments in the international system which included the advent of reconnaissance satellites and ICBMs that reduced the importance of American bases in Pakistan and elsewhere, the Sino-Soviet split, and the Sino-Indian border conflict, 1962. The United States began to manifest some fascination for nonalignment and decided to strengthen India's security to counterbalance China. This was bound to evoke the displeasure of, and protest from, Pakistan which felt the United States was pursuing policies which adversely affected an ally, i.e. Pakistan.[44]

More specifically, with John F. Kennedy's election as president of the United States in 1960, things took a new turn affecting Pakistan's relations with the United States, China and, of course, India. Kennedy's election ushered in a new era in Indo–U.S. relations. To cement closer ties with India, the United States brought in a series of amendments to the United States Mutual Security Act to facilitate the flow of arms to neutrals like India, causing anxiety and heartburn in Pakistan.[45] By 1962, India had signed the first of what became a series of military agreements with the Soviet Union. Moreover, the Sino-Indian conflict of 1962 saw the United States rush huge amounts of arms as aid to India.

Pakistan reacted by voicing genuine concerns about a military imbalance in the region that had tilted the scales substantially in favor of India. Appalled at the behavior of its Western allies, Pakistan moved closer to China and hoped to receive its assistance in the event of any act of aggression against her.[46] Consider the notable trends in Pakistan's foreign policy: "continued friendship towards aid-giving West, with political reservation; normalization of relations with the Soviet Union and friendly attitude toward China; and cultivating friendship with Afro-Asian countries."[47]

Amid these changes in the external environment, the United States and United Kingdom tried to resolve the Kashmir dispute by prodding the adversaries into a dialogue. In December 1962, an Anglo-American mission led by Duncan Sandys of Britain and Averell Harriman of the United States visited New Delhi and then Islamabad. These visits persuaded the governments to start talking to each other about Kashmir. A series of talks, held subsequently in various cities of both countries, produced inconclusive results.[48]

With respect to international organizations, the UN remained deadlocked on the issue. In fact, Khan vented his frustration over the UN's inability to conduct the plebiscite as promised after the first war in 1947–48 and saw no point in appealing to the world body. This factor later influenced his calculations about intervening in Kashmir.[49]

Religious affiliations at the external level, or the influence of the great powers sharing the religion of the presumed target of intervention, might lead the intervening state to pause and reconsider its decision. No such factor based on religious affiliations operated in this case; the great powers did not have any religious interest in the Indo-Pakistani conflict. Instead, the Christian great powers witnessed a Muslim state targeting a Hindu state's Muslim population in an irredentist conflict.

At the regional subsystem level, the two major powers of South Asia are India and Pakistan. The regional balance of power did not present a clear picture in 1965, fifteen to eighteen years after both countries achieved independence. Although India could be placed on top because of its sheer size, the Indo-China War of 1962 had dented India's reputation as the dominant regional power. In fact, defeat in that war, as noted above, formed the fundamental basis of Khan's "flawed inference" of underestimating India's defense preparations. Tension continued to build.[50]

Religious affiliations at the regional subsystem level did not influence events; a single state, Pakistan, shared religious beliefs with the Muslims of Kashmir. Hence the free rider aspect for other states in South Asia (e.g., Sri Lanka, Bhutan, Nepal, Maldives) did not play a part here.

Islam's relationship to foreign policy in general terms, however, came through most directly in Pakistan's efforts toward forging close ties with Muslim states outside South Asia. At least in principle, Pakistan extended support to the cause of Muslims anywhere in the world, including the anticolonial struggles of Indonesia, Tunisia, Morocco, and Algeria. This foreign policy reinforces the general conclusion that, for Islam, there is no separation of religion and politics.[51] In the 1950s, Pakistan tried to form a platform bringing all Muslim nations together but became discouraged because other Muslim states (a) did not see Islam playing such a strategic role in their nationalist movements and (b) suspected that Pakistan aspired to leadership of the Muslim world.

Domestic role expectations reveal important effects. To begin with, Pakistan had low institutional constraints during the Khan era, a fallout from developments a few years after Pakistan was born. The Muslim League, the vanguard party that led the freedom struggle, failed to develop into a national party like the Congress Party in India. Internal dissension, along with a national and federal leadership unwilling to hold elections, led to fragmentation and a decline in the political institutions. Leaders showed scant respect for democratic institutions and parliamentary principles and conventions; they compromised their positions in asserting a leadership role. In the process, the bureaucratic-military elite came to dominate policy making and gained the upper hand, leading finally to the bloodless coup of 1958 when Khan, the commander in chief of the army, captured power.[52]

Khan promulgated a new constitution in 1962, which at first did not allow political parties to come into being. As pressure mounted for the revival of political parties, he enacted the Political Parties Act in July 1962, "which legalized the formation and functioning of the political parties with a proviso that these could neither advocate anything prejudicial to the Islamic ideology, integrity and security of Pakistan nor accept financial assistance from, or affiliate with, any foreign government or foreign agency."[53]

Under Khan, however, the system remained top heavy, with a concentration of power in the hands of the president. The bureaucracy served as the linchpin of the new setup. Khan employed a "carrot and stick" policy to dissuade political opponents from undermining political arrangements and imposed strong pressures on the dissenting press. The "organizational weaknesses and internal feuds" of opposition parties helped Khan in the aggrandizement of his powers, which saw him sweep the presidential polls at both the national and provincial levels in 1965. Thus, under such low institutional constraints, the bureaucratic-military elite had virtually complete freedom to decide on an intervention.[54]

Except for harking back to the previous failed attempt of 1947–48 to annex Kashmir, Pakistan—being a young state—had no obvious historical analogies to fall back upon. This source of role expectations is more significant for states with histories that include interventions, both failed and successful. Interestingly enough, however, we might see the strategy adopted the second time to be very similar to the one in the first instance, although at this time it had not been designed consciously by the Pakistani foreign and defense establishment. The strategy once again involved clandestine entry into the valley in small groups, with a shift to fully armed and militarily trained infiltrators.

National leadership, confined mainly to Khan and his foreign minister Zulfiquar Ali Bhutto, assumed considerable significance as a source of foreign policy role expectations and, in turn, performance. The importance of Khan in Pakistan's politics during this period led many commentators to term it as the "Ayub Khan era." Both subjective and objective factors are involved in determining leadership.

While not denying the role Islam had played in the founding of Pakistan as a separate state, Mohammad Ali Jinnah—the founder—favored a secular state. Jinnah's successors, however, failed to implement his vision and saw Pakistan's identity as an Islamic state. Although not a theocracy, all of Pakistan's constitutions (in varying degrees) have enshrined Islamic ideology as the basis of the state.[55] As a modernist, Khan tried to distance himself from orthodox Muslims. However, following the model of his Muslim League predecessors, he could not avoid upholding "the Islamic heritage of the Pakistani state." At the beginning of his rule, Khan tried to be secular, but it became difficult to keep the religious forces at bay. The constitution of 1962 had dropped "Islamic" from the "Republic of Pakistan," which had been there since the 1956 constitution. Within a year, however, fundamentalists forced Khan to reinstate that word. However, Khan never entered into an alliance with religious leaders and tried to maintain some distance from orthodox elements.

Khan, in a sense, did engage in limited political use of Islam. For example, he "seldom used the expression 'Holy Quran and Sunna' and preferred to use instead expressions such as 'basic principles of Islam' or 'the essence of Islam'."[57] In fact, the theme of Islamic nationalism is writ large in Khan's autobiography, *Friends Not Masters*.[58] "'There are,' he [Khan] had once told a Pakistani audience, 'other Muslim countries, if they leave Islam they can still exist, but if we leave Islam, we cannot exist. Our foundation is Islam.'"[59]

During Khan's era, the practical impact of Pakistani nationalism based on an Islamic ideology became multifaceted and significant. At least three components are in evidence:

> One in consonance with ideology, the sovereignty of the state rests with *Allah*, God, rather than with the people. As the minorities are not members of Millat (Islamic brotherhood) they cannot be entrusted with the power to propound and execute state policy at the highest level....
>
> Two, conversely, the Muslims inside Pakistan and across the border in India, in view of Pakistani leaders, form one nation, though citizens of two states, Pakistan and India. Pakistan, therefore, still considers the Muslims across the borders as her special responsibility and preserve. To deny that is to deny the two-nation theory and the need to create Pakistan itself. It is here that the attitude towards India crystallises itself....
>
> Three, because of its ideology, the fibre of Pakistani nationalism is very weak and Pakistan still feels psychologically insecure. The existence of a strong, powerful India in the neighbourhood further accentuates this sense of insecurity. Hence the security of Pakistan constitutes one of the chief motivating factors in the formulation of Pakistan.[60]

The views of Zulfiquar Ali Bhutto, foreign minister during the Khan regime, are informative here and point to the zeal of Bhutto in particular to pursue an aggressive foreign policy:

> If a Muslim majority can remain a part of India, then the *raison d'etre* of Pakistan collapses. These are the reasons why India, to continue her domination of Jammu and Kashmir, defies international opinion and violates her pledges. For the same reasons, Pakistan must unremittingly continue her struggle for the right of self-determination of this subject people. *Pakistan is incomplete without Jammu and Kashmir both territorially and ideologically.* It would be fatal if, in sheer exhaustion or intimidation, Pakistan were to abandon the struggle, and a bad compromise would be tantamount to abandonment; which might in turn lead to the collapse of Pakistan (emphasis added by Ganguly).[61]

Bhutto's words—then as part of the national leadership and later as prime minister of Pakistan—show a depth of commitment. Standard scholarly treatments also connect the survival of Pakistan to Islamic identity.[62]

If not Khan, Bhutto, at least at that point saw the unfinished task of adding Kashmir to Pakistan through the prism of religion. Here religion is used by the leaders as the basis of Pakistani nationalist identity. The national leadership thus generates role expectations that derive from their values and interaction with societal forces.

Ethnic domination and diversity is not as significant as religious affiliation as a source for role expectations. *The irredentist claim on Pakistan was religious and not ethnic.* Ethnicity had a tangential effect; the decision to intervene in 1965 was aided by a bureaucracy dominated by a single ethnic group. During the initial years of Pakistan, Mohajirs (refugees who came from India) predominated in the government and bureaucratic leadership. Within a decade, however, the domination of a single ethnic group—the Punjabis—came to be the defining feature of Pakistani politics, bureaucracy, and military leadership. Thus, decision making bodies comprised overwhelmingly of a single ethnic group made the task of formulating and implementing policies of intervention easier, with no significant opposition.

Religious affiliations at the domestic level for Pakistan are separate and distinct from ethnicity. This becomes obvious with regard to India in general and Kashmir in particular. The two concepts are distinct—a point established by recent research[63]—although scholars sometimes have placed identity and cultural attributes under the umbrella of ethnic identity.[64] We will elaborate on this distinction in explaining how religious affiliation stands out as tied overwhelmingly to Pakistan's identity and survival. As will become apparent, religious affiliation is an important dimension of Pakistan's foreign policy orientation, both with regard to India and Kashmir.

With regard to religious affiliations, the propensity to intervene in Kashmir was based on Pakistan having an affiliation with the Kashmiris, specifically, the majority Muslims of the state, based on a shared religion. Pakistan's very birth was based on a "two-nation" theory, which put forward the view that Hindus and Muslims constitute two separate nations and hence need to be divided from each other. The Muslim League, the party formed during the freedom struggle to realize such a goal, voiced fears of being crushed under the domination of the Hindu majority and, based on Islamic nationalism, demanded a separate "Pakistan" at the time of independence from Britain. The League's rival, the Congress Party, opposed that view and saw India as a secular entity. Thus, from the moment the two nations achieved their independence after the partition of India, they became rivals in terms of ideological moorings, which provided an identity to each.

Geographic and demographic realities caused Pakistan to view its claim on Kashmir—a Muslim-majority province—as legitimate. The claim became more vehement because of its irredentist nature.[65] Based on Weiner's definition of irredentism, which is "the desire on the part of a state to revise some portion of its international boundaries to incorporate the ethnic/religious/linguistic minority of a contiguous state and the territory that it occupies," Ganguly regards Pakistan's claim as that type.[66] The territory of Kashmir was not merely contiguous to Pakistan; it also had a Muslim-majority population. From Pakistan's point of view, "Kashmir needed to be incorporated into Pakistan to ensure its 'completeness.'"[67] Thus we see that the role of religion—that is, Islam—is central in Pakistani politics. Religious affiliation matters enormously because of *religious ideology*. This underscores the importance of religious affiliations in Pakistan's foreign policy performance, most notably as related to Kashmir.

Although religion served as an overarching factor in defining Pakistan's identity and foreign policy, in particular on the question of Kashmir, multi-ethnic identities within Pakistan threatened its would-be Islamic unity. The Pathans bordering Afghanistan clamored for an independent Pakhtunistan on one side and the eastern wing of Pakistan also posed a threat to the very integrity of Pakistan and, in 1971, became Bangladesh. Muslims of east Pakistan, separated from the west by about one thousand miles of Indian territory, were not considered as "good" Muslims or a safe bet for the ideology of the state coming into being as Pakistan. It was thought that Bengalis remained under the Hindu cultural and linguistic influence (most being converts from Hinduism).[68] Khan's military coup in 1958 eliminated the Bengalis from the ruling hierarchy of Pakistan.

## Conclusions

This study has used role theory in its explanatory form to account for third-party intervention in ethno-religious conflict. A theoretical framework, built in terms recommended by systemism, organizes instrumental and affective factors from the international environment, regional subsystem, and within the state as actor toward that end. The case study of Pakistan's invasion of Kashmir in 1965 has been used to assess the value of the framework in explaining foreign policy role performance.

External, regional, and domestic factors, as expected, all contribute to foreign policy role expectations and performance for Pakistan. Some factors in each category are more salient than others in the case of Kashmir—this type of diversity in cause and effect, however, is no surprise at all.

At the external level, no clear balance of power advantage accrued to either India or Pakistan as a result of preferences among the major powers. In particular, the United States had been sending what appeared to be mixed (or perhaps balanced) signals to the principal adversaries. With the UN deadlocked and religion irrelevant in this global context, the external factors combined to form what Pakistan perceived to be permissive conditions for its intervention in Kashmir.

Regional factors also tended to favor intervention. India and Pakistan stood in an apparently more equal power relationship after the former had experienced disaster in war against China a few years earlier. With no regional organization on hand to dampen conflict, and Pakistan disposed toward obtaining credit beyond the region for its support of Islam in Kashmir, once again conditions pointed toward intervention.

Domestic conditions turned out to be either neutral or favorable to intervention as well. Pakistan featured low institutional constraints and had no discouraging war-related analogies upon which to draw. Its leadership, most notably Khan and Bhutto, showed a strong connection to an Islamic ideology that emphasized irredentism vis-à-vis Kashmir. Ethnicity, the last of the domestic factors considered here, played no apparent role in the decision to intervene.

All things considered, it is possible to draw three general conclusions from the preceding summary of factors. First, as systemism would suggest, a foreign policy action such as third-party intervention in an ethno-religious conflict naturally will require a comprehensive explanation that brings in factors from across levels of aggregation. Second, religion—both on its own and in combination with other factors such as leadership—played an important part in creating a foreign policy role expectation and performance that emphasized retrieval of land occupied by Islamic brethren. Moreover, religion's role here is twofold, both in terms of a basic sense of affiliation and via Islam, an ideology that promoted such action. Third, and somewhat contrary to the last point, religion is excluded from at least some important causal aspects. More specifically, religion does not play a role at the external system level in the particular case of Kashmir.

With regard to role theory, systemism, and further research on religion and conflict, this study is just a starting point. Two priorities emerge for future study. First, and most obviously, Kashmir is a single case and must be recognized as more useful for theory-building than as a definitive finding. Thus comparative case studies and aggregate data analysis become natural priorities for future research. Second, the present study effectively explained an event at the regional level—the war in Kashmir—and from a systemist point of view—where things begin rather than end. A more complete treatment would have to explore a more comprehensive set of linkages, with the causal arrow pointing both from within the state to outside and vice versa.

Some final thoughts seem in order about the contemporary situation in Kashmir and how it relates to research findings. The natural long-term prediction, with so many factors pointing toward conflict and even military intervention, would be in the direction of continuing problems after 1965. Recent developments seem consistent with that expectation. The policy of Pakistan with respect to Kashmir in the 1990s featured a strong religious element and continuing confrontation: "Over the years the religio-political groups [in Pakistan] have become not only militant in responding toward imagined or real enemies—the 'West' or 'India'—but have also become the champions of Pakistani ideology. In this new sense Islamic sentiment in Pakistan is instrumentalized by organizing the jihad andMujahideen for Kashmir, Afghanistan and other 'Islamic causes.' "[69] One recent academic commentator refers to Pakistan's near "obsession" with retrieval of Kashmir.[70] Violent conflict over Kashmir continues to this day and includes a terrorist element that involves sponsorship from Pakistan.[71] Unfortunately, and not surprisingly, Kashmir lacks a robust civil society and militants boycott elections and urge others to do the same.[72] This does not bode well for the future, regardless of who might hold sovereignty.

Perhaps the tragic situation in Pakistan reflects larger social forces in operation today around the globe. Evidence exists that modern terrorism moves in waves, with the fourth and contemporary variant being religious in character, as opposed to preceding versions that emphasized one or more secular ideologies.[73] If this assessment is accurate—and the more than fifty thousand casualties in Kashmir since 1990[74] point in that direction—the only hope for Kashmir is the passing of time, while somehow averting the use of weapons of mass destruction by one side or the other. This is not an especially pleasant future to contemplate, but it may be the best one available.

## Notes

1. David Carment and Patrick James, "Toward a Model of Interstate Ethnic Conflict: Evidence from the Balkan War and the Indo–Sri Lankan Conflict," *Canadian Journal of Political Science* 29 (1996): 521–554. David Carment and Patrick James, eds., *Wars in the Midst of Peace: The International Politics of Ethnic Conflict* (Pittsburgh University of Pittsburgh Press, 1997); Stephen M. Saideman, "Explaining the International Relations of Secessionist Conflicts: Vulnerability Versus Ethnic Ties," *International Organization* 51 (1997): 721–753; David Carment and Patrick James, "Third-Party States in Ethnic Conflicts: Identifying the Domestic Determinants of Intervention" (paper presented at the annual meeting of the American Political Science Association, San Francisco, CA, August 2001); Stephen M. Saideman, *The Ties that Divide: Ethnic Politics, Foreign Policy, and International Conflict* (Columbia NY: Columbia University Press, 2001); Stuart J. Kaufman, *Modern Hatreds: The Symbolic Politics of Ethnic War* (Ithaca, NY: Cornell University Press, 2001); Jonathan Fox *Comparative Political Studies* (Forthcoming). "World Separation of Religion and State in the Twenty First Century" (Paper prepared for the Annual Meeting of the International Studies Association, Montreal, Canada, March 2004).

2. This point is highlighted by Jonathan Fox, "Towards a Dynamic Theory of Ethno-Religious Conflict," *Nations and Nationalism* 5, no. 4 (1999): 444; K. R. Dark, ed., *Religion and International Relations* (New York: St Martin's Press, 2000), 52; Jonathan Fox, "Religious Causes of International Intervention in Ethnic Conflicts," *International Politics* 38 (2001): 517; Jonathan Fox, "International Intervention in Middle Eastern and Islamic Conflicts from 1990 to 1995: A Large-N Study" (paper prepared for the Israeli International Studies Association Convention, February 2002), 5; Jonathan Fox, *Ethnoreligious Conflict in the Late Twentieth Century: A General Theory* (Lanham, MD: Lexington Books, 2002).

3. Fox, "Religious Causes," 54, 59.

4. Fox, "Towards a Dynamic Theory;" Jonathan Fox, "Clash of Civilizations or Clash of Religions: Which Is a More Important Determinant of Ethnic Conflict?," *Ethnicities* 1, no. 3, (2001): 295–320; Jonathan Fox, "Two Civilizations and Ethnic Conflict: Islam and the West," *Journal of Peace Research* 38, no. 4 (2001): 459–472; Jonathan Fox, "Religion as an Overlooked Element of International Relations," *International Studies Review* 3, no. 3 (2001): 53–73; Fox, "Religious Causes"; Jonathan Fox, "Civilizational, Religious, and National Explanations for Ethnic Rebellion in Post-Cold War Middle East," *Jewish Political Studies Review* 13, no. 1–2 (2001): 177–204; Jonathan Fox and Josephine Squires, "Threats to Primal Identities: A Comparison of Nationalism and Religion as Impacts on Ethnic Protest and Rebellion," *Terrorism and Political Violence* 13, no. 1 (2001): 88–102.

5. Fox, "Religious Causes," 522–523.

6. Fox, "Clash of Civilizations," 310.

7. Fox, "International Intervention."

8. Patrick James, *International Relations and Scientific Progress: Structural Realism Reconsidered* (Columbus: Ohio State University Press, 2002); Patrick James, "Systemism in International Relations: Toward a Reassessment of Realism," in *Millennial Reflections on International Studies*, ed. Michael Brecher and Frank Harvey (Ann Arbor University of Michigan Press, 2002). While systemism expresses the linkages in a *functional form* to establish whether they are monotonic or step-level, that task is left for future research.

9. Mario Bunge, *Finding Philosophy in Social Science* (New Haven: Yale University Press, 1996), 149; the presentation of systemism that follows is based primarily on James, "Systemism in International Relations," and James, *International Relations and Scientific Progress*.

10. The examples that follow are intended to show the range of possible connections within systemism rather than to advocate any specific vision of how the linkages might work in practice.

11. Stephen G. Walker, ed., *Role Theory and Foreign Policy Analysis* (Durham, NC: Duke University Press, 1987).

12. Stephen G. Walker, "Introduction," in *Role Theory and Foreign Policy Analysis*, 2–3, ed. Stephen G. Walker (Dunham, NC: Duke University Press, 1987).

13. Ibid, 2.

14. Ibid, 3.

15. K. J. Holsti, "National Role Conceptions in the Study of Foreign Policy," in *Role Theory and Foreign Policy Analysis* (Durham, NC: Duke University Press, 1987); James N. Rosenau, "Roles and Role Scenarios in Foreign Policy," in *Role Theory and Foreign Policy Analysis* (Durham, NC: Duke University Press, 1987); Walker, "Introduction"; Stephen G. Walker, "Conclusion: Role Theory and Foreign Policy Analysis: An Evaluation," in *Role Theory and Foreign Policy Analysis* (Durham, NC: Duke University Press, 1987).

16. The idea of "national role conceptions" has its limits. These conceptions include policy maker "definitions of the general kinds of decisions, commitments, rules and actions suitable to their state, and of the functions, if any, their state should perform on a continuing basis in the international system or in the subordinate regional system" (Holsti, "National Role Conceptions," 12). Furthermore, national role conceptions may be more influential than role prescriptions, although the former concept is static and offers no ideas about sources (ibid, 36).

17. Rosenau, "Roles and Role Scenarios."

18. Ibid., 46.

19. Stephen G. Walker and Sheldon W. Simon, "Role Sets and Foreign Policy Analysis in Southeast Asia," in *Role Theory and Foreign Policy Analysis* (Durham, NC: Duke University Press, 1987) 142.

20. Walker and Simon, "Role Sets and Foreign Policy," 142.

21. See notes 6, 16, 23, 25–27, and 30 for references that establish the importance of these respective factors.

22. See David Carment and Patrick James, "Internal Constraints and Interstate Ethnic Conflict: Toward a Crisis-Based Assessment of Irredentism," *Journal of Conflict Resolution* 39, no. 4 (1995).

23. To be more precise, this factor focuses exclusively on the leadership involved in foreign policy decision making, that is, the body that includes the head of state and cabinet colleagues and advisors, foreign secretary and defense secretary, ambassadors, and the heads of the armed forces, each of whom is expected to play a highly significant role in any interventionist strategy implementation.

24. Yuen Foong Khong, *Analogies at War: Korea, Munich, Dien, Bien Phu and the Vietnam Decisions of 1965* (Princeton, NJ: Princeton University Press, 1992).

25. James, *International Relations and Scientific Progress*. In a classic exposition, Waltz asserts that "the structure of a system is generated by the interactions of its principal parts" and the "units of greatest capability set the scene of action for others as well as for themselves". In other words, the great powers of the time determine international politics at the system-level: "The fates of all the states and of all the firms in a system are affected much more by the acts and the interactions of the major ones than of the minor ones.... To focus on great powers is not to lose sight of lesser ones. Concern with the latter's fate requires paying the most attention to the former.... A general theory of international politics is necessarily based on the great powers" (Kenneth N. Waltz, *Theory of International Politics* (Reading, MA: Addison-Wesley Publishing, 1979), 72–73). Gilpin reinforces that point in observing that equilibrium of the international system is maintained "if the more powerful states are satisfied with the existing territorial, political and economic arrangements" (Robert Gilpin, *War and Change in World Politics* (Cambridge: Cambridge University Press, 1981), 11).

26. Bruce M. Russett and John R. Oneal, *Triangulating Peace: Democracy, Interdependence, and International Organizations* (New York: W. W. Norton, 2001).

27. Ibid.

28. Mancur Olson, *The Logic of Collective Action: Public Goods and the Theory of Groups* (Cambridge: Harvard University Press, 1965); Todd Sandler, *Collective Action: Theory and Applications* (Ann Arbor: University of Michigan Press, 1992).

29. Douglas Lemke, *Regions of War and Peace* (Cambridge: Cambridge University Press, 2002).
30. Ibid.
31. Ibid., 49.
32. Sheton U. Kodikara, ed., *The External Compulsions of South Asian Politics* (New Delhi: Sage Publications, 1993), 18.
33. Although beyond the scope of this paper, there also are linkages to consider between the international and regional power hierarchies in terms of generating different role expectations for a state (Lemke, *Regions of War*, 51, 53).
34. Although not a part of the present study (i.e., for future research), links between the external and regional levels also can be important. For an example related to the balance of power and hierarchy, see ibid.
35. Carment and James, "Third-Party States in Ethnic Conflicts."
36. Khong, *Analogies at War*, 10.
37. Carment and James, "Third-Party States in Ethnic Conflicts," 13–14.
38. Fox, "International Intervention."
39. Jonathan Fox and Shmuel Sandler "The Question of Religion and World Politics," *Terrorism and Political Violence*, 17 (2005): 293–303.
40. Harbaksh Singh, *War Despatches: Indo-Pak Conflict, 1965* (New Delhi: Lancer International, 1991); cited in Rajesh Kadian, *The Kashmir Tangle: Issues and Options* (New Delhi: Vision Books, 1992), 130.
41. Sumit Ganguly, *Conflict Unending: India-Pakistan Tensions Since 1947* (New York: Columbia University Press, 2002), 41.
42. Ganguly, *Conflict Unending*, 41–42.
43. Ganguly, *Conflict Unending*, 45–47; Shahid Amin, *Pakistan's Foreign Policy: A Reappraisal* (Karachi: Oxford University Press, 2000), 52–56.
44. Lawrence Ziring, *The Ayub Khan Era: Politics in Pakistan, 1958–69* (New York: Syracuse University Press, 1971), 85.
45. It should be noted, however, that the United States might at times be seen as tilting toward Pakistan throughout the 1960s and 1970s, with assistance in the 1971 war over Bangladesh as one example.
46. G. W. Choudhury, *Pakistan's Relations with India, 1947–1966* (New York: Frederick A. Praeger Publishers, 1968), 252–266.
47. Ibid., 273.
48. Ganguly, *Conflict Unending*, 32–35.
49. No regional organization, such as SAARC, existed as a potential influence on both India and Pakistan in 1965. Hence no role expectations emerged from this direction.
50. Ayub Khan and Jawaharlal Nehru previously had resolved a number of issues, such as signing the Indus water treaty. Khan had tried to settle differences with India in 1959 when he suggested a joint defense regime for the subcontinent. Nehru turned down that offer.
51. Fox, "Civilizational, Religious, and National Explanations."
52. Hasan Askari Rizvi, *Military, State and Society in Pakistan* (UK: St Martin's Press, 2000), 4–5.
53. Ibid., 113.
54. Ibid., 113–117.
55. Ganguly, *Conflict Unending*, 5; Norman D. Palmer, Pakistan: *The Long Search for Foreign Policy*, Duke University Center for Commonwealth and Comparative Studies series, no. 43 (Durham, NC: Duke University, Press, 1977), 418.
56. Partha S. Ghosh, *Conflict and Cooperation in South Asia* (New Delhi: Manohar, 1995), 22.
57. Ghosh, *Conflict and Cooperation*, 22.
58. Ayub Khan, *Friends Not Masters* (London: Oxford University Press, 1966); see Sangat Singh, *Pakistan's Foreign Policy: An Appraisal* (New York: Asia Publishing House, 1970), 12.
59. Freeland Abbott, *Islam and Pakistan* (Ithaca, NY: Cornell University Press, 1968), 223–26; cited in Ghosh, *Conflict and Cooperation*, 23.
60. Singh, *Pakistan's Foreign Policy*, 13, 14.
61. Zulfiquar Ali Bhutto, *The Myth of Independence* (London: Oxford University Press, 1969); cited in Ganguly, *Conflict Unending*, 32.
62. Stephen Phillip Cohen, "Identity, Survival and Security: Pakistan's Defense Policy,"

in *Perspectives on Pakistan's Foreign Policy*, ed. Surendra Chopra (Amritsar, India: Guru Nanak Dev University Press, 1983).

63. Fox, "Towards a Dynamic Theory."

64. Donald Horowitz, *Ethnic Groups in Conflict* (Berkeley: University of California Press, 1985).

65. Sumit Ganguly, *The Origins of War in South Asia: Indo-Pakistani Conflicts Since 1947* (Boulder, CO: Westview Press, 1986), 13.

66. Myron Weiner, "The Macedonian Syndrome," *World Politics*, 23: 665–683; Ganguly, *The Origins of War*, 11.

67. Ganguly, *The Origins of War*, 11.

68. Singh, *Pakistan's Foreign Policy*, 19–20.

69. Saee Shafqat, "From Official Islam to Islamism: The Rise of Dawat-ul-Irshad and Lashkar-e-Taiba," in *Pakistan: Nationalism without a Nation?*, ed. Christophe Jaffrelot (London: Zed Books, 2002), 133.

70. Paul Wallace, "Countering Terrorist Movements in India: Kashmir & Khalistan," (Columbia, MO: University of Missouri, 2004), 7.

71. Paul Wallace, "Globalization of Civil-Military Relations: Democratization, Reform and Security" (paper presented at the International Political Studies Association, Bucharest, Romania, June 27–July 3 2002).

72. Paul Wallace, "Introduction: The New National Party System and State Politics," in *India's 1999 Elections and 20th Century Politics*, ed. Paul Wallace and Ramashray Roy (New Delhi: Sage Publications, 2003), 20.

73. David C. Rapoport, "The Four Waves of Modern Terrorism," in *Attacking Terrorism: Elements of a Grand Strategy*, ed. Audrey Kurth Cronin and James M. Ludes (Washington DC: Georgetown University Press, 2004), 61–62, 67.

74. Rapoport, "The Four Waves," 62.

# Religion as a Factor in Ethnic Conflict: Kashmir and Indian Foreign Policy

## CAROLYN C. JAMES AND ÖZGÜR ÖZDAMAR

**Introduction**

Ethnic conflicts with a strong religious component do not only have domestic or foreign causes and consequences. As a result, internationalization of ethnic conflict has become an important subject of inquiry both in terms of pure research and policy-oriented studies. In this paper, India's foreign policy related to Kashmir will be analyzed within the context of religion. The aim of this study is to apply a foreign policy approach that simultaneously incorporates domestic and external factors in an analysis of how and in what ways religious elements of the Kashmir question affect India's foreign policy. The approach, an application of "systemism," contributes to current developments in the realist school of international relations through its emphasis on the need to look at both international and state levels in combination. Earlier applications of realism, as both neotraditional and structural realism clearly demonstrate, tend to remain restricted to one level or the other. In this approach, a religious dynamic can have a domestic source yet be effectively examined in terms of international ramifications.

Religion influences many aspects of politics and society and is considered by many to be an inseparable and integral component. There are many definitions of religion in connection with social and political matters. In this study, *religion* refers to three specific characteristics of a broader concept. One of the most important effects of religion is its ability to bolster or undermine the legitimacy of governments. For example, a Marxist interpretation acknowledges the relationship between legitimacy of the state and religion, and claims that religion is a tool of dominant and opposing classes to facilitate their own political actions. Secondly, religion refers to a source of identity that meets the human need to develop a secure identity for the individual or group. Third, religion is a source of political mobilization or the organization of political activities.[1] Therefore, our definition of religion refers to an individual or group identity capable of political mobilization and affecting the legitimacy of governments and government policy.

This study begins by presenting a particular ontological approach and method of inquiry—systemism—that facilitates understanding the connection between domestic factors and external, or international, features. The section continues by presenting the theoretical premises that are related to internationalization of ethnic conflict and concomitant religious factors as synthesized from the literature. The third part of the section presents an approach to the study of foreign policy that incorporates international, state, and subnational considerations of foreign policy with religion as an essential component. The second section of the paper presents a case study of Indo-Pakistani relations over Kashmir, used to evaluate the role of religion and the explanatory power of the approach presented here. The concluding section sums up the contributions of the analytical framework, assessing the impact of each factor from the framework on foreign policies while concentrating on religion. Overall generalizations and implications for further research and policy are summarized.

## Theory and Approach

### Systemism

Ethnic conflict occurs neither wholly in nor between states. To understand ethnic conflict, factors operating within the state and beyond its borders should be taken into consideration.[2] In this part, an important alternative approach to theories of international relations is summarized. Rejecting suppositions that either holism or individualism can sufficiently represent international events, systemism suggests a midpoint in the continuum:

> The alternative to both individualism and holism is systemism, since it accounts for both individual and system and in particular, for individual agency and social structure.[3]

According to James, systemism means a commitment to understanding a system in terms of a comprehensive set of functional relationships.[4] This approach allows the study of both domestic and external factors and their relationship with each other to better understand international relations. It is appropriate for a study of how ethnic conflict influences foreign policy through a full range of linkages, including religion. That is, the connections between state-level and international factors are articulated. Domestic events interact with other domestic activities or policies *and* international factors. In the same way, international activities have both global and state-level influences. Specifically, systemism focuses on each of the following causal connections: domestic-domestic, domestic-international, international-international, and international-domestic. Especially in a study in which the relationship between domestically generated, religion-based ethnic conflict and foreign policy is sought, systemism is the most appropriate choice to comprehend both domestic and external factors and domestic-international interactions.

For example, the Kashmir case has a significant ethno-religious dimension domestically for India with interstate ramifications. Domestic ethnic and religious sources of the contention interact with both state-level factors that shape the ethnic conflict (such as political leadership) and external factors that cause internationalization. Such complex relationships can be explained effectively with a foreign policy approach based on systemism.

### Ethno-Religious Conflict

The increase in ethnic conflicts around the world is a reality. The conflicts that arise from ethnicity-related factors now are as important as issues that substantially determine the course of international relations, such as political and economic globalization, the balance of power, regionalization, terrorism, and the spread of weapons of mass destruction.

Ethnic conflicts can have an important religious dimension. Religion is potentially a very important element of ethnicity; in fact, some ethnic groups have their primary origin in religion.[5] The salience of religion to ethnicity is illustrated in Kashmir. The identification of an ethnic group is determined by common perceptions among its members. Conflict among these groups carries an ethnic quality to it. If there is a primary religious difference among the conflictual parties, ethnic conflict can assume a specifically religious dimension—labeled by Fox as "ethnoreligious" conflicts.[6] Kashmir is a prime example of this type of conflict.

There are several definitions of ethnicity, ethnic conflict, and ethno-religious conflict. We have presented some definitions about ethnic and ethno-religious conflicts on which there is a fair consensus. However, there is no consensus among students of ethnic conflict as to the causes of these conflicts. To a certain extent, agreement exists that some combination of economic, political, and psychological factors can explain ethnic conflict.[7]

However, the consensus ends there. Depending on the cases studied, various explanations are put forward by scholars, diverse theories are created, and evidence from different cases is used to support these theories. Yet since the aim of this study is to evaluate the role of religion between ethnic conflicts and foreign policy, studies on the internationalization of ethnic conflict will receive primary focus.

Recent studies on the internationalization of ethnic conflict suggest that ethnic conflict may lead to violent, often unmanageable, interstate differences.[8] However, just as consensus cannot be reached on the causes of ethnic conflict, there is no consensus as to how ethnic conflict is internationalized. Is ethnic conflict sub-nationally generated, then externalized? Do ethnic conflicts weaken state structures and thus invite external intervention, or is it a more complex interaction?

First, Carment and James suggest that irredentist conflicts, among which Kashmir can be included, tend to be the most violent kind of ethnic strife.[9] The potential for conflict in such irredentist, ethnic conflicts holds a particular danger since the situation can escalate into war between the nuclear-armed states of India and Pakistan.

In their most recent study, Carment and James present four hypotheses about the problem of internationalization.[10] First, weakened state structures invite external predation and, in turn, conflict escalation. The Serbian case at the beginning of the 1990s and the Somalian case in the late 1970s support this hypothesis. Either Pakistani or superpower involvement in the Kashmir conflict also might support this hypothesis. The second hypothesis is that international organizations (both governmental and nongovernmental) serve as vehicles for external meddling by states that are attempting to intervene on behalf of their brethren. This hypothesis could be supported by United Nations (UN) involvement in India, and Kashmir in particular. The third hypothesis is that the shift in the ethnic balance of power within a state will produce escalation. The Kashmir case does not support this hypothesis as well as the example of Yugoslavia at the beginning of the 1990s.[11] The last hypothesis is about international factors such as global and regional integration; the more integrated the target state, the greater the likelihood of ethnic conflict escalation as a form of backlash against rapid change. According to Carment and James, this proposition is supported by the Yugoslavian case, in which rapid changes in the 1990s were observed in eastern Europe. In each of these cases, an ethnic conflict had international dimensions.

Midlarsky reaches a similar conclusion.[12] Midlarsky considers two instances of ethnic conflict prior to World War I, Bosnia and Macedonia, reaching the conclusion that ethnic conflict can escalate into full-scale interstate war, then regional war, and even a global war. According to Midlarsky, ethnic conflicts are more likely to internationalize when they are related to the balance of power among rival states, as was the case prior to World War I.

Another major theoretical contribution to the understanding of ethnic conflict is Alexis Heraclides's study.[13] Heraclides bifurcated state motives for involvement in an ethnic conflict. Whether partisan or mediatory, states have instrumental (utilitarian) and affective reasons to intervene in ethnic strife. Instrumental motives include international political considerations, economic gains, domestic political motives, and military gains. On the other hand, affective reasons are related more to justice; humanitarian considerations; ethnic, religious, racial, or ideological affinity; and personal relationships. When these motives exist, interactions among factors influence the internationalization of conflicts. In other words, the international system can influence subnational wars in three different ways: by diffusion and encouragement, by isolation and suppression, and by reconciliation.

A final point to be mentioned leading to the internationalization of ethnic conflict is the security dilemma. According to Kaufman,[14] once violence reaches the point at which ethnic communities cannot rely on the state to protect them, each community mobilizes to take responsibility for its own security. This leads to the intervention of other states, usually as a help to the ethnic group in need of these aids, hence leading to the internationalization of the conflict. On the other hand, Van Evera suggests that ethnic conflict creates security dilemmas for both ethnic groups and neighboring states that result in spiral effects, international conflict, and external intervention.[15] For example, the Kashmir problem between India and Pakistan has resulted in a classic example of a security dilemma that eventually escalated into nuclear rivalry.

These studies support the belief that ethnic conflicts can have international dimensions, influencing relationships among states and even being capable of causing a full-scale war. Not every ethnic conflict causes interstate conflict, but some obviously do. What role, then, does religion play in the internationalization of ethnic conflict?

The next section introduces a foreign policy approach in which ethnic and religious factors have connections to the policies of other nations as well as international-level and state-level factors that influence foreign policy. As our case of Kashmir suggests, ethnic conflict, including the role of religion, has substantial influence over the foreign policy of India in particular, but also that of Pakistan. The goal of the foreign policy approach used in this study is to better explain these connections.

## Foreign Policy Approach

The foreign policy approach developed for this study aims to articulate how the Kashmir conflict has influenced India's foreign policy. The approach is adapted from McGowan and Shapiro's classic work on comparative foreign policy studies.[16] There are two reasons why this approach is taken as the basis for this study. First, the choice of factors fit well into the nature of foreign policy studies. That is, the external and subnational components employed give a comprehensive picture, introducing an interdisciplinary understanding of history, religion, economics, sociology, anthropology, psychology, and political science. Second, by introducing these factors, it provides a comprehensive framework for applying a system-oriented approach to the study of foreign policy, with a potential for rigorous comparative studies.

Additions and alterations to McGowan and Shapiro are made to better understand the origins of domestic-level religious factors that experience internationalization. A subnational dilemma within a given state can have an impact on the foreign policy of that state as well as others. For example, conflictual relations among groups with ethno-religious identifying characteristics exist in India. Dealing with events in India's state of Jammu and Kashmir is daily fare for national leadership. However, what occurs in Kashmir is not the sole concern of Indian politicians. External links to other states (such as Pakistan) in addition to the environment of the international system (such as post–cold war unipolarity) will have ramifications on India's foreign policy. None of these elements in isolation provide a complete picture.

The approach has three main sequential steps. Part 1 consists of domestic-level factors that have been included to provide greater understanding of sources of conflict at the state and subnational level (see Table 1). They represent the interaction among state-level domestic factors with subnational sources of conflict, in this case those with an ethno-religious characteristic.[17] At the state level, eight different factors are considered: individuals, elites, politics, government, economics, linkages (trends in a decision maker's past policy behavior), analogies (comparisons to past events), and culture.[18] The assumption is that there exists a two-way, domestic-level interaction of domestic and subnational factors outside of, and perhaps prior to, interaction at the international level. For example, state-level factors refer to India, while the subnational elements apply specifically to Kashmir in order to assess the region's influence on Indian foreign policy. The goal at this step is to pinpoint initial ethno-religious sources of conflict between the Kashmir region and the national government in New Delhi.

**Table 1.** Factors of explanation for comparative foreign policy decisions

| Domestic factors | Subnational factors | International influences | State-level responses |
|---|---|---|---|
| individuals | ethno-religious issues | policies of other nations | individuals |
| elites |  | other international factors | elites |
| politics |  |  | politics |
| government |  |  | government |
| economics |  |  | economics |
| linkages |  |  | linkages |
| analogies |  |  | analogies |
| culture |  |  | culture |

Part 1
Domestic origins of ethno-religious conflict

Part 2

Part 3

Original framework by Patrick J. McGowan and Howard B. Shapiro, *The Comparative Study of Foreign Policy: A Survey of Scientific Findings* (Beverly Hill; CA: Sage Publications, 1973).

The resulting interactions between the state and subnational groups have two subsequent main connections. The first point of influence is on the policies of other nations and other international-level factors. In turn, international responses and the foreign policies of other states subsequently influence the original domestic-level factors, repeated at this point in the approach to represent international-to-domestic connections (individuals, elites, etc.). In other words, events within India triggered responses from other states and international institutions, which in turn produced feedback and affected aspects of India's domestic affairs. It is at this point that a state's political or governmental factors, for example, are assessed in terms of having an impact on its own foreign policy. In other words, this approach incorporates external and international responses to an initial domestic situation before it attempts to understand ultimate foreign policy patterns.[19] While the link between domestic and international politics is not new, this approach provides a structure well-suited for further rigorous and comparative studies.

Applied to the Kashmir conflict, this approach has the potential to explain a variety of domestic- and international-level relationships. The balance of this paper will concentrate on one: ethno-religious factors. In the following two sections, Indian foreign policy regarding the conflict in Jammu and Kashmir is presented. Specifically, India's policies toward the subnational and ethno-religious troubles in Jammu and Kashmir are investigated, with reference to Pakistani and international influence on the ultimate Indian foreign policy.

## Indian Foreign Policy—The Case of Kashmir[20]

Understanding why Indian foreign policy has been affected by domestic factors so extensively is an important area of inquiry. Religion-based conflicts have been shown to be a source of more conflicts in Asia than in any other region of the world.[21] The aim of this section is not to address this question broadly; rather, the goal is to analyze religious factors that are influential in determining Indian foreign policy. Several factors are pertinent, such as the multiethnic and religious character of the subcontinent, India's efforts to balance the authority of the central state over ethnically and religiously diverse federal states, and Pakistan's policies toward these same minority groups in India, particularly in Kashmir. No state is able to pursue a foreign policy that is independent of domestic pressures, especially those that originate from ethnic and religious subgroups. India and Pakistan are particularly vulnerable to these forces.[22]

Kashmir is considered one of the most likely places on earth to spark a major conflict.[23] The origin of the Kashmir conflict between India and Pakistan dates back to the partition of the British colonial empire after World War II. There are five large regions in the state of Jammu and Kashmir that were incorporated under a single administration in the mid-nineteenth century. As a result, the state of Jammu and Kashmir was the largest among the 562 princely states that constituted the empire before 1947. Although Kashmir is treated as a homogenous unit, it is actually the opposite in terms of demography, religion, culture, ethnicity, and language.[24]

The policies of princely states were affected by the British plan to divide the colonial empire into two independent states: India and Pakistan. Princely states were given the chance to choose which country to join. Kashmir, however, chose not to join either of them. Maharajah Singh, Kashmir's ruler at the time, sought avenues to independence. Opposing his ambitions were both India and Pakistan, whose respective leaders claimed Kashmir should belong to their union. Eventually Singh, afraid of a Pakistani intervention, decided to call for Indian troops. The immediate solution recommended by the UN was a cease-fire and a plebiscite to determine the future of Kashmir. The following succession of intense conflicts and India's unwillingness to hold a plebiscite has shaped the status of modern Kashmir.

Analyses of the origins of the dispute over Kashmir predominantly suggest that both countries claimed Kashmir because of their nation-building strategies. For the elite of newly independent India, the possibility of a Muslim majority in Kashmir choosing to live and prosper within a primarily Hindu state was a symbol of secular nationalism and state-building. This was the long-term goal of Jawaharlal Nehru, first prime minister of India. However, for Pakistan (and its first leader Mohammad Ali Jinnah) the primary defining characteristic of the nation of Pakistan was Islam. In other words, Pakistan's leadership believed Kashmir represented the impossibility of secular nationalism in the region. Therefore, Kashmir and its Muslim citizens must be part of an Islamic homeland.[25]

How has the situation in Kashmir affected Indian policy? Traditionally, the analysis of the foreign policy of India focuses on two contextual frameworks. The pluralist, regional hegemony thesis suggests that India's postindependence policies have been characterized by a persistent accumulation of power by the central state to control rising demands from an increasingly pluralist society. Centralization has led to the militarization of the Indian state, the use of force to repress domestic dissent, and rising hegemonism in relations with its neighbors. The second framework is a neo-Gramscian one suggesting India's main purpose after independence has been the neutralization of the "subaltern" or dominated classes. Both theories reach the same conclusion. The increase in centralized power within domestic politics leads to growing hegemonism in the international sphere.[26]

The two approaches to the analysis of Indian foreign policy hold valid insights. However, their weakness in terms of incorporating the domestic and international factors shaping the Indian foreign policy suggests the usefulness of a novel framework developed by Maya Chadda.[27] According to this perspective, Indian foreign policy is directly influenced by the religious and ethnic diversities and the incomplete nation-building in both India and the subcontinent in general. Chadda asserts that in South Asia, India seeks a degree of overarching power that would give it "relational control." India's foreign policy objective is to maximize freedom of action and widen available options in foreign policy so that outcomes can be influenced in its own favor.

More specifically, India's foreign policy is greatly influenced by ethno-religious divides on the subcontinent and neighboring states' involvement in Indian domestic issues. Chadda argues that India, through relational control, seeks to insulate its nation-building project from any destabilizing development in neighboring countries.[28] Specifically, India's incongruent legal, national, religious, and ethnic boundaries have led Indian policy makers to maintain relational control over neighboring states by preventing great power interference in the region. Political turmoil in contiguous states, extraregional ethnic conflicts spilling over onto the subcontinent, and displacement of (or threats to) different religious or ethnic communities could destabilize interlocking balances within India. Thus, to prevent such ethno-religious security threats, India prefers having neutral neighbors. Kashmir is a prime example of relational control in India's foreign policy due to its protracted nature and core ethno-religious aspects.

The complexity of the problem has territorial dimensions in addition to the ethno-religious factors. Apart from the religious variances, ethnic divisions between Hindus, Buddhists, and Muslim Kashmiris were exacerbated by their territorial dispersion throughout the state. Those three main problems have caused irredentist, even secessionist, demands in India, Pakistan, and within Kashmir itself.

This rivalry between two states in the subcontinent has had a substantial effect over Indian and Pakistani foreign policy. The conflict over Jammu and Kashmir has resulted in the following incidents: the 1948 and 1965 wars, the 1971 war over Bangladesh,[29] the 1990 crises, the 1999 Kargil War, and the 2002 crises.

For India, the Kashmir conflict is definitely a two-dimensional issue. First, ethnic conflict has domestic causes. Subnationally it is related to the success or failure of Indian domestic policies. Second, externally the conflict is linked to the subcontinental rivalry between India and Pakistan.[30] However, this division does not suggest a foreign policy for India that is isolated from domestic concerns.

The foreign policy approach presented here has the capability to better explain relationships between foreign policy and the religious and ethnic conflicts concerning Kashmir. In order to demonstrate the approach's usefulness, the focus of this next section will be on India's policies toward Pakistan. The connections between domestic and international factors provide a substantial analysis of Indian foreign policy.

With further concentration on the role of religion, the ways each factor has had an impact on foreign policy will be addressed.

### Part 1 of Table 1—Initial Domestic and Subnational Factors

In this approach, domestic factors are studied as sources of ethnic conflict in a given region. Ethnic and religious variances, territorial claims by domestic groups, and economic and governmental factors are the original contributors to the ethnic problem. In Indian-held Kashmir, the main source of conflict has been religious and ethno-secessionist claims of the groups that live there. The dominant population (about two-thirds) is Muslim, while there are Hindus and Buddhists concentrated in the northern part of the state. In both the Indian and Pakistani sides of Kashmir, the overall population is predominantly Muslim. However, in the region of Jammu, Hindus are a 66 percent majority, and in Ladakh, Muslim and Buddhist populations are roughly even.[31]

A full history of how these groups organized, became pitted against each other, and their specific claims are the concern of another study. However, many domestic factors have resulted in long-term instabilities for Kashmir; a mix of ethnic, religious, and territorial battles; irredentism; hypernationalism; and economic reform and turbulence leading to protracted interstate and intrastate conflict.[32]

A review of the politics of identity in Kashmir reveals the importance of ethnoreligious divides on domestic and foreign policies for India. Kashmiri identity is shaped by pairs of conflictual groups, including Muslims versus Hindus and Islamic radicals versus Kashmiri nationalists who desire at a minimum autonomy, if not full independence.[33] However, this study asserts that the most influential identity and the source of conflict in Jammu and Kashmir has been religious, specifically Islam.

Domestic factors, in terms of their combined interaction in part 1, are closely connected to the two sets of international factors in part 2. That is, substate causes of ethnic conflict interact with individual, elite, political, governmental, economic, and cultural factors that shape the conflict. It is at this point that the ethno-religious problem becomes internationalized, as depicted in part 2 of Table 1. The rise in

Islamic identity has the constant potential to cause trouble among Muslim residents in Jammu and Kashmir. This atmosphere causes India to feel more threatened and less secure. In response to this increased sensitivity to Islamic insurgents in Kashmir, the area has come under increasingly greater scrutiny by the central government. Discussions concerning Jammu and Kashmir are more numerous in New Delhi and there has been a greater tendency to intervene and micromanage affairs at the expense of regional autonomy. Policies toward Jammu and Kashmir have also grown more hard-line in nature.

### *Part 2 of Table 1: Pakistan's Policies*

The slogan of "Islam in danger" and Pakistan's religious influence over the region have the potential to stir religious sentiments at any given time. For example, the 1963 incident in which the hair of the prophetMuhammad disappeared from Srinagar's holy Mosque of Hazaratbal, although taking place in India, led to serious riots among Muslims in Kashmir and worsened Indo-Pakistani relations. More recently, developments in and around Kashmir have strengthened Islamic identity, resulting in substantial changes in Indian foreign policy: a general inspiration derived from the Islamic Revolution in Iran, the emergence of militant Islamic groups fighting against the Soviet occupation in Afghanistan, and the enormous increase in religious schools (madrassas) that has strengthened Islamic fundamentalism in the region.[34] In the last couple of years, the Taliban regime's rule and Al Qaeda's involvement in Afghanistan strengthened Islamic influence throughout the region as far as Pakistan and India, influencing Kashmiri secessionism. Growing Islamic fundamentalism has become such a great force in the region that even Pakistani leader Pervez Musharraf stresses repeatedly the importance of U.S. aid for reforming the educational system in Pakistan in the war against terrorism. According to the Islamonline news section, Pakistan has more than ten thousand madrassas that provide free education, food, and board to poor children.[35] These schools allegedly are connected to the Taliban forces in Afghanistan and insurgents in Kashmir.

Pakistan's ultimate foreign policy goal vis-à-vis India is an irredentist policy—to gain the territory of Jammu and Kashmir from India. Pakistan's irredentist foreign policy has been put into practice as support for insurgent movements in Kashmir. As a consequence, Indian foreign policy has been affected profoundly, hardening against Pakistan.

It is not surprising that since its establishment Pakistan's foreign and domestic policies, such as defense buildups and economic agendas, have been dominated by its relationship with India. There are two overriding concerns for Pakistani leadership: (a) the perception since partition that India is a threat to Pakistan's existence and her territorial integrity and (b) concern about India's secular politics in the subcontinent. Pakistan considers secularism as the greatest threat to its raison d'etre—Islam. These concerns are understandable considering relations between the two states, and the past Indian armed intervention into Bangladesh in its successful bid for independence from Pakistan in 1971.[36]

As a result, Kashmir may well have become a more important issue for Pakistani than Indian leaders. The Bangladeshi partition, in particular, resulted in a desire to control all of Kashmir. According to Prabha, there are four main reasons that Pakistan wants to conquer Kashmir: (a) it would enable Pakistan to regain the confidence of the Muslim population in the region, (b) the conquest of Kashmir would further strengthen the autocratic state structure of Pakistan, (c) it would help settle down other problems with Sindh and Baluchistan and secure territorial integrity of the country,[37] and (d) if Jammu and Kashmir is acquired, then Pakistan can search for a national ideology based on socioeconomic factors, rather than relying so heavily on Islam.

The political processes to gain territory in Kashmir started right after the partition in 1947. Former Pakistani leader Jinnah used various political means, including sending delegates, offering privileges and even independence to Kashmiri leaders in attempts to convince them to join Pakistan peacefully.

Pakistan has used various conventional foreign policy tools to attempt to acquire Jammu and Kashmir, including warfare, international organizations, political processes, diplomacy and propaganda, and foreign aid.[38] Theoretically, warfare is supposed to be the last resort that states use in international relations. However, for the Indo-Pakistani relationship, this doesn't seem to be the case. In the little more than five decades since independence, India and Pakistan have engaged in four distinct wars—1947, 1965, 1971, and 1999. The 1947 war was an apparent success in that Pakistan acquired the part of Kashmir that it still controls today, "Azad Kashmir," or Free Kashmir. The last three attempts were all failures and did not result in an advantage to Pakistan.[39]

Although it was India who first brought the problem to the UN, Pakistan also used international organizations to hold plebiscites in Kashmir or to engage in international mediation. Pakistan also used diplomacy and propaganda to create good publicity within the international community. These efforts focused on British and Islamic nations.

However, none of these efforts ended in a favorable way for Pakistan, neither through bilateral nor multilateral diplomatic attempts. The main reason behind these failures was the Simla Agreement of 1972 signed after the 1971 Indo-Pakistani War, which resulted in the separation of Bangladesh. According to this agreement, Pakistan accepted that any negotiation about Kashmir should be bilateral between India and Pakistan. The implication of this article on Indo-Pakistani relations is that India has never considered any other diplomatic option for the settlement of the dispute after this agreement. Also, this agreement has been used by India as a weapon against further Pakistani efforts to internationalize the conflict. India effectively has used the agreement to prevent interference by other states such as the United States, China, or other Muslim nations.

The last point to be mentioned is the foreign aid that Pakistan has received from the United States and Arab nations. Indian policy makers have alleged that Pakistan transferred some military capabilities to the insurgent groups of Kashmir, although there is little or no evidence to support the accusations. As for nonconventional efforts, India has accused Pakistan of supporting terrorism. Especially since the end of the 1980s, when Pakistan has been experiencing political turmoil, it is blamed by India for supporting terrorist groups in Kashmir.

The significant point about these efforts has been that Pakistan has attempted to use religion as a tool of foreign policy to create positive publicity about its claims to Kashmir. Since the partition, Pakistan has used anticolonialist and Muslim-solidarity views to color its foreign policies. The country has based its foreign policy substantially on its Muslim identity. Politically, Pakistani officials have supported the Palestinian people as well as anticolonial movements in North Africa. In economic matters they have sought the support of richer Gulf states.[40] Concerning Kashmir,

Pakistan has sought the support of all Muslim nations. As a result, the more religiously oriented Arab countries of the Middle East have articulated support for Pakistan against India and their hope of seeing the "salvation" of the Kashmiri Muslims. In addition, Indian nationalists still allege that some rich Muslim countries financially support Kashmiri insurgencies. A recent quote from the Pacific News Service is illustrative:

> Sheikh Issues Fatwa Over Kashmir: Sheikh Faysal Mawlawi, the deputy chairman of the European Council for Fatwa and Research, has issued a fatwa—a non-binding ruling in accordance with Islamic law—in case of war between India and Pakistan. According to Mawlawi, it is the duty of all Muslims to support Pakistan. He said that if there is an Indo-Pak war, the reason would clearly be Kashmir, and the Kashmiris want to be attached to Pakistan, which is an Islamic country.[41]

There are three main options for Pakistan to strengthen its territorial and national security in the near future. Two of them are interconnected: democratic liberalization and the pursuit of regional cooperation. The third option, based upon Islam, has been dominant in the past few decades. The Islamic option has two aspects. The external aspect is to build even closer ties with other Muslim nations such as Iran and Turkic states in central Asia and to support stability and peace in Afghanistan. However, there are great uncertainties to this option. First, there are great doubts about the regime in Iran and the situation in Afghanistan after the UN-led occupation in 2001–2002. Second, the Turkic republics of central Asia are ideologically and culturally closer to Turkey and its secularity. Subnationally, the Islamic approach poses serious dangers to the stability of Pakistan. The growing extremist, Wahhabite type of Islam is a great threat to the Pakistani government.[42] Any analysis of the future of Pakistani foreign policy must take into account the substantial changes caused by the military coup in 1999 and the events following the September 11 attacks in the United States. These include the United States' increasing involvement in Asian politics, the continuing war on terrorism, and Pervez Musharraf's support for the U.S.-led search for Al Qaeda militants in the region. Pursuing the Islamic option will not be hampered because of consideration of U.S. interests and influence in the region. In addition, Pakistani policy makers seem to recognize the threat of extremist political Islam against the Pakistani state both in subnational and external security matters. Thus it might be expected that Pakistan will pursue more regional cooperation options in the near future, including the avoidance of main crises with India.

To summarize Pakistan's fit into this foreign policy approach, ethno-religious realities and events in the Indian state of Jammu and Kashmir prompted foreign policy responses from Pakistan, an external participant, which in turn elicited responses from India in the form of internationalized, or foreign, policy.

### *Part 2 of Table 1—External Factors: The UN, the Cold War, and Alliances*

Domestic problems within Indian Kashmir are perceived as a threat to the founding principles of Pakistan and have led to Pakistan's involvement in the Kashmir dispute. Related to this internationalization problem, the UN and the cold war superpowers became involved in the Kashmir conflict at the international level. The UN first was brought in by India in a complaint about Pakistan's aggressive actions over Kashmir that led to the 1947–48 war. In the developments of the following decade, Pakistan's alliance with the United States brought a cold war dimension to the conflict that forced India to collaborate with the Soviet Union. These domestic causes of ethnic strife led to the internationalization of the conflict, influencing states at the system-oriented, or international, level.

International factors influencing the Kashmir conflict have included the UN's involvement after 1948, Pakistan's alliance with the United States and involvement in U.S.-sponsored military organizations such as Southeast Asia Treaty Organization (SEATO) and Central Treaty Organization (CENTO), India's establishment of close ties with the Soviet Union in response to cold war superpower rivalries and, for the last two decades, the increasing rise of Islamic ideologies and governments in the region.

The Kashmir situation was brought to the UN by India in 1948 with the hope that the UN would condemn Pakistan's aggression. After several debates, two resolutions were passed. The first, proposed by India, was to halt the ongoing war, the second, proposed by Pakistan, recommended a plebiscite for Kashmir. Both of these efforts by theUNto bring a solution to the conflict failed—Pakistan continued to occupy Free Kashmir and the promised plebiscite was never held. Since that time, India consistently has argued against the internationalization of the conflict and rejected further involvement by international organizations.

The second international source of change involved Pakistan's alliances. For example, Pakistan and the United States became allies, and Pakistan also joined SEATO and CENTO. Perceived as a cold war balance of power move, India declared that Pakistan's alliances, in particular with the United States, were a threat to its security. In response, Nehru declared that a plebiscite in Kashmir would be impossible, thereby reconfirming India's claim to Kashmir. Seen at the international level, India's policy toward Jammu and Kashmir was in response to a neighboring state's decisions on allies, even though there was no direct connection to the Kashmir dispute.

More recently, beginning with the 1980s, India has become increasingly vulnerable to the influence of Islam in the subcontinent and neighboring regions. The Islamic Revolution in Iran, the Soviet invasion of Afghanistan, and the rise of Muslim identity and resistance in the region have become important issues to consider for India in making foreign policy moves. There have been multiple consequences. Pakistan was the main conduit for the transfer of arms to mujahideen resistance against the Soviets and also became the headquarters for a fundamentalist Sunni group, *Hezb-e-Islami*, under Gulbuddin Hekmatyar. Especially with the global transformation in the 1990s, Pakistan's five-decade-long aim to have a plebiscite in Indian-occupied Kashmir has found increased international support. Considering the strategic Islamic crescent in the region that India faces, the Kashmir issue (and a more powerful rival Islamic ideology) have become even more important in shaping Indian foreign policy. Islamic mobilization in Kashmir, increasing violence in and near critical holy sites, and rising numbers of Hindu-Muslim riots in India should be analyzed in this framework as well.[43] India has also felt the fear of disintegration even more with the recent rise of Islam. And religion does not shape foreign policy of a nation only in one direction: external-to-subnational or foreign-to-domestic connections are as important as the subnational-to-external forces in making foreign policy. In the Indian example, besides the domestic ethno-religious influences on Indian foreign policy, systemic and regional changes related to the rise of Islam as an alternative ideology alter Indian perceptions and actions in international relations.

As this foreign policy approach helps explain, ethnic conflicts with domestic origins may have an influence over system-level alliances. This can occur because of the severity of a conflict, the potential for escalation, the structure of the system, and existing alliances. The result often entails further reaction among domestic components of the foreign policy making processes.

*Part 3 of Table 1: Individual and Elite Factors*

Indian bureaucratic and military elites have been strong supporters and protectors of the founding principles of national secularism in India. In this sense, considering the partition process and Kashmir's symbolism for secular India, Indian elites have had a strong commitment to the secular principle; as such they have been both the architects and implementers of India's foreign policy toward Pakistan. Their substantial influence has been seen in the hard line taken against Pakistan with reference to Kashmir and the development of a nuclear program.[44]

Religious variances of the subcontinent shape considerably the way individual Indian leaders and elites approach Kashmir as both a domestic and a foreign policy issue. For example, the rather idealist secular nationalist approach typically ignored how important communal and religious differences in India really are. The dream was that all ethnic and religious groups in India would choose a better life within the Indian nation, initially considered to be the best option in the region. Instead, after three decades of ethno-religious conflicts, the Indian elite changed their minds and policies. It has become recognized that domestic minority groups have been, and most likely will continue to be, a challenge to Indian unity. Added to this is the recognition that ethno-religious ties to peoples in neighboring countries at times has led to conflict at the interstate level. Two results are evident. Domestically, the Indian political elite has approached nation-building strategies in a more centrist manner. In addition, foreign policy toward regional powers, in particular Pakistan, has become increasingly more aggressive.

It is clear that, over time, individual leaders and elites have sought different solutions for similar problems. For Nehru, one of the founders of independent India, Kashmir rightfully belonged to India as a symbol of secular nationalism. In the first decade of the conflict, Nehru declared that a plebiscite was possible, yet he wanted to retain bilateral negotiations with Pakistan as an option. Although his policy had changed after Pakistan's alliance with the United States, it can be argued that he assumed a somewhat compromising posture.

However, in the late 1960s and early 1970s Indira Gandhi took a hard line against Pakistan. She centralized the federal system of India and took power away from local governments. In addition, she was one of the architects of India's policy toward Pakistan and Bangladesh and the 1971 war over Kashmir took place under her leadership. Indira Gandhi's decision to intervene militarily in Pakistan's civil war was a fundamental departure from the Nehruvian approach to international politics.[45] Therefore, it can be argued that she was more hawkish than Nehru in relations with Pakistan. Taking yet another foreign policy turn during the late 1970s and early 1980s, Rajiv Gandhi tried to increase cooperation and encourage negotiations about Kashmir with his Pakistani counterpart, Benazir Bhutto. Although it did not produce substantial results, Rajiv Gandhi's policies were an obvious change and created some hope for the future.

Within the framework of relational control with neighbors in the region, the transition from Nehruvian secular nationalism and pluralism to centralization of the Indian state led to a substantial decline in the autonomy of Kashmir to control religious and ethnic divisions peacefully. Both Indira and Rajiv Ghandi violated at least two fundamental principles of Indian political unity: they sought to replace the National Conference, the biggest regional party in Kashmir, and played "fast and loose" with the modern Indian state's commitment to secularism.[46] Taking a harder line against such a critical ethno-religious movement produced catastrophic results. In the short term they deepened alienation and encouraged separatism, terminating the political processes in Kashmir and Punjab and thus jeopardizing India's security in the region. In the long term these compromises weakened the union and helped to polarize India along ethno-religious lines. These developments led to the rise of the Hindu nationalist Bharatiya Janata Party (BJP) that in turn increased violence in Kashmir and Punjab.

All these developments led to the weakening of the Indian state and concomitant loss of the relational control of India over its neighbors. The primary reason for this low point in Indian politics was the leaders' changing policies: "Mrs. Gandhi, not unlike the figures in a Greek tragedy, was driven to actions that led to her own demise. Rajiv too fell victim to a similar spate of ethnonational violence."[47]

*Part 3 of Table 1: Political and Governmental Factors*

When secular nationalists came to power in India in 1947, they were committed to three principles: secularism, federalism, and democracy. For them, the empire-state of India was the same as the nation-state of India, and the newly independent India should resemble the ancient Indian multinational empire. However, the problems that they encountered in such a massive country were numerous, including communal divides, multiple sovereignties, and ethnic and linguistic divisions. In the 1980s, after forty years of ethnic conflicts, Indian public opinion was in favor of centralization and the politicians who pursued it. Growing frustration with ethnic and regional nationalism could no longer be contained in India. Frustration caused an increase in Hindu nationalism and, as a consequence, secular nationalists also had to take a centralist stance.[48]

The important characteristic of Hindu nationalism is its religious nature. It is a kind of religious ethno-nationalism aimed at consolidating and reinforcing the Hindu *rashtra*, or Hindu nation. This movement, also called *Hindutva*, or Hindu nationalist ideology, argues that the Indian state is tinged with Indian religion and culture.[49] *Hindutva* suggests showing less tolerance to minorities, such as Muslims and Christians, that are not fully loyal to the Indian state or assimilated into Hindu society. *Hindutva* ideology has been actively involved in communal conflicts in India.

The main political organization of Hindu nationalism has been the BJP. Although *Hindutva* ideology has been present in Indian politics for a long time, the BJP could claim votes from it only in the 1990s. The last decade witnessed the rise of the BJP and Hindu nationalism and the decline of the Congress Party and secularism in India. Since the 1996 elections the BJP has become stronger and defeated the Congress Party in successive elections.[50] The BJP defended the centralization of the Indian state to unite India on the basis of the Indian majority. They suggested even a harder line against Pakistan and claimed the cultural scope of India stretches from Afghanistan to Sri Lanka. The extreme strand of Hindu nationalism is expansionist and statist in external affairs and prefers authoritarian control over domestic groups. The more moderate strand of Hindu nationalism is more ambivalent about India's borders. However, proponents support a tough and security-oriented foreign policy, with an uncompromising stance against Pakistan over Kashmir.[51] However, after coming to power, Prime Minister Vajpayee, from the moderate wing of the BJP, has pursued the second option and has not closed all channels of communication with Pakistan on the Kashmir question. Other than continuing the nuclear program, Vajpayee pursued a moderate foreign policy. In particular, his visit to Pakistan in January 2004 was a groundbreaking incident for Indo-Pakistani relations. However, Vajpayee's own moderate stance in foreign policy does not mean all Hindu nationalists share his views.

Over time, Hindu nationalism has had a twofold effect on the Kashmir issue. First, centralization of the Indian polity has resulted in increased tensions in Kashmir. Second, Kashmiri politics themselves have become more vulnerable to centrist views. Both of these issues have exacerbated the relationship with Pakistan. For instance, Pakistan has accused India of ignoring human rights in Kashmir, including the right to self-determination. In one instance, corrupt local elections in 1989 resulted in political turbulence in Kashmir, leading to another serious crisis between India and Pakistan. Diplomatic measures by the foreign ministers dispelled the crisis short of war; however, tensions remained and increased toward the end of the decade.

Political and governmental factors have probably been among the most important factors determining India's foreign policy. Because of the historical legacy of the British empire and the partition process, what traditionally were domestic issues have had a direct and extensive influence over Kashmir and Pakistan, producing serious foreign policy consequences. The rise of both Hindu nationalism throughout India and Islam in areas such as Kashmir with significant Muslim populations have brought ethno-religious factors more to the forefront of Indian foreign policy with, for example, an Islamic Pakistan.

*Part 3 of Table 1: Economic Factors*

The literature on Kashmir does not consider the economic dimension as a significant source of the conflict.[52] Kashmir simply has little substantial economic value for either India or Pakistan. The economic and demographic facts show that Jammu and Kashmir is not a privileged region of India. It accounts for 6.7 percent of India's landmass but less than 1 percent of its population, due chiefly to the mountainous topography and a low ratio of arable land. The primary economic sector is agriculture, employing 80 percent of the workforce, while small-scale manufacturing is second. Jammu and Kashmir is one of the poorest of Indian states according to most economic indicators (e.g., per capita income, food production, and power consumption). The literacy rate is well below the Indian average of 36 percent. The state's economy is stagnant and suffers seriously from infrastructure problems. The only growing sector is the public sector, thanks to patronage politics.[53]

Kashmir simply has little substantial economic value for both India and Pakistan. The ethno-religious conflict and secessionist movement has, however, prompted increasing federal support for Kashmir, and an increasingly large burden for the Indian central government. Jammu and Kashmir largely depends on transfer payments from the central government, which account for almost half of the state government revenues (which are composed of 10 percent loans and 90 percent grants).[54]

Of course, this is not to suggest that economic factors have no impact on the conflict. A general premise is accepted in ethnic conflict literature that poverty, combined with ancient hatreds or power imbalances between different ethnic and religious groups, may very well be a factor exacerbating ethno-religious violence. However, economic deprivation in Kashmir has no apparent critical influence on Indian or Pakistani foreign policies. It has almost no strategic economic importance, such as natural resources, nor a developed economy with an educated population. Overall, the economic factor has had little effect.

*Part 3 of Table 1: Linkage Factors and Analogies*

In terms of linkage factors, Pakistan's past behavior has constituted a substantial reference point for Indian policy makers. Considering Pakistan's aggression over five decades and its commitment to gaining territory from India, it should not be surprising that Pakistan's actions often are perceived as a threat to Indian territorial unity. A cursory review of Indo-Pakistani relations would reveal that Indian perceptions have been shaped by Pakistan, such as the latter's continued irredentist policy toward Kashmir. Analogies certainly affect Indian foreign policy. The experience of the original partition cautions Indian leaders, who wish to avoid another division of the Indian union. Similar linkages and analogies over time have been among the factors that have shaped India's foreign policy.

*Part 3 of Table 1: Cultural Factors*

Cultural factors have had a considerable impact upon the Kashmir conflict and foreign policy of India. Actually, cultural factors overlap when evaluating any of the other factors. Traditionally, cultural pluralism has been one of India's guiding principles, even though during the 1980s it was understood to be a growing impediment to political stability. Patterns of national identity constructed by India's founding elite have acted as an independent state regarding policies on Jammu and Kashmir. India has been strongly committed to the principle of secularism. Strengthening Hindu nationalism in the wake of Kashmiri turmoil and political turbulence has, in turn, influenced secular nationalists to take a harder line in Kashmir and against Pakistan.

Specific emphasis should be given to ethno-religious aspects of Indian culture. As mentioned above, the very foundation—or partition—of India and Pakistan was based on the religious identifications of the two main ethnic groups of the subcontinent: Hindu and Muslim. These two groups created the political organizations that facilitated the liberation from British rule between the two world wars. As British rule had begun to break down, differences between Hindus and Muslims became more pronounced. While Hindus proposed the unity of the entire subcontinent under a single government, the Muslim League defended the division of the empire along ethno-religious lines. The vitality of the religious dimension in understanding Indian domestic politics, foreign policy, and specific stances on Kashmir stems from the fact that, after all, India and Pakistan were created according to ethno-religious differences and conflicts. Unfortunately, ethno-religious politics, interstate conflicts, and sub-national violence on the subcontinent are even more relevant today than in 1947.

It is not the intention here to suggest that there is a given relationship between differing religious groups and conflicts in a society. There are examples, such as China, in which we observe a less violent coexistence of various ethnic and religious groups. This kind of differentiation can, however, serve to identify some communities as not only separate, but adversarial. This attitude, known as communalism in India, has become a defining factor in the Kashmir conflict since 1989.[55]

Over the past five decades, growing communalism in India, spurred on by domestic and external conflicts, has resulted in the rise of political parties with ethno-religious identifications. The Hindu national movement, represented primarily by the Rashtriya Swayamsewak Sangh (RSS) and the BJP, have risen while secular nationalist political parties (such as the Congress Party that founded Indian politics) have lost ground and at times have been forced to lead a minority government. In 1998, the Congress Party was supplanted when the BJP led a national coalition government. The Indian polity, tired after five decades of ethnic and religious strife and the rejection of Nehru-style secular nationalism, simply turned to a nationalism defined by the Hindu majority. As a result, policies toward Pakistan concerning Kashmir have become more rigid, more uncompromising, and more dangerous.

Culture, as both a domestic and an international factor and defined in a large part by religion, is critical to understanding Indian foreign policy, particularly as it pertains to Kashmir. Since the two main adversarial groups within Kashmir are defined primarily by religion, this factor sheds more light on the protracted conflict with Pakistan than secularists would care to admit.

## Conclusion

The Kashmir problem is the symbol of the unresolved conflict of communal loyalties and secular politics. Pakistani governments, one after another, characterize it as "the unfinished business of partititon" by which they mean that, in view of its Muslim majority, the state and certainly the valley should belong to Pakistan.[56]

Religious dynamics are the products of historical legacies; they shape governmental and political structures, affect the policies of other nations, shape individual leaders and elites, and help us in understanding the cultural side of the foreign policy coin. Especially in the developing world, where the exercise of power often is legitimized on religious grounds, the masses mobilized with communal consciousness and power structures can easily be drawn together by ethnic and religious ties, including ethno-religious factors, thus strengthening explanations about politics and foreign policy.

The foreign policy approach presented here, based on a system-oriented approach, provides further understanding of the relationship between domestic factors and foreign policy as it concerns India and Kashmir. It helps to illustrate how, in the case of Kashmir, ethnic conflicts may become internationalized and determine a substantial part of a country's foreign relations. It helps to clarify domestic-level factors, such as religion, and international-level factors, such as Pakistan's foreign policy, and their combined effect on India's foreign policy.

A system-oriented approach can be used to better understand subnational and external relationships. Domestic, or state-level factors such as religious differences, have profoundly shaped the foreign policy patterns of India. Ethno-religious conflicts originating in Kashmir are as important, if not more so, than structural or international-level factors in explaining some foreign policy decisions. In this case, a domestic religious factor in India has served as the impetus for Pakistani and UN involvement, subsequently promoting a foreign policy response by India.

Since foreign policy cannot be analyzed successfully without paying special attention to domestic factors, the approach presented here provides a systematic way to study various domestic- and international-level factors and a variety of causal relationships among them. Using domestic factors and structures such as religion, culture, leaders, factors, and government (with specific reference to the ontological approach known as systemism), this study provides a robust example of a foreign policy approach that is able to clarify a more complete picture of international politics. Specifically, the emphasis on religion and the endeavor to understand how religious factors shape foreign policy decisions in different domains of polity and society gives a special strength to the approach.

Lastly, from a theoretical perspective, this study justifies the notion that realism as a dominant paradigm of international relations literature can be applied to the study of domestic and international structures. In other words, the foreign policy goals of states often have ethno-religious dynamics that play an important role in policy formation. This is not to claim that states do not consider security concerns as primary or that national interests are not defined by power-related issues. Rather, insight into what defines national interest (and how a state pursues it) is more complex than what traditional realism has argued. As is seen in the case of Kashmir, ethno-religious divides, historical legacies, and nation-building strategies have affected both the domestic and foreign policies of India.

Additional applications of the approach are recommended. Religion as a domestic factor resulting in the internationalization of a conflict can be the focus of concentration for a variety of comparative studies. Beyond the concentration on religion, other state-level factors can be placed under more intense study and analysis. As mentioned earlier, the precise effect that international-level factors, responding to initial state-level and subnational events, can have on a state's specific foreign policy processes would be a natural extension to this and other comparable studies.

## Notes

1. Jonathan Fox and Shmuel Sandler, "Quantifying Religion: Toward Building More Affecting Ways of Measuring Religious Influence on State-Level Behavior," *Journal of Church and State* 45, no. 3 (2003): 559–588.

2. David Carment and Patrick James, "Third Party States in Ethnic Conflict: Identifying the Domestic Determinants of Intervention," in *Ethnic Conflict and International Politics: Explaining Diffusion and Escalation*, ed. Steven E. Lobell and Philip Mauceri (New York: Palgrave, 2003), 11–34.

3. Mario Bunge, *Finding Philosophy in Social Science* (Chelsea, MI: Yale University Press, 1996), 264.

4. Patrick James, "Systemism and International Relations: Toward a Reassessment of Realism," in *Millennial Reflections on International Studies*, ed. Michael Brecher and Frank Harvey (Ann Arbor: University of Michigan Press, 2002), 131–144.

5. Jonathan Fox, *Ethnoreligious Conflict in the Late Twentieth Century: A General Theory* (Lanham, MD: Lexington Books, 2002).

6. Ibid., p. 70.

7. David Carment and Patrick James, "Ethnic Conflict at the International Level," in *Wars in the Midst of Peace: The International Politics of Ethnic Conflict*, ed. David Carment and Patrick James (Pittsburgh: University of Pittsburgh Press, 1997), 1–10.

8. David Carment, "The Ethnic Dimension in World Politics: Theory, Policy and Early Warning," *Third World Quarterly* 15, no. 4 (1994): 551–582.

9. David Carment, "The International Dimension of Ethnic Conflict: Concepts, Indicators and Theory," *Journal of Peace Research* 30, no. 2 (1993): 139–150; David Carment and Patrick James, "Internal Constraints and Interstate Ethnic Conflict: Toward a Crisis-Based Assessment of Irredentism," *Journal of Conflict Resolution* 39, no. 1 (1995): 82–109.

10. 2003.

11. Debate exists about the demographics of Kashmir. The accuracy of census figures has been disputed. In addition, some question whether the original populations during the 1947 partition are more or less relevant than current percentages of religious groups as they pertain to Pakistan's irredentist claims or Kashmiri independence. Manus Midlarsky, "Systemic War in the Former Yugoslavia," in *Wars in the Midst of Peace: The International Politics of Ethnic Conflict*, ed. David Carment and Patrick James (Pittsburgh: University of Pittsburgh Press, 1997), 61–81.

12. Manus Midlarsky, "Rulers and the Ruled: Patterned Inequality and the Onset of Mass Political Violence," *American Political Science Review* 82, no. 2 (1988): 491–509; Manus Midlarsky, "Communal Strife and the Origins of World War 1," in *The Internationalization of Communal Strife*, ed. Manus Midlarsky (London: Routledge, 1992), 173–188.

13. Alexis Heraclides, "Secessionist Minorities and External Environment," *International Organization* 44, no. 3 (1990): 341–378.

14. Chaim Kaufman, "Possible and Impossible Solutions to Ethnic Civil War," in *Nationalism and Ethnic Conflict*, ed. Michael Brown et al. (Cambridge: The MIT Press, 2001).

15. Stephen Van Evera, "Hypotheses on Nationalism and War," *International Security* 18, no. 4 (1994): 5–39.

16. Patrick J. McGowan and Howard B. Shapiro, *The Comparative Study of Foreign Policy: A Survey of Scientific Findings* (Beverly Hills, CA: Sage Publications, 1973).

17. McGowan and Shapiro include religion within the cultural factor, considering it one of the three most important, along with ideology and race (ibid., 45).

18. In state-level factors, establishment and societal components from the original approach are excluded. We believe the establishment factor is covered to a great extent in the "elites" factor as it represents the institutional features of foreign policy making. Similarly, societal factors from the original approach are not included because economic variables provide us with the necessary discussion of what societal factors are supposed to explain, in terms of economic inequalities and social modernization. On the other hand, the "analogies" factor in the state-level points is added to McGowan and Shapiro's approach for the sake of consistency.

19. A key component of future study using this model would be to add inquiry into effects on the decision making process that result from the inclusion of external and international factors. In addition, there are sure to be both domestic and international influences from the foreign policies themselves, serving as feedback to the original state and subnational situation, foreign policies of other states, and international elements. For the purposes of this initial study, the concentration is restricted to the initial foreign policy results.

20. The reader will note that the nuclear capabilities of these two states are mentioned only occasionally. It is our assumption that, in most instances, the effects of nuclear force structures would be similar on foreign policy considerations such as conflict escalation, regardless of the source of a crisis—religion, economics, political turmoil, and so forth. However, nuclear capability could be considered a point of inquiry as a domestic factor, with the intent of observing subsequent foreign policy processes and decisions. See Carolyn C. James, "Nuclear Arsenal Games: Coping with Proliferation in a World of Changing Rivalries," *Canadian Journal of Political Science* 33, no. 4 (2000), 723–746.

21. Jonathan Fox and Carolyn C. James, "Regional Propensities for Religious Violence, American Public Perception and the Middle East," (paper presented at the International Studies Association Midwest Conference, St. Louis, Missouri, 2002).

22. Maya Chadda, "From an Empire State to a Nation State: The Impact of Ethno-Religious Conflicts on India's Foreign Policy," in *Dilemmas of National Security and Cooperation in India and Pakistan*, ed. Hafeez Malik (New York: St. Martin's Press, 1993), 207–229.

23. Andrew Scobell, "Flashpoint Asia: The Most Dangerous Place?" *Parameters* 31, no. 2 (2001), 129–133.

24. Sumit Ganguly, *The Crisis in Kashmir: Portents of War, Hopes of Peace* (Cambridge: Cambridge University Press, 1997).

25. Sumit Ganguly and Kanti Bajpai, "India and the Crisis in Kashmir," *Asian Survey* 34, no. 5 (1994), 401–416.

26. Maya Chadda, *Ethnicity, Security and Separatism in India* (New York: Columbia University Press, 1997).

27. Ibid.
28. Ibid.
29. Although the primary reason for this conflict was not Kashmir itself, India's intervention was meant to weaken Pakistan in order to gain more concessions at the war's conclusion, including concessions involving Kashmir.
30. Sumit Ganguly and Kanti Bajpai, "India and the Crisis."
31. Mushtaqur Rahman, *Divided Kashmir: Old Problems, New Opportunities for India, Pakistan, and for the Kashmiri People* (Boulder, CO: Lynne Rienner, 1996); Reeta Chowdhari Tremblay, "Nation, Identity and the Intervening Role of the State: A Study of the Secessionist Movement in Kashmir," *Pacific Affairs* 69 (1996–97).
32. Sumit Ganguly and Kanti Bajpai, "India and the Crisis."
33. Maya Chadda, *Ethnicity, Security and Separatism*, 71.
34. Ibid.
35. Islamonline News Site, "Pakistani Education Minister on U.S. Visit to Secularize Schooling," http://www.islamonline.net/english/news/2002-03/10/article24.shtml (accessed March 2002).
36. Kshitij Prabha, *Terrorism: an Instrument of Foreign Policy* (New Delhi: South Asian Publishers, 2000).
37. In Sindh and Baluchistan—two southern provinces of Pakistan—local governments face problems with the central administration on issues such as sharing sovereignty and the exercise of authority. Controversy still exists concerning whether or not it was fair and legal that the two provinces joined Pakistan during the partition.
38. Kshitij Prahba, *Terrorism*.
39. Sumit Ganguly, *Conflict Unending: India-Pakistan Tensions Since 1947* (New York: Columbia University Press, 2002).
40. Kail C. Ellis, "Pakistan's Foreign Policy: Alternative Policies" in *Dilemmas of National Security and Cooperation in India and Pakistan*, ed. Hafeez Malik (New York: St. Martin's Press, 1993).
41. The News International, "Sheikh Issues Fatwa over Kashmir," May 30, 2002, http://news.pacificnews.org/news/view article.html?article_id=434 (accessed April 2, 2005).
42. Maya Chadda, *Building Democracy in South Asia: India, Nepal, Pakistan* (Boulden, CO: Lynne Rienner, 2000).
43. Maya Chadda, *Security and Separatism*.
44. Chadda,"From an Empire State." While India must consider China, in particular, in terms of nuclear balance or deterrence in the region, Pakistan's arsenal was created almost entirely in response to a perceived threat from India.
45. Ibid.
46. Maya Chadda, *Security and Separatism*.
47. Ibid., 144.
48. Maya Chadda,"From an Empire State."
49. Mitsuhiro Kondo, "Hindu Nationalists and Their Critique of Monotheism: The Relationship between Nation, Religion and Violence," in *The Unfinished Agenda: Nation Building in South Asia*, ed. Mushirul Hasan and Nariaki Nakazato (New Delhi: Manohar Publishers and Distributors, 2001).
50. Partha S. Ghosh, "The Congress and the BJP: Struggle for the Heartland," in *Political Parties and Party Systems*, ed. Ajay K. Mehra, D. D. Khanna, and Gert W. Kueck (New Delhi: Sage Publications India, 2003), 224–243.
51. Maya Chadda, *Building Democracy*.
52. Tremblay, "*Intervening Role*"; Rahman, *Divided Kashmir*; Ganguly, *Conflict unending*; Ganguly and Bajpai, "India and the crisis"; Chadda, "From an Empire State."
53. Tremblay, "*Intervening Role*"; Rahman, Divided Kashmir.
54. Tremblay, "*Intervening Role*".
55. Ainslie Embree, "Kashmir: Has Religion a Role in Making Peace?" in *Faith-Based Diplomacy: Trumping Realpolitik*, ed. Douglas Johnston (New York: Oxford University Press, 2003), 33–75.
56. T. N. Madan, "Religion, Ethnicity and Nationalism in India," in *Religion, Ethnicity and Self Identity*, ed. Martin E. Marty and R. Scott Appelby (Lebanon, NH: University Press of New England, 1997), 53–71.

# Forgiveness and Reconciliation: The Religious Dimension

## YEHUDITH AUERBACH

What is the role of religion in conflicts? If one surveys the ancient as well as the recent history of bloody confrontations between believers of rival religions, one could hardly avoid the conclusion that "religion, having so often inspired, legitimated and exacerbated deadly conflicts, cannot be expected to contribute to their peaceful transformation." Appleby, who refutes this notion, contends that "a new form of conflict transformation—'religious peace building'—is taking shape on the ground, in and across local communities plagued by violence."[1] This argument is also presented and validated by other scholars of the role of religion in conflict.[2]

In this paper we will probe the potential contribution of religion to conflict termination through the conceptual prism of *forgiveness*. Before getting into the main argument, I will review some of the recent developments that have questioned the conventional, "realist" assumptions about the "rules of the game" in the international arena, and which necessitate a new approach.

One witnesses these days a plethora of contradictory developments taking place in the international arena since the end of the cold war. On the one hand there is a significant increase in violence and hostilities, either in the form of sanguinary ethnic wars (e.g., in the Balkans) or gruesome terrorist acts by Islamic zealots,[3] followed by reprisal wars by the attacked states. On the other hand, there are increasing efforts at redressing past evils and enhancing justice and peace among nations and groups— particularly in the form of apologies and requests for forgiveness. Many of these apologies have been exchanged between nations involved in World War II. Examples of this include the following: *The Czech–German Declaration of Mutual Relations and Their Future Relations* issued in January 1997, whereby the two countries apologized for past grievances caused by each of them to the other's population;[4] the Russian apology to the Polish people for the murder of fifteen thousand Polish reserve officers in Katyn; Poland's president Lech Walesa asking for Israeli forgiveness in the Israeli Parliament in May 1991, and Austrian president Frantz Vranitsky apologizing to the Jewish people for the Austrian participation in the Holocaust in July 1991.[5]

Another type of apology is put forward by a nation-state apologizing for its misconduct to the group that was the object of the transgression. An example of this kind is President de Klerk's apology in August 1996 to the black majority in South Africa for the brutal violation of their rights under apartheid rule.[6] Israeli Prime Minister Barak made a similar, though less reverberant, apology in September 1997 to Israel's non-European "Eastern" immigrant communities for their sufferings caused by misdeeds of the Labor party when in power. In some cases the apology is accompanied by an offer of compensation for past injustices, e.g., the apology and compensation offered by the Reagan administration to Japanese–Americans who had

*171*

been interned during World War II. Some countries (e.g., Australia, New Zealand, and Canada) are investigating ways and techniques of compensating their indigenous populations.

Mass media, which has become a major method of shaping public opinion, contributes to the increasing impression that apology is the order of the day. Press pages and television screens are replete with pictures of this or that world leader offering his apologies for past evils which his country was responsible for in one way or another. Thus, American presidents Bill Clinton and George W. Bush have used their televised visits to Africa to apologize to their hosts for the slavery of African natives by Americans, and the English prime minister Tony Blair has asked the Irish people to forgive England for turning a blind eye to their suffering during the grand famine of 1840. "It almost seems that apology has become an international fad," concludes one of the most astute observers of these recent developments.[7]

Another attempt to redress past injustice and bring about peace within damaged societies is truth commissions. This technique is usually based on a kind of an informal understanding between a majority group that has previously been subjected to the oppressive rule of a minority group, and the minority (now afraid of reprisals). According to this agreement, perpetrators confess their crimes and in return receive immunity from prosecution. The best-known example of such a commission is the Truth and Reconciliation Committee (TRC) in South Africa initiated by Nelson Mandela and chaired by archbishop Desmond Tutu.[8] Similar commissions have been established in Argentina, Chile, El Salvador, Honduras, Rwanda, Uruguay, and recently Peru.

Yet another effort at providing guarantees for justice and truth is the establishment of an international judicial system aimed at trying war criminals. The latest examples are the War Crime Tribunal set up following the Balkan wars and the International Criminal Court already approved by the majority of the international community.

These examples may corroborate the thesis that we are entering a new era of enlightenment. Proponents of this thesis argue that, "as the so-called realism of the cold war vanished, the UN, NATO and individual countries struggled to define their places in a world that is paying increased attention to moral values."[9]

The interpretation of international phenomena depends, of course, on one's worldview or paradigm. And the realists or neorealists will not relinquish their case that easily. But even the most convinced realist cannot deny the authenticity of Bush's moral rage against terrorist organizations. By the same token, realists will acknowledge—with due disgust—the religious zeal that motivated the terrorist acts in the United States as well as in the Middle East and Spain. It may be that all the seemingly contradictory occurrences cited above have sprung from one and the same source, namely the failure of "track one" diplomacy to bring about peace and justice and the subsequent growing awareness, on both sides of the civilization gap, that the rational and relativistic approach which has dominated the international arena since World War II should be replaced with some kind of a value-based system.[10] Unfortunately, this thirst for justice, morality and (one would argue) more religiosity in the world has brought about the "clash of civilizations."[11] This much-debated clash is not only evidence of the tensions and differences between Muslim tradition on the one hand and Judeo-Christian legacy on the other, but also points to the "ambivalence of the sacred."[12] The longing for the "sacred," argues Appleby, is both the source of the best of human deeds as well as the engine for the most evil and destructive deeds. In the name of religion, people have been murdered and eliminated throughout history, but a deep religious feeling is (presumably) one of the motivating forces behind the growing movement toward the pursuit of justice, democracy, and human rights as well as the recent "fad" of forgiveness and apology in international relations.

This paper focuses on "forgiveness" as one of the most conspicuous expressions of the growing role of religion in conflict transformation. The main questions put forward are the following: What is the role of forgiveness in reconciliation? Is forgiveness a necessary condition for reconciliation between former enemies? Is it sufficient for bringing about real and stable peace between them? To what extent and how does religion affect the reconciliation via forgiveness process?

In trying to cope with these questions I will juxtapose two pairs of concepts—*material conflicts* and *conflict resolution* on the one hand versus *identity conflicts* and *reconciliation* on the other. I will argue that *forgiveness is a necessary though not sufficient condition* for bringing about reconciliation in conflicts that are *identity conflicts*. *Material conflicts*, however, are more amenable to "track one" diplomacy, which has traditionally strived to resolve conflicts rather than to bring about reconciliation between former enemies. In *identity conflicts*—where there is need for forgiveness—religion will help in bridging the gap of rancor and vengeance only if the sides to the conflict share similar religious convictions regarding forgiveness. Otherwise religion will be irrelevant or could even hamper the reconciliation process.

The key concepts in this paper are therefore *identity conflict, material conflict, conflict resolution, reconciliation,* and *forgiveness*. The first sections of the paper will present and illustrate these concepts. Following that, I will analyze the role of religion in reconciliation via forgiveness in identity conflicts.

## Identity Conflicts and Material Conflicts

International conflicts vary in intensity, duration, the number of players, and a host of other parameters. One crucial dimension for distinguishing between conflicts is the kind of issue around which they have evolved. Looking at conflicts from this angle one can differentiate between *material conflicts* and *identity conflicts*. In the case of material conflicts, the dispute is mainly about material and dividable assets such as oil, territory, and the like. The dispute may be bitter, long, and hard to resolve. Strong emotions may be felt on all sides. Often the conflict escalates into acute crises and sanguinary wars. It may take many efforts, including the intervention of a third party, until the rivals get to the negotiation table, let alone to an agreement. But each side knows that resolving the conflict is only a question of how to divide the coveted assets and pay the minimal price. The conflict will terminate when it reaches a point when both rivals believe that the costs of continuing the conflict are higher than the benefits, and that the benefits of stopping the hostilities are greater than the costs.

While identity conflicts may also have a material dimension, the core bone of contention in this kind of conflict is *identity* and the feeling, of at least one of the sides, that the other has usurped their legitimate rights. These rights include (since the end of the nineteenth century, and more so after World War I) claims for national self-expression and, ultimately, the establishment of a sovereign nationstate. When the fulfillment of these claims involves bloodshed and sacrifices, the ground is prepared for the creation and inculcation of a moral/religious ethos that lends the battle for national independence an aura of a holy war—where the good are entitled and obliged to defeat the bad.

Reflecting about the links between conflict, the search for identity, and religion, Gopin mentions: "Especially in conflict-ridden situations, the tight relations between identity, personal [as well as national, Y. A.] legitimacy and the drive to create religiously unique cultural expression is high." This search for a unique and exalted identity at times of conflict, which Gopin calls "negative identity," "tends to focus on what makes me the most different precisely when I feel the most mortally and existentially threatened by an enemy."[13] The intensifying effect of religion on conflicts is not limited to the premodern era, when religion played a central role in the lives of people and served as the exclusive focus of loyalty, but is also evident in modern identity conflicts that evolve around (secular) symbols of nationhood and political sovereignty. In this kind of conflict, religion—often cynically used by secular leaders to mobilize public support—serves as a rationalization rather than as the rationale for a holy war. To be sure, the "clash of civilizations" takes place in a "postmodern" era when the authentic thirst for religiosity, partly caused by the failures of modernity to provide better lives to peoples of the third world, is easily used by charismatic leaders (like bin Laden) to wage war against the big (United States) or small (Israel) Satan. Once religion enters into the picture, be it as cause or as pretext, the conflict "tend(s) to be more intractable due to the non-bargainable nature of the motivations behind [it]."[14] Religious rhetoric (used fervidly by this kind of leader) stirs up the public, propels the other side to react in a similar vein, and consequently lessens the chances for a rational dialogue between the parties. The identity conflict which "is usually nourished by a powerful sense of injustice on the part of the victimized nation or identity group," tends to be passionate and intense. "The historic wounds are felt as assaults on the self-concept and therefore ultimate safety and security of the victim group."[15] Religion is then offered both as rationalization for the suffering and as a source for consolation and hope for days of glory.

These two kinds of conflict are "ideal types" in the Weberian sense. Hence, real conflicts are usually mixed cases where material and identity issues are inextricably interwoven. Sometimes a conflict starts as an identity conflict and evolves into a material conflict or vice versa. The Israel–Egypt conflict is an interesting case of various passages from one ideal type to another. From 1948 to 1967 the relations between the two countries fitted quite well into the "identity conflict" profile. As a matter of fact, there were no genuine feelings of animosity or rancor between the two peoples, but presenting Israel as the "big demon" that was directly and exclusively responsible for the calamity of the Palestinians, served the Egyptian leaders' Pan-Arab ambitions. Following the occupation of the Sinai Peninsula by Israel in 1967, it seemed that the conflict was gradually assuming "material" characteristics, as the demand for returning the Arab soil became the main Egyptian condition for conflict resolution. However, the 1967 Khartoum declaration whereby the Arab countries (led by Egypt) pledged "no peace with Israel, no recognition of Israel, no negotiation with Israel" and the linkage made between the territorial demands and the "rights of the Palestinians in their homeland"[16] made it clear that the perception—or more accurately, the presentation—of the Israel–Egypt conflict as an identity conflict was still predominant in Nasser's strategic thinking. It was not before Sadat's startling visit to Israel in 1977, and his notorious saying that 70 percent of the conflict was merely psychological, that the conflict genuinely shifted from the "identity" to the "material" pattern. This act opened the way to conflict resolution and to normalization. Voices against the agreement with Israel have been heard in Egypt since then, particularly from the Egyptian intelligentsia who, on the whole, deny Israel's legitimacy as a nation-state. However, Egyptian interests as perceived by President Mubarak have prevented thus far the deterioration of Israel–Egypt relations into the identity conflict pattern.[17] In contrast, the continuous bloodshed between Israelis and Palestinians demonstrates the difficulties of the two peoples in breaking the chains of their respective "victim ethos," and the resulting tragic consequences. This is a clear case of an identity conflict.[18]

Each of these two conflicts, having different sources and characteristics, demand a different mode of conflict termination. The material conflict, which originates in and persists because of risk versus chance calculations, may be ended through a series of "track one" diplomacy steps, which conclude with "conflict resolution." The identity conflict, which has been fueled by feelings of injustice and victimization, demands more than a formal accommodation and needs "forgiveness" and ultimately "reconciliation." I will proceed with a short juxtaposition of "conflict resolution" versus "reconcilation" and then elaborate on the role of forgiveness in reconciliation.

## Conflict Resolution and Reconciliation

Conflict resolution as a means of ending rivalries between nation-states has mainly been examined within the framework of the realist paradigm, which has long dominated the study of international relations. According to this approach, conflicts erupt over material interests and are nourished by the belief of each side that the continuation of the hostilities will bring about tangible profits. When pushed, by realistic power calculations, to terminate their conflict, the rivals will direct their efforts at resolving the conflict—usually through compromise and contractual agreements.

Scholars who wished both to understand the process and to contribute to its realization developed the "conflict resolution" concept as a vehicle for this double outcome.[19] The concept was defined and elaborated within the limited contours of the relevant era. According to Kriesberg, the conflict resolution approach "presumes that conflicts are never wholly zero-sum...consequently there is the possibility of...an integrative outcome whereby all parties gain much [but not all, Y. A.] of what they need or want."[20] Studied from a cognitive perspective, conflict resolution is defined as a "political process through which the parties in conflict eliminate the perceived incompatibility between their goals and interests and establish a new situation of perceived compatibility."[21]

Following the end of the cold war, the concomitant growing cooperation between nations and peoples in the Western hemisphere, and the increasing number of apologies and acts of forgiveness throughout the world, scholars of conflict and conflict-ending strategies have gradually shifted their focus from "conflict resolution" to concepts such as "reconciliation" and "forgiveness" that reflect more correctly the spirit and practice of the "new age."[22]

The concept of reconciliation has a much broader meaning than conflict resolution. It involves psychological processes, both cognitive (e.g., shared political narratives) and emotional (e.g., healing, empathy), and thus adds an important element to the analysis of conflict termination. True, socio-psychological contributions have been introduced into the study of conflict and conflict resolution for over the last thirty years.[23] However, the socio-psychological approach has usually focused more on the *process* than on the *outcome* of conflict resolution. Scholars like Kelman, Burton, and Fisher are deeply convinced that "track one" diplomacy (based on techniques such as mediation and negotiation) is a deficient conflict-ending instrument. They suggest that the parties to a conflict, and particularly third parties that offer their services to the combatants, make use of "track two" techniques (such as interactive workshops) as vehicles for narrowing the psychological and cultural gap between the protagonists.[24]

While reconciliation scholars mostly concur that "reconciliation is both a process and an outcome,"[25] they tend to put greater emphasis on the *outcome* aspect of reconciliation. Reconciliation, often used interchangeably with "stable peace," is considered "the long-term goal of any process of conflict resolution."[26] Kriesberg views reconciliation as a "relatively amicable relationship typically established after a rupture in relations involving one sided or mutual infliction of extreme injury."[27]

Kriesberg describes the four steps that former rivals take on the way to reconciliation: "they acknowledge the reality of the terrible acts that were perpetrated; accept with compassion those who committed injurious conduct, as well as acknowledging each other's sufferings; believe that their injustices are being redressed and anticipate mutual security and well-being."[28]

The last phase marks, in fact, the culmination of the reconciliation process and embodies the hopes for trust, respect, and harmony that motivated both the study of reconciliation and its practice by former enemies.

Kriesberg notes that full and complete reconciliation is almost never accomplished between former enemies. Nonetheless, he encourages rivals to mobilize their efforts toward this goal since "the failure to carry out any measure of reconciliation endangers the stability in relations between former enemies."[29]

While reconciliation, according to this school of thought, is a prerequisite for stable peace in *all* conflicts, one can think of cases where former protagonists have reached the stage of "stable peace," whereby "neither side considers employing force,"[30] without taking genuine steps toward reconciliation.[31] Former rivals in material conflicts who have decided to terminate their conflict usually do not strive for more than the cessation of hostilities and the settlement of their dispute in a rational way. Generous, unexpected reconciliation steps may signal the readiness of one of the parties to get into a "normal" conflict-resolution process rather than a willingness to fully reconcile with the enemy.[32] Once conflict resolution has been reached and a peace agreement (or some equivalent formal document) signed, full reconciliation may remain a noble goal worthy of lofty hopes and restless endeavors (usually by non governmental organizations [NGOs]) rather than a realistic target to which the former rivals mobilize their political efforts. Given the realistic nature of the material conflict and the rational, "cost-benefit" characteristics of the mechanisms used in its termination, forgiveness seems almost irrelevant to the conflict resolution or reconciliation processes.

By contrast, the antagonists in an identity conflict, separated by gaps of mistrust, anger, hostility, and feelings of victimhood, could be pushed by pragmatic considerations to resolve their conflict and normalize their relations—or at least attain some kind of "peace without reconciliation." But this peace will be deficient "because it forfeits the advantages of reconciliation—the repaired and renewed relationships that are essential to the reconstruction of political life, the economy, and a strong civil life."[33] This is particularly true for relations between partners in an intrasocietal conflict, but applies as well to antagonists in any identity conflict whose past memories of suffering and injustice need repair and restoration. The way to the fulfillment of such needs is by no means simple, but can be smoothed with the help of a common cultural foundation provided by religion. Even if the parties are divided by different (and sometimes rival) religions, they usually share some similar beliefs that can serve as a spiritual bridge over their actual quarrels. The recognition that all human beings are potential sinners whose lives are geared to please an almighty God should eventually open their hearts toward compassion and forgiveness to their victimizers. If they fail to mobilize their efforts to this noble end and try to circumvent the process of asking and giving genuine forgiveness, the way toward full reconciliation might be blocked.[34]

In the first of the two following sections I will introduce the concept of forgiveness and the debates in the literature regarding its virtue and feasibility. In the subsequent and last section I will focus on the relation between forgiveness and religion.

## Forgiveness

Forgiveness is typically defined as "the forswearing of resentment, the resolute overcoming of anger and hatred that are naturally directed toward a person who has done an unjustified and non-excused moral injury."[35] According to Shriver, the transaction of asking for and giving forgiveness presupposes the following:

- "[Recognition of] the commission of an *evil* act by one agent against another"
- "the willingness of offenders to acknowledge their offenses... this is the *repentance* side of the transaction"
- "moral forgiveness begins with the memory of immorality, with moral *judgment*"
- "to forgive... *is to value the hope of relation repair*"
- "forgiveness always involves a certain *forbearance*, a step back from revenge"
- "it... involves some degree of *empathy* with the one who has committed the wrong"[36] (emphasis in original).

The six components outlined above are not of equal importance or difficulty. The sine qua non for forgiveness seems to be the recognition on both sides to the conflict that one side has committed a crime against the other. Forgiveness is only possible when the sides involved in the conflict acknowledge that an injustice has been done and agree upon the identity of the victim and the perpetrator.

In the literature there is some vagueness concerning the similarities and differences between *forgiveness* and *apology*. *Forgiveness* seems to be broader than apology, incorporating both the request for forgiveness made by the perpetrator and the victim's response. It thus has the connotation of a transaction. *Apology*, on the other hand, seems to denote only the action of asking for forgiveness. For the present discussion I'll refer to these two concepts interchangeably, relying on authors like Tavuchis, who actually suggests that the one incorporates the other: "one who *apologizes* seeks *forgiveness* and redemption for what is unreasonable, unjustified, undeserving and inequitable"[37] (emphasis is mine).

Tavuchis differentiates between four modes of apology: from one to one (individual to individual); from one to many (individual to collectivity); from many to one (collectivity to individual); from many to many (collectivity to collectivity).

The mode that is most relevant to the discussion of the role of forgiveness (or apology) in the process of reconciliation between societies is the fourth—from many to many. True, in most cases it is one person (usually the leader) who makes the apology speech, but in fact he is apologizing on behalf—though not always with the full approval—of his people, and he addresses his plea to the many, namely to the other people.

The collective apology differs from the individual apology in its tone and style. It is not as spontaneous and emotional as the bid for forgiveness addressed by one person to another. Being "a diplomatic accomplishment,"[38] it tends to be "couched in abstract, remote, measured and emotionally neutral terms."[39]

This qualitative difference notwithstanding, the collective apology—like the individual apology—is an act of expressing remorse and asking for forgiveness, and as such it is regarded as "a prelude to reconciliation" between offenders and victims.

There is disagreement regarding the psychological merits of forgiveness. Psychotherapeutically, it has been argued that resentment is a legitimate and healthy way of expressing self respect[40] that makes people "feel alive and wards off the threat of emptiness."[41]

The moral dimension of forgiveness has also been the focus of continuing discussions. Haber challenges the morality of the demand to forgive and give up resentment and claims: "A lack of resentment on this or that occasion is evidence of a moral failing."[42] He rejects the positions of philosophers such as Nietzsche, Spinoza, and William James who have, in one way or another, loathed remorse and repentance and argues: "It is morally wrong to forgive a wrongdoer unless the wrongdoer has repented her misdeed. In the absence of repentance forgiveness betrays a lack of self-respect."[43]

Archbishop Tutu, who was deeply involved in the work of the TRC in South Africa, rejects the allegations against forgiveness and lauds its moral and purifying power: "In forgiving people are not being asked to forget. On the contrary it is important to remember, so that we should not let such atrocities happen again. Forgiveness does not mean condoning what has been done. It means taking what happened seriously and not minimizing it.... Forgiveness is not being sentimental... Forgiving means abandoning your right to pay back the perpetrator in his own coin, but it is a loss that liberates the victim."[44]

Tutu considered the TRC in South Africa (based on the idea of forgiveness, though asking for forgiveness was not a condition for immunity) to be a "flawed commission," but sees "in this flawed attempt... a possible paradigm for dealing with situations where violence, conflict, turmoil and sectional strife have seemed endemic." Tutu does not differentiate between inter- and intra-societal conflicts and calls upon the antagonists in the Israeli–Palestinian conflict to emulate the South African model.[45]

But forgiveness as a mechanism for terminating a conflict has its limits, particularly in cases of conflicts between states. "Factors associated with forgiveness that act to restore order in civil cases are largely absent in international cases" argue Long and Brecke.[46] Asking for forgiveness in the context of intractable and sometimes bloody interstate conflicts may seem "extreme and perhaps paralyzing."[47] The plea for forgiveness may be perceived as an act of humiliation and subsequently hurt the pleading state's status. On the other hand, the victim who is asked to grant forgiveness may feel that "to forgive is to relinquish the victim role and the rewards that go with it" such as "the power to induce guilt, to demand apologies and reparations or to seek punishment of the perpetrator."[48]

The literature dealing with forgiveness in the context of international or intra-national conflict does not fully agree about the causal link between the act of forgiveness and the process of reconciliation. Some would argue that reconciliation brings upon and facilitates forgiveness and healing.[49] Others hold that forgiveness is a step toward reconciliation. Among those who see forgiveness as a phase in the process of reaching genuine reconciliation there are still some differences regarding the nature of this phase. Is it a necessary *and* sufficient condition for reconciliation? There are scholars who claim that forgiveness is not a necessary condition for reconciliation, relying on cases like the reconciliation between West Germany and Israel.[50] I will argue that forgiveness is important, and in some cases—most notably when a crime of the scale of the Holocaust has been committed—necessary for a *full and genuine* reconciliation between former enemies. If no real effort at achieving forgiveness is made, reconciliation is doomed to be partial and vulnerable. In some cases, most paradoxically when forgiveness is most needed, the way to forgiveness may be hampered.

Forgiveness is, therefore, a *necessary—though not always possible*—and not sufficient condition for *full* and *perfect* reconciliation between former adversaries. Forgiveness is only possible if and when the two sides that engage in the process of reconciliation agree about the crime committed by one of them, and about the identity of the perpetrator. In many of the ongoing conflicts that attract world attention (e.g., the Israeli–Palestinian conflict), the contradictory arguments about the identities of the criminal and the victim are one of the most serious stumbling blocks on the way to reconciliation. Every side has its version of the dispute and cultivates its own historical narrative. The conflicting narratives serve as the cornerstones of the respective collective identities and are, therefore, almost immune to change. If the sides have come to agree on the issues of crime, perpetrator, and victim, most of the work toward conflict resolution has already been done. Then and only then can the reconciling sides enter into a process of forgiveness in order to achieve full and perfect reconciliation.

However, there are cases where the assertions about the nature of the crime and identity of the perpetrator are beyond dispute. In most cases of genocide, or even of less brutal wrongdoing toward indigenous inhabitants, there is no doubt about the share of guilt. These are the cases where forgiveness is most needed, but also hard to undertake. Israel–Germany relations following the Holocaust is an example of such a case. When the two states wished to enter into negotiations for the sake of reparations, the Israeli prime minister demanded a clear and unequivocal acknowledgement of the German responsibility for the crimes committed by the Nazis. Chancellor Adenauer circumvented Ben Gurion's demand, setting an example for all other chancellors to come. Nevertheless the two states signed the Reparation Agreement, and since then relations have gradually warmed and become "normal," some would argue "special,"[51] but full reconciliation has not been achieved nor has a genuine bid for forgiveness been made.[52]

Asking for and granting forgiveness in cases of genocide and other heinous crimes of that scale raises a host of intriguing questions: Are all crimes forgivable? Is there no danger that cheap and easy forgiveness will lead rather to the perpetuation of evil instead of eradicating it? Do survivors have the right to forgive in the names of the dead victims? And alternately, should and can the descendants of perpetrators ask for forgiveness in the names of their late fathers?

This is the place where religion can play a crucial role. To the extent that the antagonists share the same religious convictions regarding forgiveness, the chances for forgiveness and reconciliation are enhanced. However, incompatibility in the religious tenets regarding forgiveness will make it hard for the sides to get into a genuine forgiveness process and will have, therefore, a negative impact on reconciliation. In the last section I will examine the role of religion in furthering or halting the forgiveness and reconciliation processes. I'll limit myself to a short discussion of the three monotheistic religions.

## Forgiveness, Religion, and Reconciliation

Forgiveness is a religious concept prevalent in the three monotheistic religions, but it is much more accentuated in Christianity.[53] The centrality of forgiveness in these religions stems from three basic tenets common to all of them: (1) God created the world, (2) human beings are created in the image of God and, therefore, (3) should follow his steps: "Thou shalt keep the commandments of the Lord thy God, and walk in his ways."[54]

In the Old Testament, forgiveness is represented as one of the basic qualities of God. It emanates from his love for his people and is given to sinners as a gift.[55]

Forgiveness between man and God is possible because man is aware of his own weakness vis-à-vis God and is, therefore, not afraid of being humiliated through his plea for forgiveness. No power calculations are involved in this story. Giving pardon does not diminish God's power, and man does not feel patronized by receiving it—as is often the case when one human being grants forgiveness to another, thus placing himself morally above the transgressor. The person that atones for his sins knows that God loves him and wants him to repent.

Forgiveness between human beings is more complicated and treated differently by the three religions. A quick glance at references to forgiveness in the three monotheistic religions will reveal the potential for misunderstanding between antagonists that consider forgiveness as a way to reconciliation.

Forgiveness is one of the cornerstones of Christian theology. It should be given unconditionally to friends and enemies alike independently of the magnitude of the crime or the behavior of the perpetrator. The idea of unlimited forgiveness is linked, in the Christian tradition, with the notion of original sin. Since all human beings are conceived in sin and therefore doomed to a sinful life, they are entitled to forgiveness.[56]

Christianity teaches its believers to cherish love and mercy and to express these noble feelings through forgiveness to their enemies. The devout Christian is required to follow the example of Jesus, who forgave his enemies on the cross, without even waiting for them to ask for forgiveness.[57]

Judaism is less tolerant toward sinners. The rabbinical tradition believes that man is a free agent, fully capable of overcoming his inherent tendency toward evil, and therefore accountable for his deeds. Judaism "is more concerned with justice than with forgiving incorrigible sinners, whereas Christianity...talks more of forgiveness as an act of grace, given even to the undeserving and not yet repentant, than of justice."[58]

Judaism has strict rules regarding forgiveness. Forgiveness can be asked only from the victim himself, and only the victim can forgive. Maimonidis says: "Sins between one man and his fellow, such as striking, cursing, or stealing are never forgiven until one pays up his debt and appeases his fellow. Even if he returns the money he owes he must still ask for forgiveness."[59] According to Rambam (Maimonidis), there are three essential stages in the process of *teshuvah* (repentance). Firstly, the sinner has to confess the sin, thereafter the person is requested to repent their wrongdoing, and finally the person must undertake not to repeat such sins.[60] The wrongdoer shall confess to the sin in front of the community and must compensate the victim. Only after having fulfilled these requirements is the transgressor entitled to forgiveness.

*Teshuvah*—repentance—is the sine qua non for forgiveness. Without *teshuvah* there is no forgiveness. Repentance paves the way to forgiveness and ultimately to reconciliation. Judaism puts greater emphasis on *teshuvah* than on forgiveness. The story of God forgiving the children of Israel for the sin of building a golden calf is brought forward by Christianity as well as by Judaism as the ultimate lesson about forgiveness. While the Christian tradition depicts God as a model of absolute mercy and forgiveness, Judaism uses the same verses to teach its believers the limits of forgiveness. Following Moses's request, God forgave his people, but forgiveness is not unconditional. "God is...controlling his anger in order to give the wicked an opportunity to repent....If...the wicked do not repent they will not be forgiven."[61] The children of Israel are taught to emulate God's behavior and forgive the wrongdoer only if and when the person repents.

The idea of repentance is a recurring motif in Jewish thought. The prominent Jewish thinkers Rabbi Abraham Yitzhak Hacohen Kook and Rabbi Yosef Dov Halevi Soloveitchik imbue *teshuvah* with the halo of truth, love, and light and elevate it to the highest degree of religious accomplishment.[62]

In Islam, forgiveness has been given major attention. Tawba (repentance), like its Jewish equivalent *teshuvah*, is a demanding process consisting of three phases identical to those requested by the Jewish law[63] and considered a necessary condition for *Ghufrān*—forgiveness granted by God to the repenting sinner.[64] The rituals of *sulh* (settlement) and *musalaha* (reconciliation), usually performed within a communal framework, are meant to end conflicts among believers and establish peace through acknowledgement and forgiveness of the injuries between individuals and groups.[65]

Within each of the three monotheistic religions one can find a mixture of different ideas regarding forgiveness, some of which are quite similar to those found in the "sister" religions. Thus, Jewish proponents of forgiveness would applaud King David for forgiving his foe—Shimei, the son of Gera—who had cursed him and thrown stones at him in the course of Absalom's rebellion against his father.[66] On the other hand, those Christians who are not at ease with the message of instant forgiveness will find in the New Testament warnings against cheap and easy forgiveness.[67] However, the discrepancy between Christianity and the two other Abrahamic religions regarding the prominence of forgiveness should not be ignored and can be summarized as follows: while Judaism and Islam highlight the idea of repentance and justice, Christianity emphasizes the importance of mercy, love, and forgiveness. This difference may hamper understanding and, consequently, halt the reconciliation process between parties of different religious convictions.

An example of such an incongruity is provided by Simon Wiesenthal. Wiesenthal shares a past dilemma, when he was unable to forgive a Catholic former Nazi soldier who, on his deathbed, begged and felt entitled to forgiveness for his terrible crimes against Jews.[68] Fifty-three people, among them philosophers, theologians, authors, and religious authorities have tried to cope with Wiesenthal's disturbing question: "What would I have done [if I were in Wiesenthal's place]?" All the Jewish respondents answered that Wiesenthal was right in not granting forgiveness to the Nazi soldier. All those who said they would have forgiven were non-Jewish (one Buddhist and the others Catholics). It is of course not surprising that the Jewish interlocutors would concur with their fellow Holocaust survivor. Still, the impact of religion goes beyond ethnic solidarity and is evident in the answers of most participants. For example, one of the respondents, a Catholic priest, said: "My whole instinct is to forgive. Perhaps that is because I am a Catholic priest. In a sense I am in the forgiving business. I sit in a confessional for hours and forgive everyone who comes in, confesses, and is sorry."[69]

Wiesenthal's report sheds light on the difficulties in building a bridge of forgiveness between victims and victimizers who are set apart not only by the immediate past, but also by their ancient religious traditions and myths. For many Jews, Germany is the live embodiment of their mythological foe Amalek—whose remembrance they were ordered to "blot out...from under heaven."[70] The lesson for descendants of the Jews murdered by the Nazis seems, therefore, straightforward; forgiving Germany—Amalek's equal—is a sin, and therefore strictly forbidden.

Incompatibility in religion is not the only (or even the main) reason for the lack of forgiveness, and consequently of genuine reconciliation, between Israel and Germany.[71] But it appears to be another obstacle on the way of these two countries toward healing and rapprochement.

Forgiveness in that case is specifically hard because the wrongdoers (those required to ask for forgiveness) were Christians (Adenauer himself was a devout Catholic) trained to think in terms of unconditional forgiveness, while the victims (those expected to grant forgiveness) are Jews who have been taught that nothing less than full repentance warrants forgiveness. By contrast, the path to forgiveness and subsequent reconciliation between Germany on the one hand and both Poland and the Czech Republic was lubricated with a similar religious approach to forgiveness (Christian and mainly Catholic). Furthermore, both cases (unlike the German–Jewish case) display a kind of "victimhood symmetry," as the expulsion of Germans from Poland and from the Czech Republic at the end of World War II, though not comparable to Germany's aggression against these two countries, justified reciprocal acts of forgiveness.[72]

Another example of successful forgiveness because of a similarity in religious and cultural background is the South African case. In this case the victims' Catholic upbringing converged with the already-existing tendency toward compassion and harmony in the African *ubuntu* weltanschauung.[73] This cultural-religious infrastructure has, arguably, played a significant role in the prevention of bloodshed and vengeance following the ascendance to power of the African National Congress (ANC) in 1994.

These examples bolster Gopin's conclusion that "forgiveness can only play a crucial role in conflict resolution...when it is placed in the context of individual cultures."[74] When the sides to the conflict share similar attitudes regarding the value, importance, shape, and contents of forgiveness they are ready to embark on the long and difficult journey toward forgiveness that culminates in reconciliation. The greater the cultural-religious gap between the groups, the smaller their chances to reach this goal.

## Conclusion

This paper has focused on "forgiveness" as one of the most conspicuous expressions of the growing role of religion in conflict transformation. The main questions put forward were: What is the role of forgiveness in reconciliation? Is forgiveness a necessary condition for reconciliation between former enemies? Is it sufficient for bringing about real and stable peace between them? To what extent and how does religion affect the reconciliation via forgiveness process?

In trying to cope with these questions I have juxtaposed two pairs of concepts: *material conflicts* and *conflict resolution* on the one hand, *identity conflicts* and *reconciliation* on the other. In the case of material conflicts, where the dispute is mainly about material and dividable assets, the conflict will terminate through traditional conflict resolution techniques. Identity conflicts, however, are harder to solve through "track one" diplomacy because they involve deep-seated hatred originated in the feeling, of at least one of the sides, that the other has usurped legitimate rights. Identity conflicts, this paper argues, need "track two" diplomacy, and most of all forgiveness in order to reach reconciliation. Forgiveness, basically a religious concept, is a necessary though not sufficient condition for bringing about reconciliation in identity conflicts. To the extent that the sides to the conflict share similar religious convictions regarding the nature of forgiveness, religion will contribute to reconciliation through building a bridge of common spiritual beliefs over the gap that has separated the antagonists. But if the contenders hold different, let alone conflicting, tenets regarding forgiveness, religion may hamper the reconciliation process.

A quick glance at the three monotheistic religions points to significant discrepancies in their approaches toward forgiveness. While Judaism, and to some extent Islam, see repentance as a sine qua non for forgiveness, Christianity highlights mercy and love, and teaches its believers to ask and grant forgiveness without preconditions. These differences may widen the gap between the parties to an identity conflict that wish to resolve their conflict and reach full and genuine reconciliation.

While forgiveness has been presented in previous writings[75] as the magic remedy for protracted conflicts between damaged societies and belligerent peoples, this paper emphasizes its limits. The power of forgiveness as a means for reconciliation is contingent, on both the role of religion in a specific conflict and the similarity between the approaches of the relevant religions to forgiveness. Thus, this paper takes a middle ground between those who argue for greater integration of religious elements in the process of reconciliation[76] and others who stress the potential contribution of religion to the intensification of conflicts.[77]

The arguments put forward in this paper need to be tested in historic and actual cases of identity conflicts. The Israeli–Palestinian case could serve as a suitable example for such a test.

## Notes

1. R. Scott Appleby, *The Ambivalence of the Sacred: Religion, Violence and Reconciliation* (Lanham, MD: Rowman and Littlefield, 2000), 7.

2. For example, see Mohhammed Abu Nimer, "Conflict Resolution, Culture and Religion: Toward a Training Model of Interreligious Peacebuilding," Journal of Peace Research 38, no. 6 (2001): 685–704; M. Gopin, *Between Eden and Armageddon* (New York: Oxford University Press, 2000); M. Gopin, *Holy War, Holy Peace* (New York: Oxford University Press, 2002).

3. E.g., the mega-terror events in the United States—September 11—and Spain—March 11, 2004—and the many terror acts in the Middle East.

4. Vladmir Handle, "Czech-German Declaration on Reconciliation," *German Politics* 6, no. 2 (1997): 150–67.

5. Joseph V. Montville, "The Healing Function in Political Conflict," in *Conflict Resolution Theory and Practice*, ed. D. J. Sandole and H. van der Merve (Manchester: Manchester University Press, 1993), 122–23.

6. Louis Kriesberg, "Coexistence and Reconciliation of Communal Conflicts," in *Handbook of Interethnic Coexistence*, ed. E. Weiner (New York: Continuum, 1998), 186.

7. Donald W. Shriver, "Forgiveness: A Bridge Across Abysses of Revenge," in *Forgiveness and Reconciliation*, ed. R. G. Helmick, S. J. Petersen, and R. L. Petersen (Philadelphia: Templeton Foundation Press, 2002), 163.

8. Dezmond Tutu, *No Future without Forgiveness* (New York: Doubleday, 1999).

9. Elazar Barkan, *The Guilt of Nations: Restitution and Negotiating Historical Injustices* (New York: Norton, 2000), xvi.

10. On the need for "track two" (non-official) diplomacy to compensate for the shortcomings of the regular "track one" diplomacy, see John Paul Lederach, *Building Peace: Sustainable Reconciliation in Divided Societies* (Washington DC: Institute of Peace Press, 1997); Joseph V. Montville, *The Arrow and the Olive Branch: A Case for Track Two Diplomacy; The Psychodynamics of International Relations* (Lexington, MA: Lexington Books, 1990).

11. Samuel P. Huntington, "The Clash of Civilizations?" *Foreign Affairs* 72, no. 3 (1993): 22–49.

12. Appleby, *Ambivalence*, 7.

13. Marc Gopin, *Between Eden and Armageddon*, 63.

14. Jonathan Fox, "Religion and State Failure: An Examination of the Extent and Magnitude of Religious Conflict from 1950 to 1996," *International Political Science Review* 25, no. 1 (2004): 58.

15. Joseph V. Montville, "Religion and Peacemaking," in *Forgiveness and Reconciliation*, ed. R. G. Helmick, S. J. Petersen, and R. L. Petersen (Philadelphia: Templeton Foundation Press, 2002), 101.

16. Moshe Dayan, *Story of My Life* (Jerusalem: Edanim Publishers, in collaboration with Tel Aviv: Dvir Publishing House Yediot Aharonot Edition, 1976), 512.

17. For a description of Israel-Egypt relations vis-à-vis the "stable peace" and "reconciliation" concepts see Y. Bar Siman-Tov, "Israel-Egypt: Stable Peace?" in *Stable Peace among Nations*, ed. Arie M. Kacowicz et al. (Lanham, MD: Rowman and Littlefield, 2000), 220–38; William J. Long and Peter Brecke, *War and Reconciliation: Reason and Emotion in Conflict Resolution* (Cambridge: MIT Press, 2003).

18. On the role of "victim" ethos and narratives in sustaining intractable conflicts in general and the Israeli–Palestinian conflict in particular, see Daniel Bar-Tal, "Societal Beliefs in Times of Intractable Conflict: The Israeli Case," *International Journal of Conflict Management* 9 (1998): 22–50.

19. For example, Kenneth E. Boulding, *Conflict and Defense: A General Theory* (New York: Harper and Row, 1962); L. A. Coser, "The Termination of Conflict," *Journal of Conflict Resolution* 5 (1961): 347–53; Ronald J. Fisher, *International Conflict and Behavioral Science* (New York: Basic Books, 1964); Kalevi J. Holsti, "Resolving International Conflicts: A Taxonomy of Behavior and Some Figures on Procedures," *Journal of Conflict Resolution* 10 (1966): 272–96; and Evan Luard, *The International Regulation of Frontier Disputes* (London: Thames and Hudson, 1970).

20. Louis Kriesberg, *International Conflict Resolution* (New Haven: Yale University Press, 1992), 9.

21. Daniel Bar-Tal, "From Intractable Conflict through Conflict Resolution to Reconciliation: Psychological Analysis," *Political Psychology* 21, no. 2 (2000): 354.

22. For example, Lily Gardner-Feldman, "The Principle and Practice of 'Reconciliation' in German Foreign Policy: Relations with France, Israel, Poland and the Czech Republic," *International Affairs* 75 (1999): 333–56; Louis Kriesberg, *Constructive Conflicts* (Lanham, MD: Rowman and Littlefield, 1998); Montville, "Healing Function," 112–27; Robert L. Rothstein "Fragile Peace and Its Aftermath," in *After the Peace: Resistance and Reconciliation*, ed. Robert L. Rothstein (Boulder, CO: Lynne Rienner, 1999), 223–47.

23. For example, John W. Burton, *Conflict and Communication* (London: Macmillan, 1969); J. W. Burton, "Conflict Resolution as a Function of Human Needs," in *The Power of Human Needs in World Society*, ed. Roger A. Coate and Jerel A. Rosati (Boulder, CO: Lynne Rienner, 1988), 187–204; Ronald J. Fisher, "Methods of Third Parties Intervention," in *The Berghof Handbook of Conflict Transformation*, ed. Norbert Ropers, Martina Fischer, and E.

Manton (Berlin: Berghof Center for Conflict Management, 2001), 1–27; Herbert C. Kelman, "An Interactional Approach to Conflict Resolution and Its Application to Israeli–Palestinian Relations," *International Interactions* 6, no. 2 (1979): 99–122; Herbert C. Kelman, "Social-Psychological Dimensions of International Conflict," in *Peacemaking in International Conflict: Methods and Techniques*, ed. J. William Zartman and J. Lewis Rasmussen (Washington: United States Institute of Peace Press, 1997), 191–237.

24. For an updated summary of the social-psychological approach to conflict resolution, see Herbert C. Kelman and Ronald J. Fisher, "Conflict Analysis and Reconciliation," in *Oxford Handbook of Political Psychology*.

25. Ervin Staub and Daniel Bar-Tal, "Genocide Mass Killing and Intractable Conflict," in *Oxford Handbook of Political Psychology*, ed. David O. Sears, Leonie Huddy, and Robert Jervis (New York: Oxford University Press, 2003), 732.

26. Rothstein, "Fragile Peace," 237.

27. Kriesberg, *Constructive Conflicts*, 351.

28. Ibid., 352.

29. Ibid., 354.

30. Alexander L. George, "Foreword," in *Stable Peace among Nations*, ed. Arie M. Kacowicz et al. (Lanham, MD: Rowman and Littlefield, 2000), xiii.

31. E.g., the peaceful, but far from friendly, relations between Israel and Egypt following the 1979 peace agreement and improved, but not really reconciled, relations between the United Kingdom and Argentina following the signing of a series of bilateral agreements in 1990.

32. E.g., Sadat's visit to Israel in November of 1977 and Menem's benevolent visit to England in 1998.

33. Appleby, *Ambivalence*, 194.

34. Ibid., 195–96.

35. Jeffrie G. Murphy and J. Hampton, *Forgiveness and Mercy* (Cambridge: Cambridge University Press, 1998), 15.

36. Donald W. Shriver, "Is There Forgiveness in Politics? Germany, Vietnam and America," in *Exploring Forgiveness*, ed. R. D. Enright and J. North (Madison: University of Wisconsin Press, 1998), 133.

37. Nicholas Tavuchis, *Mea Culpa* (Stanford: Stanford University Press, 1991), 17.

38. Ibid., 100.

39. Ibid., 102.

40. Jean Hampton, "Forgiveness, Resentment and Hatred," in *Forgiveness and Mercy*, ed. Jeffrie G. Murphy and Jean Hampton (Cambridge: Cambridge University Press, 1988), 35–87.

41. Montville, "Healing Function," 120.

42. Joram Graf Haber, *Forgiveness* (Lanham, MD: Rowman and Littlefield, 1991), 83.

43. Ibid., 103.

44. Tutu, *No Future*, 271–72.

45. Ibid., 281–82.

46. Long and Brecke, *War and Reconciliation*, 111.

47. Lily Gardner-Feldman, "Practice of 'Reconciliation,'" 335.

48. Julie Juola Exline and Roy F. Baumeister, "Expressing Forgiveness and Repentance: Benefits and Barriers," in *Forgiveness: Theory, Research and Practice*, ed. Michael E. McCullough, Kenneth I. Pargament, and Carl E. Thorsen (New York: Guilford Press, 2000), 147. For further discussion of obstacles on the way to forgiveness in the international arena see Yehudith Auerbach, "The Role of Forgiveness in Reconciliation," in *From Conflict Resolution to Reconciliation*, ed. Y. Bar Siman-Tov (New York: Oxford University Press, 2004), 149–75.

49. John P. Lederach, "Beyond Violence: Building Sustainable Peace," in *Handbook of Interethnic Coexistence*, ed. Eugene Weiner (New York: Continuum, 1998), 236–45; Ervin Staub, "Genocide and Mass Killing: Origins, Prevention, Healing and Reconciliation," *Political Psychology* 21 (2000): 367–82.

50. Gardner-Feldman, "Practice of 'Reconciliation,'" 333–56.

51. Lily Gardner-Feldman, *The Special Relationship between West Germany and Israel* (Boston: Allen and Unwin, 1984).

52. For the detailed story of the Reparation Agreement and its impact on Israel-Germany relations see Yehudith Auerbach, "Foreign Policy Decisions and Changing Attitudes" (Doctoral dissertation, The Hebrew University of Jerusalem, 1980), Yehudith Auerbach,

"Ben-Gurion and Reparations from Germany," in *David Ben-Gurion: Politics and Leadership in Israel*, ed. Ronald W. Zweig (London: Frank Cass, 1991), 274–92.

53. Shriver, "Forgiveness in Politics," 134.
54. Deut. 28:9.
55. Elmer, William, John Smitt, "Sin and Forgiveness in the Old Testament" (doctoral dissertation, Drew Theological Seminary, 1943), 230, 376.
56. Solomon Schimmel, *Wounds Not Healed by Time: The Power of Repentance and Forgiveness* (New York: Oxford University Press, 2002), 57.
57. Tutu, *No Future*. For an excellent review of the literature regarding both the Christian and Islamic approaches to forgiveness, see the appendix to Dan Bar-On, "When Are We Expecting Parties to Reconcile or to Refuse to Do It? The Specific Triangle of Jews, Germans, and Palestinians" (paper presented at the Workshop on Reconciliation, Leonard Davis Institute for International Relations, Jerusalem, February 2001).
58. Schimmel, *Wounds Not Healed*, 64.
59. Rambam, *Mishneh Torah, Hilchoth Teshuvah*, 2, 9–10.
60. Rambam, *Mishneh Torah, Hilchoth Teshuvah*, 1, 1.
61. Schimmel, *Wounds Not Healed*, 30.
62. Rabbi Avraham Y. Hakohen Kook, *Orot Hateshuvah* [The Lights of Repentance], (Jerusalem: Rabbi Kook Institute, 1994); Pinchas H. Peli, *On Repentance: From the Oral Discourses of Rabbi Joseph B. Soloveitchik* (Jerusalem Education Department of the World Zionist Organization, 1974).
63. "The Encyclopedia of Islam," *EI²*, New ed. Vol 10 (Leiden: Brill, 2000), 385.
64. "The Encyclopedia of Islam," *EI²*, New ed. Vol 2 (Leiden: Brill, 1991), 1078.
65. George E. Irani, "Islamic Mediation Techniques for Middle East Conflicts," http://www.biu.ac.il/soc/besa/meria/journal/1999/issue2/Jv3n2a1.html
66. 2 Samuel 19:23.
67. For elaboration of this point see Schimmel, *Wounds Not Healed*, 83–85.
68. Simon Wiesenthal, *The Sunflower* (New York: Schocken, 1998).
69. Theodore M. Hesburgh, in Ibid., 169.
70. Deut, 25:17–19.
71. For elaboration of that point see Auerbach, "Role of Forgiveness."
72. Gardner-Feldman, "Practice of 'Reconciliation.'"
73. Tutu, *No Future*, 31–32.
74. Gopin (note 2) 190.
75. For example, Shriver, "A Bridge," and Tutu, *No Future*.
76. Like Appleby, *Ambivalence*, and Gopin (note 2).
77. Like Fox, "Religion and State Failure."

# Index

*Achdut Havoda* 88
Afghanistan 145, 159, 161, 162
Africa 15, 20
African Americans 40, 116–17, 123, 124
African National Congress 182
afterlife 41, 44, 48
Al Qaeda 5, 46, 159
al-Aqsa intifada 97
Al-Aqsa Martyrs' Brigades (*Kata'ib Shuhada al-Aqsa*) 97–8, 103–4, 104–5
Al-Aqsa Mosque 84, 97, 98–9
allegory 52
Amalek 66
America *see* United States of America (USA)
American Jews 115–16, 116–17, 126
apartheid 171
apologies 171–2, 177–8
Appleby, S. 40
*Arab American Republicans against Bush* organization 113
Arab Revolt (1936–9) 59
Arafat, Y. 100–1
Ashkenazi Jews 80
Asia 20, 157
authentic religion 41
Azad Kashmir 160

balance of power 136–7, 137–8, 153, 154
Bangladesh 145, 159, 160
Begin-Sadat Center for Strategic Studies 1
belief systems 2, 18
Beyer, P. 12
Bhagavad Gita 52
Bharatiya Janata Party (BNJ) 164–5
Bhutto, Z.A. 143, 144
Bible 51–2
Bloc of the Faithful (*Gush Emunim*) 83
BNJ *see* Bharatiya Janata Party
boarding schools 89
Bosnia 153–4
Buddhism 53
Bunge, M. 152
burial sites 99

causes of conflict *see* conflict causes
Central Treaty Organization (CENTO) 140, 162
Chadda, M. 157
chi-squares 47, 52–3

China 141
Choudhury, G.W. 141
Christianity 51, 53, 139, 180, 181, 183
church attendance 14
civilizations: classification of countries 31; and cultural identity 18; importance of religion **15**; and role of identity 2
clash of civilizations 5, 18, 42, 46, 77
Clinton Framework for Final Status Agreement (Israel–Palestine, 2000) 85
coalition politics 84–6
collective apologies 178
commanded wars 63
communalism 167
comparative foreign policy studies 154–6
compensation 171
compromise 80, 81, 85, 86, 139, 174
conflict causes 17–18, 40, 41–2
conflict intensity *see* intensity
conflict resolution 173, 174–5, 179, 183
conflict studies: African American study 40–1; and authentic religion 41; civizational conflict 42, 44; conclusions 45; place of extremism 40, 43; and religious legitimacy 39–40; role of language 42; the Serb-Bosnian conflict 42–3; significance of elites 41–2, 43–4; value conflicts 44; view of the afterlife 41, 44, 48
conflict-culture nexus 17
Congress Party (India) 144–5, 167
Congress (USA) 118–20, 121–2; 105th (1997–8) 123, 127; 106th (1999–2000) 123–4, 124–5, 127–8; 107th (2001–2) 124, 125, 128
constructivism 2, 18
Correlates of War Dataset 42
corrupted religion 41
cosmic war 43
cultural conflicts **19**
cultural differences 13, 18, 42
cultural imperialism 13
cultural pluralism 91
cultural studies 11
culture-conflict nexus 17

*dat* (religion) 77
*dati-leumi see* national-religious Judaism
DeLay, T. 115
democracy 16, 20, 22, 116

*187*

Democratic Front for the Liberation of Palestine (DFLP) 101
democratic liberalization 161
deterrence 67
diasporas 8, 13
dictatorships 41, 138
diplomacy 172
discretionary wars 63, 64
discrimination 40, 48
doctrine 2–3
domestic policies 7, 156, 162, 167–8
doves 80, 81, 85

economy 13, 16, 22, 23
education *see* religious education
Egypt 174, 175
elections 84
elites 41–2, 43–4, 138, 142, 163–4
*eretz Israel* (land of Israel) 68
ethnic conflicts: and the balance of power 153, 154; domestic causes 158; and internationalization 151, 153, 158; and intra-ethnic compromise 139; and irredentism 153; overview 152–4; role of state motives 154; substate causes 158
ethnicity 144, 146, 153
ethno-nationalism 86, 89, 90
ethno-religious conflicts 133, 152–4, 163, 166
ethnocentricism 78, 86–7, 91–2
evangelicalism 118
exile 59
extremism 40, 41, 43, 83–4, 89, 161

Fatah: affiliated institutions 101; compared to Hamas 97, 102; founding document 102; involvement in violence 99; relationship between nationalism and religion 99–103; relationship with Islam 100, 107, 108–9; secular politics 106–7, 107–8
Feinstein, Rabbi M. 61
folk religion 40
forbearance 177
*Foreign Affairs* 18
foreign policies: conclusions 167–8; decision making *155*; and impact of religiosity 2; importance of domestic policies 156, 162, 167–8; of India 151, 156–8; influence of religion 7, 133; Israeli 83; of the NRP 88; of Pakistan 141, 143; relevance of international/state scene 151; role analysis 133, 135–6, 143; role of the elites/masses 8; studies 154–6
forgiveness: and apologies 177; in Christianity 180, 181, 183; conclusions 182–3; and healing 179; and humiliation 178; in identity conflicts 175; international examples 171; in Islam 181; in Judaism 180, 183; moral dimension 178; overview 171, 173, 177; and repentance 181; role of religious traditions 180–2
Fox, J. 39–40, 174
Free Kashmir 160
freedom of speech 16
*Friends Not Masters* (Khan) 143
functionalism 7
fundamentalism 6, 13
funding 83, 89

Gandhi, I. 163
Gandhi, R. 163
genocide 179
*ger toshav* (resident alien) 80
Germany 181, 182
globalization 12
Gopin, M. 174
Goren, Rabbi S. 62
Great Britain *see* United Kingdom
grievances 40
group identity 17
Gurr, T. 39
*Gush Emunim* (Bloc of the Faithful) 83, 84, 89

*Habad* movement 79
*halacha* 59, 62, 77, 78–80, 83
halachic discourse: effect on national-religious conscripts 70; importance of Maimonidean template 63–4, 65, 66; intellectual/practical implications 69–71; and low intensity warfare 67–8; mediums of transmission 62–3; participants 60–1; and preemptive war 67; and rules of engagement 66–7; Sabbath observance 68; significance 70–1, 71–2; traditional view 61–2
Hamas 97, 99, 102, 103
*Hapoelei Agudat Yisrael* (ultra-Orthodox Jewish group) 79
*haredi* society *see* ultra-Orthodox Judaism
al Hasan, H. 106–7
hawkishness: conclusions 83, 88, 90, 91–2; and ethnocentrism 86–7; overview 77; in Pakistan 163; in politics 84, 85; and public opinion 88; relationship to religion 78, 80, 81, 82, 86–90; role of history 87–90
Henderson, E. 42
*Herut* party 88
Herzog, Rabbi I. 65
*Hezb-e-Islami* (Sunni group) 162
Hindu nationalism 164–5
Hinduism 52, 53, 55, 164–5, 166
historical analogies 138–9, 142–3
Holocaust 179
Holy Land 68

holy wars 41, 174
House of Representatives (USA) *see* Congress
housing 90
human rights 5, 81, 165
humiliation 178
Huntingdon, S. 5, 18, 42

identity: as an increasing cause of conflict 19; and discrimination 48; and ethnic groups 17, 153; and fundamentalism 13; and modernization 12–13; Muslim 160–1; negative 174; relationship to the revival of religion 11; and religion 2, 18, 44, 144–5, 151–2; view of social sciences 4
identity conflicts: conclusions 183; definition 173–4; distribution **20**; over time **19**; relationship to material conflicts 174–5; role of history 174
identity-oriented definition: of religious conflict 45, 46–7, 49, 51, 55
ideology 139, 145
Inbar, E. 60
India: and the BNJ 164–5; conclusions 167–8; conflict intensity 53; foreign policy 151, 156–8, 159; hegemonism 138, 157, 162; importance of elites 43–4, 163–4; influence of Islam 162; and Kashmir 156–7, 159–60, 165–6, 166–7; and Pakistan 143, 145–59, 163, 167; policy of Indira Gandhi 163; rise of communalism 167; role of secular nationalism 164–5, 166; significance of the Indo-China War 142; and the Simla Agreement 160; and the Soviet Union 162
individual apologies 178
Indo-China War (1962) 142
Inhofe, J. 126
intensity: conclusions 53, 55; and Islamic minority groups 52; of religious conflicts 39, 42, 47, *48*, 50; and type of religion *54*
International Criminal Court 172
international relations theory: and the clash of civilizations thesis 5, 40, 77; conclusions 9–10; position of religion 1, 4–6; view of scholars 5–6; and the Westphalian system 6, 7, *see also* systemism
internationalization: conclusions 167; of ethnic conflict 151, 153, 158–9; influencing subnational wars 154; overview 153–4; role of the UN 161–2; and security issues 154
Internet 13
interventionism 133, 135–6, 139
intifadas 67, 89
intrastate conflicts: and economic growth 22, 23, 24; and mountainous terrain 22; and national resource dependence 22; and population 22, 23; significance of religion *21*, 23; and time since last conflict 22–3
Iran 161
Irish famine (1840) 172
irredentism 145, 153, 159
Islam: concept of jihad 51; conflict intensity 53; influence in India 162; in Kashmir 158; levels of religiosity 15; nationalist role 102, 143; in Pakistan 3, 142, 143, 145, 157, 159–60; pragmatic use 106, 108, 142, 143; in religious interventions 139, 145; and responsibility of moderate Muslims 41; role of identity 13; stereotype 52; as a tool of mobilization 3, 7, 9, 41–2, 107; versions of 5, 43; view of forgiveness 181; in Yugoslavia 42–3
Israel: armed forces 86; Congressional discussions 123–5, 127–8; education system 91; foreign policy 83; political culture 84–6, 89, 92; as a postmodern country 90–1; probit analysis of support *122*; role of the peace process 77; support of USA 114, *120*, *121*, *see also* Israeli–Palestinian conflict
Israel Defense Force (IDF) 60, 62, 67, 70, 71–2
Israel–Egypt conflict 174
Israeli–Palestinian conflict: as an identity conflict 175; and forgiveness 179; land rights 80; overview 78, 98–9; as a religious war 97
issue-orientated definition: of religious conflict 44–5
*ius ad bellum*: conclusions 71–2; importance of the Holy Land 68; mediums of transmission 62–3; participants in the debate 60–1; rediscovery of ancient texts 69; rules of engagement 66–7; significance of the Maimonidean template 64, 65, 66; traditional frameworks/terminology 63

Japanese civilizations 15
Jewish academies (*yeshivot heseder*) 71
Jewish law (*Mishneh Torah*) 63
Jewish learning (*yeshivot*) 62
jihad 51, 97
Ali Jinnah, M. 143
Judaism: American 115–16; conclusions 91–2; conflict intensity 53, 55; definition 77; discretionary war 63, 64; distinction from religion 77; on forgiveness 180–2, 183; importance of Maimonidean template 63–4, 65; on mandatory war 63, 64; orthodox tradition 77; overview of factions 79–80; on the peace process

80–1; political elections 84; public opinion surveys 81–3; role of the government 64; on the significance of territory **82**; view of war 59; views on self-defence 60, 61, 66, *see also* national-religious Judaism; ultra-Orthodox Judaism
judicial systems 172
justification *see* legitimacy

Kashmir 139–45; conclusions 145–7, 163, 167–8; conflict origins 156–7; cultural factors 166–7; economy 165–6; geographic/demographic realities 145; reasons for the Pakistani invasion 139–40, 144; relevance of ethnicity 153; religious identities 158; role of Hindu Nationalism 165; as a security issue 154; significance of shared religion 144, 145; terrorism 160, 161
*Kata'ib Shuhada al- Aqsa see* Al-Aqsa Martyrs' Brigades
Kennedy, J.F. 141
Kever Yosef 99
Khan, A. 140, 142, 143
Khartoum Declaration (1967) 174
Knesset 64, 84
Kook, Rabbi Z.Y. 65, 80
Kriesberg, L. 175, 176

land *see* territory
language differences 42
Lantos, T. 115
"Laws of Kings and Their Wars" (Maimonides) 63, 65
leadership 144
legitimacy: distinction from motivation 7; and grievance formation 40; manipulation of religion 3, 7, 9, 41–2, 44, 139, 174; role of religious education 40; use of religion in foreign policy 133
liberalism 86, 90
liberalization 161
Likud 85

madrassas (religious schools) 159
Maimonides 59, 63, 64, 65, 66, 68–9
mandatory wars 64, 65, 66, 67
mass media 172
material conflicts 173, 174–5, 176, 183
*Meimad* (political party) 80, 81, 84, 86
*mekhinot kedam tzevaiyot* (military academies) 71
messianism 43, 79, 80, 88
military academies (*mekhinot kedam tzevaiyot*) 71
military elites 142
military service 62, 70, 71
*Millennium* 5–6

Minorities at Risk Dataset 40
*Mishneh Torah* (Jewish law) 63
mobilization 3, 151, 174
modernity 11, 12, 174
modernization 11, 12–13, 39
modernization theory 4, 12
Mohajirs 144
Montville, J.V. 174
morality 3–4
*Morasha* 84
mosques 103
motivation for conflict 7, 8, 9, 18, 72
Mujahideen 146
multi-ethnicity 139
multilateralism 137
*musalaha* (reconciliation) 181
Musharraf, P. 159
Muslim League 142, 144, 166

National Conference (Kashmir) 164
national leadership 139, 144
national religiosity 14, 15, 16, *17*, 20, 23
National Religious Party (NRP, Israel) 84, 85, 88
national-religious Judaism: beliefs about the state of Israel 68, 87; compared with other forms of Judaism 61–2, 79, 80; conclusions 91–2; and extremism 89; in military conflicts 70, 71; view of political elections 84
nationalism: in defining conflict causes 46; and Hinduism 164–5; and Islam 102, 143; and religion in the Fatah 99–103; secular 164–5, 166; in speechmaking 100–1
NATO *see* North Atlantic Treaty Organization
Nazism 181–2
negative identity 174
*Neturei Karta* Jewish sect 79
New Testament 52
normalization 174
North Atlantic Treaty Organization (NATO) 138
Northern Ireland 43, 46
NRP *see* National Religious Party
nuclear programmes 163

obituary notices 105–6
offensive-defensive actions 67
Old Testament 51–2, 180
Operation Gibraltar (1965) 139
Operation Peace for the Galilee (1982) 67
Oslo Accords (1993) **82**, 85
*Oz Ve Shalom/Netivot Shalom* (peace movements) 80

Pakhtunistan 145
Pakistan: alliances 162; and China 141;

conclusions 145–7, 167–8; constitution of 1962 143; domestic role expectations 142; foreign policy 141, 143, 144, 160–1; and India 143, 145–6; involvement of UN 161–2; irredentism 145, 159; Islamic nationalism 143, 144, 145, 146, 157, 159–60; political use of Islam 3, 143, 160–1; relations with USA 140–1; relationship with Kashmir 139–40, 145, 156–7, 159–60, 165–6, 166–7; rise of Ayub Khan 140, 142, 143; and systemism 140–5; use of diplomacy 160, *see also* Kashmir

Palestine Liberation Organization (PLO) 79

Palestinian Authority (PA) 99

Palestinian–Israeli conflict: as an identity conflict 175; and forgiveness 179; land rights 80; overview 78, 98–9; as a religious war 97; and state building 108

peace process: and ethnonationalism 86; and hawkishness 83; ideal/reality of 41; importance of state funding 83, 89–90; and Judaism 77, 80–1, 89; levels of religiosity 78; as a means of preventing conflict 40; position of various religious factions 85–6; pragmatic approach 78, 79; research overview 78; role of suppression 41; significance of territory 80; violence against 83–4; without reconciliation 176–7

Peres, S. 85

plebiscites 162

political elites 8

Political Parties Act (Pakistan, 1962) 142

political regimes 16, 23

political science 4, 6

politics 84–6, 142, 143

population 22, 23–4

postmodernization 78, 90–1, 92

preemptive strikes 67

PRIO Armed Conflict Dataset 47

Punjabis 144

Rabbi Moses ben Maimon *see* Maimonides

Rabin, Y. 77, 84

Rachel's tomb 99

Rapport, D. 43

Rashtriya Swayamsewak Sangh (RSS) 167

reactive-defensive actions 66

realism 151, 168

reconciliation: conclusions 183; facilitating forgiveness/healing 179; and genocide 179; and identity conflicts 173; importance 175–6; view of Judaism 181; without peace 176–7

reconnaissance units (*sayarot*) 70

refugee flows 13

regime types 23

regional subsystems: and balance of power 137–8, 140, 141–2, 162; and global integration 153; and religious affiliations 142

relative deprivation theory 39

relevance of religion *49*, 50, 51

relevance variables 46–7

religion: definitions 2, 151

religiosity 2, 40–1, 78, *see also* national religiosity

religious affiliations: and the balance of power 138, 141; and the regional subsystem 142; role in international relationships 137; significance of Kashmir 144–5

religious conflicts: conclusions 53, 55; identity-oriented definition 45, 46–7, 49, 51, 55; importance of religious affiliations 144–5; issue-oriented definition 45–6; problems in defining 45, 49; relevance of religion 17–18, *49*, 50, 51; role of religious education 48; and territorial conflicts 48, *see also* conflict studies; intensity

religious differences: as a cause of conflict 11, 18, 20, 24, 42; conclusions 42; effect on conflict post Cold War 23; and ethnolinguistic differences 42; and intrastate conflict *21*; and problems with compromise 18; research overview 23

religious education 40, 48, 91, 159

religious elites 8

religious hierarchy 48

religious ideology 145

religious legitimacy *see* legitimacy

religious peace building *see* peace process

religious revival theory: conclusions 14, 17, 23, 24–5; importance of economic conditions 16; and religion in the West 13; significance of civilizational belonging **15**; survey of importance of religion *14*; variables used 14

religious rhetoric 174

repentance 177, 180–1

repression 40

republicanism 86, 87, 88, 89, 90

resident aliens (*ger toshav*) 80

resource dependence 22

responsa 63

role analysis 133

role expectations: domestic 142; effect on foreign policy 143; and ethnic diversity 144; and historical analogies 138–9; national leadership 144; and regional balance of power 137–8; and role performance 135–6

role theory: advantages of 135; conclusions 146; Kashmiri example 140–5; and systemism 134–9; use in explaining ethno-religious interventionism 135–6

Rosenau, J. 135–6
Rummel, R. 42

SAARC *see* South Asian Association of Regional Cooperation
Sabbath 68
the sacred 172–3
salutations 101
*sanhedrin* 64, 65
Sara and Simbha Lainer Chair in Democracy and Civility 1
satellites 141
*sayarot* (reconnaissance units) 70
SEATO *see* Southeast Asian Treaty Organization
secularism 39, 163, 164–5, 166
secularization theory 4, 6, 12
security 154
self-defence *see ius ad bellum*
Sephardi Jews 79
September 11th, 2001 7
Serb-Bosnian conflict 42–3, 153
settlements (*sulh*) 181
settlements (territory) 80, 81, 83–4
*shabiba* (youth movement) 101
Shach, Rabbi E.M. 79, 86
Sharon, A. 84
*Shas* (Jewish religious party) 79, 85
Shriver, D.W. 177
Simla Agreement (1972) 160
Six Day War (1967) 79, 88
slavery 172
social control 7
social sciences 1, 2–4, 9–10
sociology 4, 6
*Sociology* 6
Somalia 153
South Africa 172, 178, 182
South Asian Association of Regional Cooperation (SAARC) 138
Southeast Asian Treaty Organization (SEATO) 140, 162
sovereignty of states 5
Soviet Union 141, 162
*The Spirit of the IDF* 71
stable peace *see* reconciliation
State Failure Dataset 45
state funding 83
*Strategic Moves* (Fatah website) 102–3
suicide bombers 3
*sulh* (settlement) 181
systemism: conclusions 145–7, 167–8; definition 152; functional relations **134**; and India's foreign policy 151; overview 133–4, 151–2; and role theory 134–9

technology 13
Temple Mount 97, 99
territory 48, 79–80, 81, 83–4, 157–8, 166

terrorism: messianic 43; in Pakistan 146, 159, 160; view of the USA 172; and war 45
*teshuvah* (repentance) 180–1
theocracy 107, 109, 143
theology 40
Tito, J.B. 41
tourism 13
track one diplomacy 172, 173, 176, 183
track two diplomacy 176, 183
tradition 12
TRC *see* Truth and Reconciliation Commission
Treaty of Westphalia (1648) 5, 6
truth commissions 172
Truth and Reconciliation Commission (TRC, South Africa) 172, 178
Tutu, Archbishop D. 178

UK *see* United Kingdom
ultra-Orthodox Judaism: conclusions 91–2; and hawkishness 87; key tenets 79; politics 89–90; role in the peace process 85; significance of state funding 83; view of political elections 84; view of the Six Day War 88
UN *see* United Nations
unilateralism 137
United Kingdom (UK) 141
United Nations (UN) 137, 140, 141, 153, 161–2
United Nations (UN) Charter 107
United States of America (USA): antiabortion issue 43; and Arab Americans 113; conclusions 125–6; defending sovereignty 46; and evangelicalism 12, 118, 126; importance of race 124, 125; influences on foreign policy 113, 115, 125; involvement in Kashmiri dispute 140, 141, 145; overview of research 114–15, 118–20; and Pakistan 140–1, 159, 160, 162; relationship with Israel 114, 124; religious beliefs 114, 117–18; role in Asian politics 161; role in world peace 137; support for Israel 115–18, *120*, *121*, 126; view of Al Qaeda 5; view of Catholics 117; view of Israeli–Palestinian conflict 115–18; view of terrorism 172, *see also* African Americans; American Jews; Congress
Uppsala Conflict database 19
US State Department 5
USA *see* United States of America

Vajpayee, A.B. 165
value conflicts 44
variables 46, 47
*ve-ezrat* (to assist) 66–7

victim ethos 175
violence: in Christianity 51–2; conclusions 45, 53, 55; in Hinduism 52, 55; in Islam 51; in the Israeli–Palestinian conflict 97, 98–9; in Judaism 53, 55; levels in religious conflicts 39, 42, 44, 47; and the peace process in Israel 83–4; research overview 45–7

Wailing Wall riots (1928–9) 98
Walker, S.G. 135
war 19, 45, 59, 154
War Crime Tribunal 172
war criminals 172
War of Independence (Israel, 1948–9) 66
the West 13, 14, 15, **16**
Westernization 13

Westphalian system 5, 6
Wiesenthal, S. 181–2
world values surveys 29–30
World War II (1939–45) 171, 172
Wye Agreement (Israel–Palestine, 1998) 85

*yahadut* (Judaism) 77
yeshiva 99
*yeshivot heseder* (Jewish academies) 71
*yeshivot* (Jewish learning) 62
Yom Kippur War (1973) 66
Yosef, Rabbi O. 79–80, 81
Yugoslavia 41

Zionism 61, 62, 80, 98
Ziring, L. 141